THE
PLEASURE
OF THEIR
COMPANY

Howard Taubman, *c.* 1952.

THE
PLEASURE
OF THEIR
COMPANY

A REMINISCENCE

HOWARD
TAUBMAN

AMADEUS PRESS
Reinhard G. Pauly, General Editor
Portland, Oregon

Designed by Susan Applegate
Printed in the United States of America

AMADEUS PRESS
The Haseltine Building
133 S.W. Second Avenue, Suite 450
Portland, Oregon 97204-3527 U.S.A.

Library of Congress Cataloging-in-Publication Data

Taubman, Hyman Howard, 1907–
    The pleasure of their company: a reminiscence / by Howard Taubman.
        p.   cm.
    Includes index.
    ISBN 0-931340-78-0
    1. Taubman, Hyman Howard, 1907–   . 2. Theater critics—United States—Biography. 3. Music critics—United States—Biography.
    I. Title.
    PN1708.T38 1994
    791'.092—dc20
    [B]   94-21716
                                                                          CIP

For Lori,
my wife,
whose devotion sustained me
during long months of illness

Contents

Acknowledgments

I AM INDEBTED to members of my family for invaluable help. My son Philip, deputy national news editor of *The Times*, got an essential batch of photographs from the archives of *The Times* for use as illustrations. He had indispensable help from Al Siegal, assistant managing editor, and Bob Medina of *The Times* Archives Department. My older son, William, despite his duties as the Bertrand Snell Professor of Political Science at Amherst College, found time to seek a publisher for this book and to make the initial contact with Amadeus Press. And my wife, Lori, transmitted the script to disks on a word processor.

I also want to express my gratitude to Karen Kirtley, editorial director of Amadeus, who prepared the manuscript for publication. Karen was unfailing in her expressions of delight in the book.

Thanks are also due to Reinhard Pauly, general editor of the press. Coincidentally, our paths crossed in 1945 when I covered the surrender of the German armies in Italy for *Stars and Stripes*, and he, a young U.S. Army officer, served as interpreter and translator of the surrender document.

I owe a debt of gratitude to Arthur Ochs Sulzberger, Jr., for permitting me to quote from some of the editorials and from some of my reviews in *The Times*.

I am thankful to Harriet Van Horne for coming to my defense as a television critic for the *World-Telegram* and for permitting me to reprint her column.

I thank Mrs. Eleanor Cousins for granting me permission to quote from an article by Robert Shayon, in my defense vis-à-vis David Merrick, and for writing that her late husband, Norman, editor of the *Saturday Review*, would have been delighted to grant permission.

I owe thanks to Richard N. Hunter, lawyer for the executor of the Alfred Lunt Estate, for permission to use a letter Lunt sent me long ago. I should add that when we phoned Actors' Equity to ask for the name of the executor of the estate of Alfred Lunt, an unknowing young man told us, "We have no one listed by that name." Alas, *sic transit gloria mundi.*

I thank June K. Goodman of the Marian Anderson Award Fund for permission to reprint material I wrote for one of its programs.

I thank *The New Yorker* and Ed Fisher for permission to reprint Ed's cartoon and for waiving any fee that would be expected.

I am grateful to Nuala Cuddy for sending a photo of Emmet Dalton and his wife Alice.

And I thank David Golding, my *Stars and Stripes* editor, for coming up with a photo of me in Army uniform and another of Ingrid Bergman and Roberto Rossellini.

Howard Taubman
Redding, Connecticut
June, 1994

1

Introduction

I NEVER KEPT a diary or a journal. I assumed, arrogantly no doubt, that I would remember what was worth remembering. Not quite true unless, of course, one is Marcel Proust, who forgot nothing and whose imagination subtilized and enriched every recollection. In setting down these recollections of men and women whom I was fortunate enough to encounter and even know, and of events I reported—some of which I was involved in—I have relied largely on memory, reinforced by recourse to scrapbooks of pieces I wrote for *The New York Times* in more than four decades and to my books and many articles for magazines. There were also some letters, mostly those I sent home while I was in the Army during World War II.

Even if I felt self-important enough to undertake an autobiography, told with chronological precision, I would realize that way lies boredom, for me as well as others. Old folks tend to reminisce about their lives and careers as if they were subjects that must absorb all in range of their voices. How foolish not to notice the suppressed yawns. I remember a few ancient friends and colleagues who, though they had lively tales to tell, managed to burble on and on. One endearing exception was my colleague of long ago Noel Straus, who would bring up out of the depths of his memory precise recollections of exquisite nuances of performances he had heard before the turn of the century. His absorption in music was so complete that he would speak of the time when he "heard Pavlova dance."

I never saw, let alone heard, Pavlova dance, but when I was a boy of high-school age, growing up in a working-class home in New York City, I began to frequent the summer concerts at Lewisohn Stadium. The New York Philharmonic, even before it merged with the New York Symphony to become the Philharmonic-Symphony, played every night *al fresco*, except when there was a rainstorm, and even tried to carry on if the showers came midway in the program and were not heavy enough to endanger the instruments. The orchestra was seated on a wooden platform in front of a band shell about where the 50-yard line would be opposite the stadium. The stadium was a long, concrete crescent-like structure with hard, backless rows of seats rising to what seemed like a dizzy height far from the musicians. Between the orchestra and the stadium, on what was the playing field for the football teams that represented City College in the fall, were rows of folding chairs, and directly in front of the orchestra there was an enclosure with tables and chairs to accommodate officialdom, generous patrons and the press. The price range was $1 for a chair on the field, 50 cents for the front and center sections of the stadium and 25 cents for the upper reaches.

I cannot recall how often I sat in those upper reaches. On nights when there was not a glamorous soloist, it was not crowded; one was not disturbed if one moved down to a 50-cent location after the program was well along. When the soloist was renowned, every seat in every section would be taken; it was important to get there early to have any kind of decent spot in the 25-cent area. I can still recall rushing past the older concertgoers carrying cushions to ameliorate sitting on concrete and the stately walkers who knew they had reserved chairs on the field.

The acoustics at Lewisohn Stadium were not good, and whether the management resorted to amplification or not, what we in our 25-cent aerie heard was bound to be distorted. Add the hazard of occasional airplanes flying low over the field and we found heart-stopping moments in a noble slow movement obliterated, and a great full-voiced climax reinforced needlessly by the roar of motors. As if these disturbances were not nuisance enough, fire engines or ambulances would race by with sirens screeching.

Nevertheless it was wonderful music—Bach, Mozart, Haydn, Beethoven, Schubert, Brahms, Wagner and so on and so on. It mattered a little that the playing was sometimes ragged and tired—but not much. For one who had had to do with a small collection of Caruso records played at home on a modest phonograph, this opportunity to hear a good deal of the symphonic repertory

The New York Philharmonic rehearsing for a concert at Lewisohn Stadium in 1936.

was a treasurable boon. I used to muse, perched high up in the stadium, how marvelous it would be to attain the unreachable goal of a chair on the playing field. I did not dream that some day I would be sitting up front at a press table as a member of the Music Department of *The Times*.

One gets lucky. I was often lucky. At Cornell University, which I was able to attend thanks to a four-year tuition scholarship—the annual tuition fee was $400—I had to work to pay for my room and board. Among my jobs—part-time waiter in a fraternity house and dishwasher at the college infirmary—was an assignment to help Professor Otto Kinkeldey of the Music Department sort out and distribute tickets for the annual concert series. Kinkeldey, who became the occupant of the first chair in musicology at an American university, treated me as a kind of protégé, lecturing me incessantly about music and manners. I believe I learned something of both from him. His friend and colleague, an even more formidable presence on the Cornell campus, Professor Lane Cooper, intimidating even when he thought he was being friendly, taught us to observe simply and accurately. At the initial session in his course on Middle English, which meant Chaucer, Beowulf and other early worthies, he held up the textbook he had assigned and demanded to know what was the first thing we had seen. Some of us attempted elaborate answers, and he broke in impatiently, "The color of the binding, of course!" Another, gentler professor, Robert Sibley, brought me up very short with a comment he wrote on a theme paper I had submitted: "Probably you are complacently aware that you write pretty well."

The most modest, sweet-natured teacher I had, Professor Leslie Nathan Broughton, taught me something about humility. I took a course in Wordsworth with him. As I look at that sentence, I wonder, *Does anyone these days spend a whole semester in a course devoted to Wordsworth?* True, I studied the tragedies of Shakespeare with Joseph Quincy Adams, who became the first head of the Folger Shakespeare Library in Washington, and the comedies with William J. Strunk, whose book on style E. B. White helped to convert into a classic. But Wordsworth? My only excuse was that I liked poetry. At any rate, instead of a final exam, Professor Broughton requested a term paper. I undertook to read and write on "The Excursion," the poet's last and endless work. I waded through the poem, filling a notebook with notes, but my reach exceeded my grasp. At term's end I found that, what with requirements for other courses, I had no time to write the term paper. I decided to throw myself on Professor Broughton's mercy—to ask for a postponement. I explained that I had gone through the poem and showed him my notebook with its voluminous notations. He turned its pages carefully, smiling faintly as he went along. Then he stood up, came around to where I sat, patted me gently and said, "We'll consider the course complete. Now, my boy," he said, and the faint smile was shaded with a touch of sadness, "there are two of us who have read 'The Excursion.'"

My luck held when I got out of college. I was in the class of 1929, a phrase that became a synonym for the miseries that befell its members as the stock market crashed and the terrible Depression years ensued. I had done occasional pieces as a college correspondent for the New York *Post,* then a full-size, reputable newspaper owned by Cyrus H. K. Curtis, whose enormously successful publications included the *Saturday Evening Post* and the *Ladies' Home Journal.* Having taken a full load of credits in previous semesters, I was able to ask for a leave in the second half of my junior year and worked on the *Post* as a copy editor in the Sports Department at $30 a week, to me a munificent sum. I was promised a permanent job when I graduated. But in June of 1929 the *Post* was not hiring. *The Times* in those days ran a current-events contest at a number of colleges, a written test with a prize of $150 to the winner. I took the test, won it and was able to leave Ithaca with—*mirabile dictu*—most of my debts paid. I also had the foresight to ask Professor Robert Cushman, who administered the test, if he could give me a letter of introduction to someone on *The Times.*

It was addressed to Captain H. I. Brock, a courtly oldtimer in the Sunday Department, who had helped to manage contest details from New York. When I presented it to the Captain, who was near retirement, he remarked that he knew hardly anyone in the News Department and had no influence. But he picked up the phone and called the city editor, David H. Joseph, and urged him enthusiastically, as if he knew and was convinced of my worth, to see me. Reluctantly Joseph agreed. In those pre-Newspaper Guild days, *The Times*, like other newspapers, frequently used reporters on a part-time basis. With the air of a man who had little to lose, Joseph said he would give me a try. The pay would be $3.25 for an assignment; in effect, that meant $3.25 for an afternoon's or evening's work, and that work could encompass any number of assignments and stories to be written.

"Here," said Joseph, "see what you can do with this." He handed me a piece of paper that described a Swedenborgian convention going on somewhere in Brooklyn. What was a Swedenborgian convention? What was a Swedenborg? I had no time to consult a dictionary or an encyclopedia. The next day I did and discovered that he was an eighteenth-century Swedish scientist, religious leader and mystic. At the site of the meeting I asked questions but came away with only the foggiest notion of what was going on. I returned to West Forty-third Street, happy to hear that Joseph and his day-side crew of assistants had gone home. The night city editor was as indifferent to Swedenborg as I was ignorant and suggested that I give him two paragraphs, which is all I would have been able to muster in any case.

The next day when I arrived for an assignment, Joseph gave me a talking-to. "Young man," he said, "you are now working for *The Times*, not the *Post.* We like complete stories." He handed me another sheet of paper. "Maybe you can do better with this!"

I walked away and read the written assignment with bewilderment. The new Independent subway was being built, and it was cutting a large gash through Prospect Park. My job was to find out what the building of the subway was doing to the park. With even a *soupçon* of experience in the way of New York journalism, I would have known how to use the phone and call a few sources or at least to trot around to the Parks Department and get its evaluation. I could think of nothing but to go out to Prospect Park, walk the length of the trench being dug to make way for the subway and examine minutely the effects of the digging and blasting. I counted the number of trees that had been removed and the number that remained. I examined the damage done to lawns and flower beds. And I wrote a report—complete, I hoped, this time, that was like a physician's unsparing diagnosis of a traumatic ailment.

How lucky can you get? It turned out that Mrs. Ochs—wife of *The Times* publisher Adolph S. Ochs—was the president of the New York City Park Association, as was her daughter, Mrs. Arthur Hays Sulzberger, after her, and she sent a note of commendation. When Joseph showed it to me—"the best piece on the parks I've ever seen in *The Times*," it said, or something like that—he beamed. My failure with Swedenborg had been forgiven.

Indeed, impressed by the unexpected accolade from on high, Joseph and his assistants thrust assignments on me. Often I would get morning, afternoon and evening chores, which meant that I earned $9.75 for the day's work. Some weeks, working seven days in a row, I ended with paychecks of more than $65. An auditor brought this fact to the management's attention, whereupon Joseph summoned me to tell me that I had made the grade and was now to be a full-time, permanent member of the staff at a weekly salary of $40.

Through *The Times* I met a wonderful assortment of people, traveled, made friends and had matchless opportunities to observe how the world turned. There was a moment in my second year of employment when I was offered a job as the head of public relations for a national charitable organization at a breathtaking salary of $125 a week. I was sorely tempted. But by then the Depression was invading every corner of life, and I decided that *The Times* was there to stay and it was wiser to cling to a $40-a-week job than to take chances elsewhere.

Mr. and Mrs. Adolph S. Ochs, 1930.

There were other feelers for other jobs with impressive remuneration in later years, but I found it easy to turn them down. I was enjoying the excitement, the surprises and the fun of my work at *The Times*. Music, theater, the arts were at their best, endlessly exhilarating. It was a privilege to be a part of these worlds. It is a privilege to conjure up memories of some of the people who inhabited them and whom I had the great good luck to encounter.

During my time as a reporter, music critic, drama critic and critic-at-large I spent forty-two years at *The Times*, and always had the support of the owners and their top executives. As a very young music editor I decided to run an uncommissioned Sunday piece about Walter Damrosch, a powerful and influential figure in New York's musical and social worlds. It was highly critical of his work as a composer and conductor. I agreed with its evaluation. Mr. Damrosch did not. I was sent for by Edwin L. James, the managing editor. When I walked into his office he was on the phone with Mr. Ochs, vigorously defending me without asking me to explain. Years later, when there was an advertising campaign to question my experience and right to condemn a Broadway version of *Advise and Consent*, Orvil Dryfoos, then publisher of *The Times*, took the trouble to see the play and to reassure me that he agreed with my judgment.

One day I received a note from Arthur Hays Sulzberger—the *Times* publisher from 1935 to 1961—enclosing a letter to him from Alfred Knopf which said, "Dear Arthur, would you please get your music critic to do something about the ventilation in Carnegie Hall, where I tend to fall asleep?"

"What do you suggest I answer?" Mr. Sulzberger wrote me.

My reply was, "Mr. Knopf, as we all know, is a famous gourmet, and no doubt drinks fine wine with his dinner. I do not, and I have no quarrel with Carnegie Hall's ventilation, nor do I fall asleep."

Mr. Sulzberger sent my note to Mr. Knopf, who replied indignantly, "Your critic is an impertinent pup."

Mr. Sulzberger sent it along to me without comment. I hope he got a chuckle out of it.

Arthur Hays Sulzberger, 1948.

Mr. Sulzberger had an apartment of his own in the building where *The Times* was edited and printed, and he was in the habit of turning on WQXR each morning when he bathed and shaved. Repeatedly he found fault with the people at WQXR and their choice of morning music. Several of them came to me and brought a listing of all the music that had been on the station for a number of mornings.

"Would you please analyze it and give us your estimate."

They made no secret about the fact that Mr. Sulzberger had complained about "too much Mozart."

I complied with a memorandum suggesting that the programming was rather good, and my only criticism was that there was not enough Mozart. They evidently sent my memorandum to Mr. Sulzberger, who clearly remembered months later when I was in his office for a kind of informal investiture upon my appointment as chief music critic in succession to the late Olin Downes. With a tolerant, friendly smile Mr. Sulzberger asked, "Do you still like Mozart?"

My answer was, "More than ever."

Mr. Sulzberger shrugged as if to say this would be forgiven and forgotten.

He was good, indeed admirably considerate, at sharing with me the reactions he received in the mail to my reviews and commentaries. Once he sent me a manila folder full of letters complaining that I was paying too much attention to performers of dubious worth. I had written seriously about Johnny Ray and Elvis Presley and not so seriously about Liberace. I had written for *The Times Magazine* about Louis Armstrong and Duke Ellington as well as the goings on at Eddie Condon's raffish watering hole in the Village. Lester Markel, the exigent Sunday editor, a man of admirable, ferocious curiosity, as all good editors and journalists should be, tended to fall into repeated patterns when ordering articles. When he felt an urge for a piece on jazz, he asked me to do Benny Goodman. I liked Benny but was tired of writing about him. I told Markel how I felt. I should have mentioned the evening I had dinner at the home of John Hammond, great connoisseur of important newcomers and undeservedly neglected oldtimers. John's brother-in-law, Benny, marched in, cuddling a bagpipe. He was wearing a happy, mischievous grin, the kind he wore when he was perpetrating some musical impudence on the clarinet.

Markel and I compromised on the jazz figures I mentioned. I enjoyed writing about Eddie Condon, a free spirit. I attended some lively evenings of impro-

Lester Markel, Sunday editor of *The Times*, at right with arm outstretched, in the 1940s. Taubman is at left, and Seymour Peck, Markel's assistant, in the background.

Benny Goodman at Carnegie Hall, 1976.

visations at his place. When he heard that the piece was in print he asked for an early copy. I invited him to come to my office. While he was there, my phone rang. Eddie grabbed it and barked into it, "Eddie Condon's, NO reservations tonight!"

I was delighted to visit Armstrong. As we sat and chatted in his office in his home in Queens, a small, friendly white mongrel bounced around. Louis wore a towel around his head and looked like a turbaned pasha. Suddenly a malodorous stench filled the room. Louis swore at his pet, jumped up and seized a nearby atomizer for emergencies and began spraying the room. He wrote me a long letter of apology. After the piece appeared he wrote frequently, always beginning "Dear Pops."

The review that most irritated many correspondents was of a concert by Edith Piaf at Carnegie Hall. It was denounced as sacrilege. True, she was not a refined singer of *Lieder* or classic arias. In a rough, vulgar voice she sang of suffering and unrequited love, a character out of Colette. The play *Piaf,* by Pam Gems, which came to Broadway, was full of compassion. Jane Lapotaire in the title role got it right.

Edith Piaf performing in New York in 1950.

A high point of my years at *The Times*—at least from the point of view of the management—was the day *The New Yorker* printed a cartoon with my name. When the cartoon appeared, Turner Catledge, the executive editor, called me into his office to show it proudly. Evidently in his mind it was tantamount to a seal of approval. Indeed, a few weeks later there was a substantial increase in my salary.

"Howard Taubman isn't going to like it."

2

My Friend Bill Chase

M Y FRIEND Bill Chase was easy to know, yet diffident about revealing
himself. He gave of himself freely and generously, yet withheld much.
My last message from him, on the usual penny postcard, was postmarked
July 5, 1948. It read:

> You and Nora were both so kind as to write about coming up for a look at your
> old teammate. I owe you humble apologies for a foolish silence till now. You'll
> laugh at it, but I dreaded to be looked over by best friends who 'knew me when' I
> was fit for work, or even play. My remaining cottages were reserved for Lucy, who
> just now releases them. The Taubman hilltop has its lights and water on but I can't
> renew its youth or my own. Come if you are ever free, and please forgive my tardi-
> ness. This broken-down typing tells you I'm the same.—WBC

I didn't go, though I could have. I had not been to his farm in Whitefield,
New Hampshire, for more than five years, what with war service abroad, a busy
return to my duties as music editor of *The New York Times* and a sense, hinted
in the penny postcards, that he was reluctant, because physically incapable, to
resume the old close contact. I had heard that he had had grave eye trouble for
more than a year and no longer welcomed visitors with his quiet, unparalleled
openness. I didn't go—and on August 25, 1948, he died.

I can still see him—thin, bony, crooked-shouldered, hawknosed, spectacled,
wearing a jacket and a tie except on extremely hot days, often with a fedora on
his head—trundling his red wheelbarrow up the hilly country road. It would
be full of books and other treasures, which he moved constantly from cottage

to cottage. These transfers occurred when the occupants—a niece, nephews, cousins—were not there. The only house from which little was taken but to which choice additions were constantly made was Ellen's Cottage, in which guests were never invited to stay. It was being preserved with loving attention for the time that Ellen would visit, or perhaps live there.

Ellen was his daughter. I never met her. Almost fifty years after being taken on a guided tour of Ellen's Cottage, I heard from her. I never learned about her mother except that in 1907, according to the obituary article in *The Times* in August, 1948, William Bunton Chase and Elizabeth Smith of Brooklyn became husband and wife. From relatives I discovered that they parted in 1920.

We began to work together in September, 1930, when I was persuaded, nay, ordered, by Frederick T. Birchall, feisty acting managing editor of *The Times*, to move into the Music Department—"temporarily," he boomed, "for two years, laddie," and I remained for thirty. I knew early on that Bill rented a room in a West Side apartment. His first and only mention of a wife—whether he

Frederick T. Birchall of *The Times, c.* 1929.

William B. Chase, July 25, 1872–August 25, 1948.

was separated or divorced, I never found out—came as we strolled up Broadway one late afternoon and paused in front of a shop window filled with the trappings an American Indian might wear for a festive dance—headdress, fringed shirt and chaps, ornate moccasins. He studied the display with a bemused expression, and I wondered why it held him.

"Now you can see," he said, "why my marriage broke up." I could not see. "I was walking along this street years ago," he continued, "and I saw this young Indian in full regalia, staring into a window like this. I stopped and said a few words. We chatted. He was a pleasant fellow, most agreeable. Without any warning to my wife, I brought him home for dinner."

When I made my first official appearance in the Music Department, stashed away in a remote corner of the News Department floor, there was Bill to greet me.

The Music Department occupied a large, open room and was used as an overflow area to accommodate homeless staff members. Hanson Baldwin, the military correspondent, had his desk in a corner. So did John Martin, the dance critic. Harry T. Smith, the paper's linguist, was another occupant. Harry was talkative and liked to comment on whatever was being discussed. A former Socialist, he frequently irritated the conservative Hanson. We weren't a happy, well-met group, but we managed to remain polite and friendly. Harry did translations from foreign publications and commented on what he was translating, much to the annoyance of those who were trying to write. Olin Downes, the senior music critic, was off in a private office, his entrances and exits then and thereafter generally unpredictable.

Olin Downes, music critic at *The Times,* 1941.

When the newsroom was expanded by acquiring some space in the Paramount Building, a bank of offices was set up for the critics—drama, Brooks Atkinson; films, Mordaunt Hall (Bosley Crowther's predecessor); and music, Olin Downes.

Rachel McDowell, a fussy busybody who was religious editor, approached Mr. Birchall to request a private office of her own. It was said he turned her down with these words: "Downes is paid to criticize music, Atkinson, theater, Hall, movies. If I ever catch you criticizing religion, you won't worry about an office of any kind."

Benjamin Grosbayne, the other assistant critic, had his nose buried in foreign journals. By this time Bill Chase, with *Times* approval, worked about half a year, spending all summer and part of spring and autumn in New Hampshire, but he had come down a bit earlier than usual to guide and indoctrinate the young newcomer. Bill had started on *The Sun* in 1896 after his graduation from Amherst and had come to *The Times* as the number two man, first assistant critic, in the Music Department in 1916. In effect, but not officially, he was music editor.

There was a vast assortment of announcements, news releases, pleas for space and demands for attention to be examined and processed if newsworthy. They were piled in great heaps on my desk. Obviously they and their kind were to be one of my responsibilities. I was at sea and would have drowned, were it not for Bill. He had other things to do, leads to follow, people to see, but he sat beside me as we went through the fearsome accretion, patiently explaining, commenting, praising and warning. He made a point of being on hand at my arrival time for the next few weeks. Finally, in the arrogance of my twenty-three years, I assured him that I could manage the assignment on my own.

That day, as I riffled through the sheaves of papers, I made quick decisions with the authority of one in complete control. At one side I put material that might be useful, at the other important items. A vast amount I discarded. My wastebasket was full of debris. Now, after a short trip to the water cooler, I was ready to write. I glanced at the important pile. The announcement—I forget whose and what—that would lead the next day's news about music was missing. I carefully examined every item in the two piles on my desk. Not these. I did not remember putting anything away in a desk drawer but went through every drawer with increasing haste and anxiety. I fished in wastebaskets and trash cans. In my frantic search, I hardly noticed that Bill Chase, sitting in his habitual position, like a stork with one leg tucked under, had stopped tapping away at his typewriter and was watching my erratic behavior.

"Would you mind telling me," he said mildly, "what you're looking for?"

Feeling foolish and troubled, I grumbled, "Never mind, I'll find it."

He nodded amiably. "I'm sure you will, but please tell me what it is."

I finally did.

"Oh," he said, and drew several sheets of paper from a drawer. "Would this be it?" It was.

I flushed. "Where did you get it?"

He smiled gently. "In the wastebasket where you dropped it—accidentally, I'm sure." He returned to his typing and never mentioned the incident again.

He rarely explained or gave advance notice of his intentions but managed to introduce me to hosts of men and women in the business. It was all so casual. We were passing by, so we stopped in to say hello. At the Metropolitan Opera— the old brick pile on Broadway between Thirty-ninth and Fortieth Streets where the sightlines were in part abominable and the acoustics everywhere admirable—preparations for the new season were under way. I was led into the Press Office and exposed to William J. Guard, its principal guardian. The two Williams—Guard and Chase—bore a curious resemblance, a kind of Old World elegance of manner, though Guard carried himself like a *boulevardier* and talked like a *flâneur* while Chase was reserved and understated like a good New Englander. With Guard and Chase as my cicerones, in the following weeks I met everyone who mattered—Giulio Gatti-Casazza, the sphinx-like general manager; Edward Ziegler, his right-hand man; Earle R. Lewis, in charge of the box office. Once the season was under way, Bill Chase saw to it that I met even the ushers. There was no one, as I learned in the ensuing years, who could not be helpful to a journalist in need of a bit of vital information.

In fact, one of Bill Chase's page one *New York Times* stories—reporting a foul-up at the Met that made a huge difference to Lawrence Tibbett—owed its existence to a pal among the Met ushers who told Bill all about it. Tibbett, a young American baritone, had been cast as Ford in a revival of Verdi's *Falstaff,* in which the greatly admired veteran Antonio Scotti played the title role. Although Tibbett was a member of the Met, he had had little opportunity to show what he could do. Now, given a chance, he sang Ford with great intensity and impressed the audience. At curtain-call time, Scotti was sent out repeatedly alone. The audience wanted a solo call for the American and would not settle

Giulio Gatti-Casazza (at right), chief of the Metropolitan Opera, with two of his conductors *c.* 1912. Alfred Hertz (at left) led the German wing. Photograph by Mishkin.

down until Tibbett appeared alone. And how it thundered its approval! The incident got national attention, and thereafter Tibbett was a star, a role he filled with style and grace.

In my casual strolls with Bill Chase, we visited Carnegie Hall, Town Hall, the offices of concert managers, and I was introduced to many more Chase friends, all of whom could be—and many were—valuable news sources. But it was not a series of rounds designed to enhance work. Most of it, indeed, was meant to be fun. We went often to the small, comfortable apartment of a colleague, Grena Bennett, the music critic of the *New York Journal*, and immediately I had a new, warm friend. He took me to a party at the Central Park West apartment of Giovanni Martinelli, and I met a raft of opera singers chatting away in Italian. One midnight months after we had finished writing our reviews, he even induced me to go with him to see Guard. I knew that Guard was ailing; I did not realize that I was being invited to the death watch. We stood with other friends and listened to the death rattle. Later that night Guard died. I am sure that it meant a great deal to Bill Chase to be there in the final hours of a dear friend. I have to confess that this was one time when the opportunity to share a profound experience with Bill left me feeling shaken.

He took me to lunch frequently at the Dutch Treat Club, and eventually I became a member. He took me occasionally to the Players Club for lunch or dinner. From his reserved, soft-spoken manner you would have inferred that he would avoid formalized gatherings. But he was in the best sense of Samuel Johnson's word naturally clubbable. He relished the gossip and banter of cultivated people. He left *The Times* in the spring of 1935. When I heard that during his retirement he became a member of the Rotary Club in Whitefield, I thought the poor soul was lonesome up in the north country during the hard winters when his farm was not overrun with relatives and other guests. After all, his fellow members were nothing like the sophisticates in his New York clubs. And they weren't. On one of my short, off-season trips to Whitefield, he talked me into speaking at his favorite Rotary. There were about a dozen men seated around a large round table, and I babbled about life at *The Times* and the music world for about twenty minutes, boring them even more than myself. But Bill sat there clearly content: he had exposed me to a new set of friends.

With a subtle mentor like Bill Chase I began to make myself increasingly felt at *The Times*. I was producing more and more interesting stories about the world of music, and my reviews were winning approval from my superiors. In those days by-lines were rare indeed at *The Times*. The chief Washington correspondent, a star reporter or two and the chief drama, music, film and art critics were about the only writers identified in print. It was only after great pressure from Downes that the management consented to let his assistants sign their reviews with their initials. It was wise of Downes to push through this tiny reform. After all, readers as well as performers who felt themselves victimized by an unfavorable notice might assume that Downes himself had been the perpetrator.

Then came the night of a very special occasion at the Met, which, at the bottom of the Depression, was in desperate straits financially: a grand gala with all the major artists taking part for an evening that promised to be musically and socially grandiose. And musically it was truly gala. I was assigned to cover the event, and to convey the spirit of the occasion required all the skill and speed I could muster. I remember that Bill was in the office as I wrote and asked permission, as if he needed to, to read my copy before it was moved for editing. After a while he strolled off to the city room. I was much too preoccupied to notice his going and coming. Only later did I learn that he had barged in on the night managing editor and succeeded in convincing him to ignore precedent. That was how I got my first by-line.

The Depression hit us all. When I became a member of the *Times* staff in 1929, my salary was $40 a week. In view of what apple sellers and people on work relief were getting, I could not complain. I had a job and my $40 went far. *The Times*, of course, was hurting too, and presently we all took a 10 percent cut. So there I was, belaureled with my first by-line, well thought of for the quality of my work and griping to Bill Chase, among others, about my monetary regression. He sympathized, but what could be done about it?

Eventually he decided to try. One day he opened an in-house envelope, chuckled somewhat grimly and handed it to me to read. It was a memo to Birchall, arguing with some heat that he, Chase, was contributing less and less. Therefore he, Chase, with due consideration herewith proposed that X dollars should be deducted from his, Chase's, salary, and added to Taubman's. It was a closely reasoned, eloquent document, which moved the acting managing editor to equal eloquence. Across the entire page in huge letters he had scrawled one word—BALLS.

My first visit to Chase Farm took place in the early thirties. I had undertaken to help Gatti-Casazza assemble some of his memories of opera for a series to be run in the *Saturday Evening Post*. Even though he presided over one of the most prominent and publicized institutions and companies in America, Gatti was a singularly private man. He gave no interviews and held one press conference a year, when he announced his plans for the following season. In that unique meeting he had his secretary hand out a comprehensive written statement, contenting himself with only a spoken word or two, and that in Italian. He had been loath to accept the invitation from the *Saturday Evening Post* but agreed in the hope that by reminiscing and perhaps speaking out he might help the Met in its gravest crisis.

As I recounted in a preface I wrote for the book *Memories of the Opera*, published some years after Gatti's death, we held sessions morning after hot

Gatti-Casazza, 1934.

Gatti-Casazza, behind his desk, saying farewell to the press upon leaving the Met in 1935.
Bill Chase is third from left in the back row and Taubman at right in the front row. The
woman between Gatti and Taubman is Grena Bennett, music critic of the *New York
Journal.* Photograph by Carlo Edwards.

morning in his suite at the Savoy Plaza, with the windows tightly closed to avoid drafts.

Our common language was French, mine a lot worse than his, and there was a stenographer to record our conversations. With these transcripts in hand, I had to search the archives to dig up facts that could flesh out some of the sketchy memories.

The place to dig, it turned out, was the spacious attic in the largest of the Chase Farm houses, known as the Homestead. Here were Met programs going back to 1896, when Bill had begun his career as a reporter and critic. Here were stacks of old newspapers, magazines, books, all dealing with the world in which Bill had worked for decades.

I spent a couple of weeks that summer poring over these incunabula, and I came away not only with invaluable Met data but with a beginning sense of the interdependence of Chase and farm as well as their impact on so many people.

The farm had been left to Bill by his parents because, as he explained with a straight face, he had been the only son of four to leave home. The family, an old New England one, had had its roots in New Hampshire for a long time and retained them though Bill's father had set up a successful manufacturing business in Syracuse. Bill treated the four hundred acres he had inherited as a trust to be preserved and enhanced for all the Chases and collateral lines. And when he took me on a tour of the premises, I found out about Ellen's Cottage; the Brown House, which had belonged to a neighbor and which the family had purchased to serve as a base for overflow guests; the cottages of Lucy, a niece, Aurin and Austin, nephews, and Philip, a cousin. These were also used for overflow guests when their designated occupants were not in residence. Neither Bill nor I had any inkling that in 1938 mine would become the fourteenth cottage.

There were, of course, barns. The biggest became the Chase Barn Playhouse. That happened because Bill's affection for everything connected with the Metropolitan Opera and his eager reaching out to young, attractive people came together in his mind as a natural match. It must have been the next summer when I was again in Whitefield, this time on vacation, that Bill suggested we drive down to Franconia Notch, where a group of young men and women led by Beatrice Beach (later MacLeod) and Carl Allensworth, of the Yale Drama School, had launched a theater season in a hotel. They called themselves the Forty-niners because their admission charge was 49 cents. Bill took an imme-

The Chase Barn Playhouse.

diate liking to these fresh, young performers and asked them whether they would come to Whitefield next summer if he converted his barn into a theater. He knew that the Met was in the process of replacing its seats, which had been in place for fifty years, and that he could buy some of the old ones still in good condition. Buy them he did, and for years the Chase Barn Playhouse housed a lively young acting company and on some Sunday afternoons served as a concert hall.

To pay for the transformation of the barn Bill depended on his own resources. I never had any idea what they amounted to, but I am certain that he hardly ever spent anything on himself. He was rather proud of the fact that he had not needed to pay for clothes after he acquired the late Bill Guard's wardrobe. After all, they were almost the same size and build, and a bit of tinkering here and there provided him with style and quality he would never have bought for himself.

I have a penny postcard dated January, 1937, that offers a clue to Bill's budgetary attitude: "In another fortnight I'll be out of last year's debts. It's been

Bill Chase at the farm.

plain living and high thinking. Only lately I broke loose and got a dozen books, naughty and other, from New York."

He installed one of the daughters of Joe Grey, his farmer-neighbor, and her new husband in the Brown House because he relished the idea of a working farm on the old place. He wanted to make sure that Wally and Seraphine could live and work with some sense of independence, and he knew that Joe was old-fashioned enough to demand that he must be the unquestioned boss. Another postcard from Whitefield reported, "I'm tied to the farm now to save up for my cows, horses and perhaps some land, all to be bought to carry on the farm after April 1. The date, you'll agree, is appropriate for such a fool as I. Your old team-mate, WBC."

Was it nostalgia for the time when there had been a working farm on the premises that led him to install one? Or was it the need to have warm, sympathetic friends close by in the months when the place was not swarming with relatives and friends? I know how he valued company during the long, cold winter nights. I happened to pay him a brief visit early one April and was unlucky to hit a fierce cold spell, when the temperature during the night dropped to 30 below zero Fahrenheit. Before retiring in a congealed bedroom where I shivered in all my clothes under five or six blankets, I stopped to say goodnight to him in the kitchen, where he sat beside a woodburning stove. Under a single bare light bulb he was reading a book. I remonstrated that he was ruining his eyes. I remember a message on another postcard sent in midwinter: "I'm burning all but the house to keep warm." He was saving money again—out of his own hide. But why, as I looked closely, did he have a piece of cheese on his knee? Simple to explain. There was a friendly mouse who appeared every night, and when it climbed to his knee to snatch the prize it provided a nice, companionable interlude.

Bill's gentle ways extended to his professional life. Because he hated to be severe with any musician, he always tried to find something kind to say. Assigned to review the debut of the British two-piano team Bartlett and Robertson, he wrote a short piece before he saw and heard them. Since they were named Ethel Bartlett and Rae Robertson he assumed they were "charming Englishwomen." Unfortunately, Rae was a man.

If Bill had had his way I would have spent every summer vacation on the farm. Apart from wishing to see the country and the world—and my wife, Nora, and I did drive across the United States one year and make a grand tour of Europe another—I found the summers on the farm a little too hectic. Staying in the Homestead meant being a member of a house party of as many as twenty. The guests could range from a retired pugilist to Serge Koussevitzky. There was Aunt Nelly, widow of an older brother of Bill's, who fancied herself, I'm sure, a few cuts above most of the guests. She had her own chauffeur, who came with her from a town near Syracuse and who took her for a drive every afternoon through the lovely New Hampshire countryside. Never seen in informal country clothes, she always looked ready for a garden party at Buckingham Palace. "Does she ever wear anything but high heels?" Bill would mutter, and then he would scrounge to find another guest willing and suitable to accompany her on the afternoon drive.

There was Harry Rowe Shelley, well along in years, a composer who had written hymns still sung in some churches and who had been the private organist in homes like those of J. P. Morgan and George Blumenthal. When I visit the Metropolitan Museum in New York these days and enter the great paneled hall that Blumenthal had imported piece by piece from Europe and installed in his

Fifth Avenue home complete with a magnificent pipe organ, I recall the time when Shelley escorted me to that home—the Blumenthals were away—led me up to the organ loft, sat me down on the bench beside him and regaled me with Bach. At Whitefield Shelley was a delightful raconteur and an exigent guest. There was scarcely an evening—no matter what the temperature—when Harry did not request a fire in the fireplace.

A commanding, motherly woman named Margaret Connolly, who had been close to Lavina Bunton Chase, Bill's mother, presided over the mixed grill of guests. She was like a master sergeant who assigned tasks to various guests and requested a few dollars from some of us to help defray the costs of food. I did the dishes after several dinners, and it was not unlike K.P. I drew during basic training in the Army.

A lot of this was fun, but Nora and I longed for a little privacy. Bill understood without being told. He made it a point to urge us to come in the off-season. A postcard dated February, 1938, suggests, "Any time in April that your vacation permits, I want you to know that the Whitefield house is waiting for you. The furnace going, beds made and kitchen working. I am the crew and the cook." Another card dated March, 1938, says, "Take time even if you're late; you'll find the shed door unlatched, rooms swept lately and mostly empty. Maybe you can tell if a flock of visiting birds are kinglets or just plain sparrows."

That April we did come up for a week, and it turned out to be a happy one. Bill's surviving brother, known at times when he needed a little guying as Colonel Aurin, was there. He had fathered two impressive families—a daughter and three sons by his first wife and three daughters by his current one—and had retired from the family business. He was a man of many gifts, an amateur musician as well as a better-than-amateur carpenter. The 1938 hurricane had toppled some fine old trees in the Chase Farm woods, and as we sat and mused after dinner in front of a fire, Bill remarked to Colonel Aurin, "We have enough good wood lying about to build another cottage, haven't we?"

Colonel Aurin nodded assent.

Bill turned to me. "Would you come for the summer if we built you a house?"

I laughed.

Bill protested, "I'm serious. Aurin thinks it can be done and he's willing to do it."

I said I was touched by the offer and would let him know.

In May Bill informed us that the fallen trees had been milled into boards and that he was going ahead with plans to build the simplest of cabins. I replied that if it were available we would be willing to use it all of July and August. Nora would spend both months there, and I would come for my vacation and long weekends whenever possible.

Now the penny postcards arrived frequently and with some urgency. The one dated May 27: "Your July–August plans revolutionize the simple cabin. Tomorrow a small complete bath goes into the N.W. corner, kitchenette close adjoining, breakfast alcove by W. center window. Telesphore Pouquet [Bill's French-Canadian handyman] and a helper are painting now, not so gaudy, as the neatness of the finished building led us to relapse into old-fashioned white walls and green roof. Mountain views from your E. living & bedroom windows are very fine these days. Don't worry, I'm not counting my chickens before they hatch, but just 'getting ready.'"

The next postcard, dated June 2, said, "Your bath in cabin's N.W. corner and pipe to Bell barn tank's electric pump are going into final shape today. Septic tank and drain already in. Only the Grand Coulee or Boulder Dam could be more exciting at the moment. The stone wall foundations are complete around cabin and porch. Lumber for bath & bedroom partitions just arriving in a sea-going truck that is plunging over the furrow for water pipe just plowed by Wally from house to road. By this weekend it should be 'like home' on your knoll."

On another postcard a day or two later, Bill reported the reaction of Harry Rowe Shelley. "Millionaire Harry has written a most appreciative letter about the 'log cabin' he hears I'm building, and mildly suggesting a fireplace built of 'boulders and field stone.' I think he's seen too many of the great hunting lodges out West and fancies our little shack is like a Yellowstone hotel."

The first summer in the "simple cabin" was idyllic. From our knoll looking to the west and south we had glorious views of the Presidential range. The members of the Chase Barn company, which offered a fresh production each week even as it was rehearsing another play for the following week, would walk by our knoll from their theater to the Grey farmhouse, where they took their meals. They would pause to say hello and occasionally, if they were not terribly pressed for time, would loll on the grass while I played some records on a portable phonograph. I had brought a small collection—some Mozart, Beethoven and by chance, Sibelius's Second Symphony, which appealed particularly for its proclamatory theatricality. Bill heard of these spontaneously arranged concerts *al fresco*, was delighted that we had become in a way parts of his playhouse community and appeared one afternoon, sans wheelbarrow, to see and hear. He stayed briefly, pleased with what he saw but ready to leave without hearing very much. After forty years of professional concert- and opera-going, he had too many other things to do.

At the end of the summer I insisted on paying rent for the use of the "sim-

The Taubman cottage at Chase Farm.

Taubman in New Hampshire in the 1930s.

ple cabin," and we argued before he would accept what I regarded as a reasonable sum. I had arranged to have some bills forwarded to me in New York, and
one day there was a postcard with a strict injunction: "Please note—you're to
pay no more bills unless you're sure what they're for."

In the summer of 1939 Nora and I were in Europe and Bill rented the cottage on the knoll to someone else. We stayed in it again in 1940 and in 1942,
when we brought with us for Bill's approval an eight-month-old named William
Chase Taubman. I insisted on paying for additions to the house, including a
lovely sleeping porch. As usual Bill kept producing favorite pieces of furniture
taken from other houses but not Ellen's. It reached a point where we dared not
admire any object in any house but Ellen's. Within hours it would be in our
cottage. We admired particularly a Victorian sofa, feeling sure it was too large
to be accommodated in the cottage. It arrived that fall in our New York apartment.

We talked about Ellen's Cottage but not about Ellen. I heard that in his last

Nora with William Chase Taubman at three-and-a-half months.

years, Bill spent a severe winter in Ellen's Cottage. In the early 1980s there came a letter from a Mrs. Charles Adams of Greensboro, North Carolina. She and her husband had been to Amherst College for a fiftieth class reunion and had made the acquaintance of Professor William Chase Taubman, and she was writing to tell us how pleased she was to meet the man named after her father. Direct contact with Ellen at last! She wrote about her children and proposed that we all meet at Amherst at the following commencement. That meeting did not take place because someone in the family was ill. There was something I wanted to ask but preferred not to put into writing. Now I doubt that I shall ever know, if indeed she knew.

During one of the summers when we were staying in "our cottage" on the knoll, we were sitting on the porch when Bill appeared. We offered him a chair, but he seated himself on the steps. The conversation was small talk, and there were moments of silence. Clearly he had something on his mind. Then he

William Chase Taubman in 1980 with his wife, Jane, and their children, Alex and Phoebe.

pulled an envelope out of the breast pocket of his jacket and handed it to me. I looked at it and at him. He indicated he wanted me to examine the enclosure. I drew it out. It was an invitation to a wedding—Ellen's. I started to say congratulations, then looked closely at the invitation. The wedding had taken place the previous week. I did not have the heart to ask whether the arrival was the fault of the post office or deliberate. He reached out for the envelope and the invitation and without a word got up and headed slowly down the road.

Bill Chase in his last years.

3

Casals

L ONG BEFORE I met or heard Pablo Casals in person, one of the profound achievements in music-making was, for me, his playing of Bach's sonatas for unaccompanied cello, to be savored again and again on the old 78-r.p.m. records. Though he chose not to tour in the United States for some years before the start of the Spanish Civil War in 1936—there were legal complications stemming from his separation from his wife, Susan Metcalfe, an American singer, whom he married in 1914—his renown grew rather than diminished. Reports of his playing abroad, alone or as a member of a trio with Alfred Cortot, the pianist, and Jacques Thibaud, the violinist, were always laudatory, and even when gifted cellists like Gregor Piatigorsky and Emanuel Feuermann appeared on the musical scene, Casals was regarded as the greatest of them all.

Then came the Spanish Civil War, and Casals' commitment to the defenders of the republic defined him as a man of the highest integrity as well as a great musician. To those of us who anguished during those bitter battles in Spain, who feared that that war was the curtain-raiser to World War II, who fumed at the farce of non-intervention conceived and tolerated by such democratic leaders as Léon Blum of France and Franklin D. Roosevelt of the United States, who read helplessly of the Italian troops and Nazi bombers supporting Franco, Casals was a man to admire unreservedly, for he remained in Spain and did what he could to sustain the morale of his people in their struggle against the Fascists.

With the final defeat of the Loyalist forces early in 1939, the last remnants of the government of the republic, its armed forces and its more ardent and vul-

Pablo Casals in the 1920s.

nerable supporters fled from Spain. Among them was Casals. In the spring I read that he had agreed to play at the festival in Lucerne that summer. He needed to work, for he had left nearly everything in his beloved Catalonia. Moreover, the Swiss festival had become a magnet to musicians who would have no traffic with any Nazi-dominated country. Toscanini, fierce antagonist of Fascism and Nazism, parted with the Salzburg Festival after Hitler forced Anschluss on Austria in 1938, as he had parted with Bayreuth in 1933, and engaged to conduct in Lucerne.

I made up my mind to see Casals, if possible, in Lucerne. In my plans for a European trip in the summer of 1939, Switzerland was not on the itinerary, but I would rearrange my schedule if I could count on meeting Casals. I sent a request through a mutual acquaintance and got word that I did not need an appointment; all I had to do was to call him when I got to Lucerne.

I arrived by train one afternoon, phoned, and several hours later I knocked on the door of his room in a hotel overlooking the Lake of the Four Forest Cantons. The hotel dripped elegance, but not Casals' room. His pipes covered the dressing table, newspapers were strewn on the bed. A bare table, with correspondence neatly piled on one side, stood in the center of the room near a low-hanging, bare electric light. A chair was directly under the light, and leaning against it the cello. Casals had stopped practicing when he got up to admit me.

A small, round, baldheaded man in a gray cardigan and battered carpet slippers peered at me through thick glasses and ushered me into the room. He insisted that I make myself comfortable in an easy chair while he moved the cello to the bed and seated himself on the chair under the light. He lit a pipe and waited for my questions.

He had offers of engagements to play and conduct, he said, but he did not intend to go to countries that recognized Franco. However, he would play in France, which had granted asylum to him and hundreds of his fellow refugees from Spain. He talked of organizing a big event to benefit French charities, but in less than two months France was at war with Germany, and that plan came to nothing.

When the subject moved from music to the doggedness of the republic's defenders, the man was transformed. His eyes took on intensity, his figure seemed to grow bulkier. Anger and sorrow mingled in him as he discussed the tragedy of Spain and of Europe. He knew that the rout of democracy in Spain would lead to war in Europe. He lamented for what was to come as he grieved over the suffering of his Spanish friends—those who had died and those who had reached haven on the French side of the Pyrenees. At that moment he was distributing nearly everything he earned to refugees in desperate want. The letters on the table were mostly requests for help. He asked no questions but sent married men 400 francs, a couple with a child 500, a single man 200. As he read a line or two from a letter picked up at random and described the acts of his brave Catalans in the last weeks of the fighting, tears rolled down his cheeks.

I do not know how Casals managed to cling to his belief in the possibilities of decency and humanity during the years of World War II. I can only imagine that he drew solace from music, which now was entirely a private matter, and from the fellow Catalans who were too old to join the fighting against Hitler.

I did not see Casals again until the summer of 1951. His friends, led by Alexander Schneider, had persuaded him that sitting and brooding in Prades on the French side of the Pyrenees was a contribution neither to music nor to his fellow Spaniards in exile and that he must agree to a modest festival with himself a participant. Such a festival took place in 1950 in Prades, and the reports I heard from Schneider and other musicians were so glowing that I resolved to be at the next Casals Festival.

The next took place in Perpignan, where it was moved from Prades to accommodate more listeners and allow for a greater modicum of comfort than was possible in the limited facilities of a small town like Prades. The concerts devoted to Bach, Mozart and Beethoven were played in the courtyard of the Palace of the Kings of Majorca, with the final one in Perpignan's cathedral. It was a setting to cause one to forget for a while the horrors of almost two decades: a courtyard in a medieval fortress begun by the kings of Catalonia when they reigned over a large kingdom. The citadel, surrounded by three tiers of stone walls, stood high over Perpignan and commanded a dramatic view of the Pyrenees and the Mediterranean in the distance. A stage had been erected under an arcaded balcony, and floodlights played on the musicians and the stone battlements while the audience sat on tiers of benches as in a sports stadium.

I shall never forget the opening of the first concert. The musicians were assembled on the stage, their instruments, except the bulky ones, in their laps. Out walked a small, round figure carrying a cello and bow. It was Casals, now in his seventy-fifth year and looking slower but no frailer than when I had last seen him.

The audience and the musicians rose as one to salute this small, baldheaded

figure. Then he sat down and played Bach's Suite No. 1 in G for unaccompanied cello. What I wrote in *The Times* then bears repeating:

> His tone was not big, but what miracles of shading he managed to convey. It was
> as if he had searched into the heart of Bach and had brought forth his distillation
> of the essential truth of the music. This performance alone would have justified
> the trip to Perpignan.

Then he conducted, sitting down: Mozart's Piano Concerto in E-flat (K.
271), with Myra Hess; Mozart's Sinfonia concertante in E-flat major for violin
and viola (K. 364), with Isaac Stern and William Primrose, violist. Later in the
festival there were trios, sonatas, solos, concertos, arias—playing and singing to
cherish. Jennie Tourel's singing of Bach's "Erbarme Dich, Mein Gott" with
Schneider's violin obbligato; Casals and Serkin in Bach's Sonatas Nos. 1 and 2
for cello and piano; Mieczyslaw Horszowski, Eugene Istomin, Aksel Schiötz,
Clara Haskil, Marcel Tabuteau, John Wummer—these musicians and their performances joined in an occasion unique among festivals. "The animating emotion," I wrote at the time, "is love—love for music, love for Casals and love of
Casals for his musician and lay friends."

He worked untiringly, rehearsing and performing and recording. During
preparations for the ninth concert one morning, he suddenly felt faint. He
stopped, leaned forward and rested his head on the podium while his hands
clutched his knees. Members of the orchestra thought he had suffered a heart
attack. He was examined by a physician and taken to a nearby home to rest. He
slept for a few hours and awoke at 5 P.M. refreshed. Back he went to the Palace
of the Kings of Majorca to resume rehearsals and to conduct a concert that
lasted past midnight.

Remembering that day and observing some years later that after suffering a
heart attack in Puerto Rico at the age of eighty he resumed playing, conducting and teaching, one was not surprised to watch him carry on as a beloved elder
statesman of music until his death at ninety-seven. Listening to him play the
cello, a distinguished violinist whispered, "Did you note the four shades of color
he got in one bow?"

One day Myra Hess walked briskly into her hotel after a swim in the Mediterranean, and as we met, I said that she seemed to be bursting with vitality. It was
a grand swim, she said, and through it she kept thinking of all the piano concertos she would like to play with Casals.

"Was it a long swim?" I asked.

"Yes," she replied, "there were many concertos on my list."

To suggest the spirit of the festival, I can do no better than to reprint these paragraphs I wrote for *The Times* in July, 1951:

> To begin with, no one sits at Casals' feet. He does not hand down judgments from on high. He approaches music in a spirit of humility. Each composition, whether it is a piece in which he plays the cello or a work for orchestra which he is to conduct, is like a fresh adventure to him. He may know it as well as he remembers the landscape and people of his beloved Catalonia, but he does not take it for granted. Long before he began rehearsals he had examined it anew in his study, and the rehearsals and discussions with his colleagues amount to voyages of rediscovery.
>
> He rejoices in making music. There is a relaxed atmosphere at his rehearsals. His baton technique is hardly a technique. He conducts usually sitting down but when intent on a point rising and waving his arms, moving his eyes, head and body. He may or may not indicate the beat; he may shape a phrase here and there; throughout you feel that he is modeling a large conception.
>
> He takes a work like Mozart's "Eine Kleine Nachtmusik," which is a chestnut to most musicians and audiences, and breathes new life into it. He brings out the vitality and grace of its genius. It is clear that he loves it, and presently his fellow musicians re-evaluate it through his perception.
>
> Casals does not fret over technical falls from grace. A flawed note here or there does not seem to disturb him. So long as the attitude toward the work as a whole is consistent and honest, he is content. And when things go well he does not constrain his delight. He pounds his stick on the music stand; he stops to applaud; he throws kisses.

On Bastille Day there were no rehearsals or performances, and at Casals' invitation I drove to Prades to visit with him. His home was a small gatekeeper's lodge. He received me in a tiny living room with a round table at which he sat with a number of Catalonian exiles. Through a door one could see a bedroom, and on the bed lay his cello; earlier no doubt he had practiced.

He introduced his friends, among them a poet, a biographer and a former member of the Catalan Parliament. For years, he said proudly, his fellow exiles had been joining him on Sundays and holidays. Occasionally other Catalans would steal across the border to see him and bring him the news. Some who had passports to visit France were warned by the Spanish police that Casals was

an enemy of the state and must be avoided by loyal Spaniards. They came anyhow, he observed. Indeed, he had had feelers from Franco, promising everything he wished if he would return to Spain. He never did, though his remains
were interred there years after his death.

On Bastille Day the host and guests made a place for me at the table. The
talk naturally was of politics and Spain. I mentioned rumors that, like
Paderewski in Poland after World War I, Casals might be drafted to head Spain
if Franco should fall. He said that he would not agree to be president or premier in such an event but that he would not refuse to be head of a Catalan government. He speculated with remarkable prevision about what would happen
after Franco was gone. It was a miscalculation, he said firmly, that the only possible successor to Franco would be a Communist regime.

In 1957 I saw Casals once more, but this time under unhappy circumstances.
In that year Puerto Rico, where Casals was now living, undertook to launch a
festival as well as a conservatory in his honor and under his leadership. Some
weeks before the opening he had his heart attack. I had made plans to attend
part of the festival, but with the news of his illness it was suggested at *The Times*
that I need not go. I argued that Puerto Rico had invested a lot in this effort
and that it would be the right thing to attend, even if Casals could not appear.
Indeed, I wrote an article in advance urging support of the undertaking. At a
reception in the governor's palace I went through a receiving line headed by
Governor Luis Muñoz Marin and his wife, Doña Inez. When I spoke my name,
Doña Inez drew from her bodice a copy of my article, waved it proudly and
embraced me.

Casals? I was permitted a glimpse of him in his bedroom. He was being taken
care of by a lovely young woman, Martita, who had been his student and
became his wife. He recognized me, nodded to me, smiled faintly but was too
weak to talk.

Casals recovered, of course, and resumed his work at festivals in San Juan
and Prades. The next year he was well enough to come to New York and play
at the United Nations on the anniversary of its establishment. He had refused
to give concerts in the United States because the U.S. recognized Franco, but
because he believed so strongly in the U.N.'s mission, he made an exception.

I spent an hour or two with him and Martita at his New York hotel. He was
in great good humor; though fundamentally a serious man, he never lost his
appetite for laughter. With some prodding, he told the story of the time long

ago that the music-loving Queen Elisabeth of Belgium invited him to come to the palace for an evening of Beethoven trios. She played the violin, and a brilliant Conservatoire student was the pianist. They launched into a Beethoven trio, and the ensemble became ragged. The Queen, gracious lady though she was, was clearly not up to her partners. The young pianist, breathing hard, desperately whispered to the person turning pages for him, "Whom shall I follow, the Queen or the maestro?"

In New York in 1958 Casals found time to visit the Manhattan School of Music, where he was surrounded by students. He retained almost to the end his fondness and interest in young musicians. Before his heart attack he had many students; afterwards he could deal with only a few. But he went to places like Marlboro in Vermont, where he conducted and gave advice. In New York there was a young Japanese cellist who had decided to go wherever Casals went—France, Puerto Rico, the United States—to seize whatever free time could be found for lessons.

The measure of Casals' openness and warmth toward young musicians was underscored by a story told to me more than three decades ago by Russell B. Kingman, then himself a mature man of affairs. Years earlier, Kingman, as a young man, had been in Des Moines on business, and in the hotel dining room at breakfast he saw Casals. His heart, he was sure, skipped a beat. He went to the cellist's table and asked, "Are you Casals?" A nod. Stuttering, Kingman explained that he was an amateur cellist, had heard Casals whenever possible and would ask no more in this life if he could shake the master's hand.

Casals extended his. Kingman shook it and turned to go. Casals suggested a cup of coffee. Kingman mumbled something about imposing, but Casals waved apologies aside and called the waiter. After breakfast Casals asked, "Like to hear me practice?" Kingman gasped an affirmative reply. The two went up to Casals' room. The cellist took off his coat, peeled the cover off his cello and sat down as the visitor stood awkwardly and stared. "This is going to take three hours," Casals said. "Take your coat off, lie down." After the practice session Casals invited Kingman to join him for lunch. Then for a walk, then more practice, then dinner, then the concert, then supper. For Kingman, later a distinguished official of the United States Lawn Tennis Association, those were sixteen of the most exciting hours of his life.

Fritz Kreisler once declared that Casals was the best ever to draw a bow. That was generous of the violinist; it is enough to say that he was one of the best. He

Casals performing with the choir of the Manhattan School of Music in 1964. Photograph by Lee Romero.

was a thinking man's cellist. He experimented with technique. To cope with a cramp that affected the thumb on his bow hand when he played for too long a stretch, he invented a rubber thumb to ease the pressure; suddenly every cellist was using a rubber or wooden thumb. When he began to study Bach's unaccompanied cello works, he recalled, they were regarded as dry exercises, if not downright unplayable. He showed that they not only could be played but were enchanting pieces.

Because he remained steadfast in his commitment to democracy and humanism, he exercised a moral leadership he did not seek. After the war Cortot, his former music-making colleague, came to see him in Prades, hoping, as it were, for absolution after his services to Marshal Pétain's Vichy government. Casals would not shake his hand. Wilhelm Furtwängler, who remained in Nazi Germany to the end, tried to resume an old friendship, but Casals declined.

Casals had a reunion with Albert Schweitzer, another old friend, in Zurich when a number of cellists assembled for an "Homage to Casals." Casals urged Schweitzer to join him in a protest against the atom bomb. Schweitzer, Casals later told me, argued that the correct thing for the artist was not to protest but to create. Casals insisted that there were not many whose voices could be heard above the world's confused babble. Several years later, Casals said with satisfaction, Schweitzer did join a group protesting the further manufacture of nuclear weapons.

Though he would not return to Spain, Casals had good lines of communication to his native land. When he heard that the superior of the Montserrat monastery had been jailed by the Franco government for a political offense, he got in touch with a Spanish cardinal who as a small boy had been a member of a Montserrat choir that Casals had conducted, and through the cardinal sent a message to Pope Paul VI that led to the superior's release.

Aware that Casals was short of funds in his self-imposed exile in Prades, an American friend sent a young cellist to study with him and provided him with $500 to pay for lessons. The American's purpose was to enable Casals to earn money he would not otherwise accept; he hardly knew the young cellist he recommended to Casals. The young cellist became Casals' student, but Casals refused the money: he would not accept payment for obliging a friend.

In a life that spanned a century, there was an incalculable wealth of memorable images. For me these three are precious because they remind me of Casals' profound simplicity as a man and musician: walking alone on the beach beyond his house in Puerto Rico on a warm day as he held an open umbrella to keep the sun off his head, his face alive with appreciation of the scene's serenity; speaking about the composers who meant most to him and summing up, "Bach is all"; alone on the stage on the closing day of the Perpignan festival, as he played a valedictory, "The Song of the Birds," a plaintive Catalan folk song that seemed to convey all he felt about a brutalized Spain and his lost felicity.

4

A Room at the Inn?

THE PICTURE on the postcard was inviting. A squarish building of modest size flanked by palm trees with a charming dining space on a terrace, and in the distance nothing but white sand and the sparkling blue of the Mediterranean. A note scrawled by Alexander Schneider, identified only by the signature *Sasha*, said, "Two rooms reserved, milk definite." That clinched it. My wife and two sons, almost three and almost ten, could accompany me to the Casals Festival in Perpignan in June, 1951.

The card identified the building purporting to be a hotel as Le Tourbillon. My French was too limited to suggest what the name connoted; a look in a dictionary told me it meant "the whirlwind." What a fine, dramatic-sounding moniker for a place in which we expected to spend the three weeks of the festival. I felt grateful to Schneider, who as Pablo Casals' close friend had played a vital role in organizing the festival and who was determined to persuade a *New York Times* representative to attend.

It must be remembered that in 1951 the famous festivals drew a knowledgeable, moneyed elite. The widespread use of the jet airplane was still some years away, and the development of its jumbo offspring was even farther in the distance. The practice of arranging tours that guaranteed accommodations and tickets for performances was still in the offing. Rooms in good hotels at glamorous festival sites were limited, and one had to scramble, even if one was a *Times* critic intent on writing about the festival, to be assured of a decent place to bed down.

43

The problem was even stickier when I attended my first Salzburg Festival in 1935. Compared with my next visit in 1951, when new accommodations had been provided, 1935 was almost impossible. Nora and I thought we were lucky to find a small room in a tiny place that had the temerity to call itself a Gasthaus, not far from Getreidegasse, where the house in which Mozart was born remains a prime attraction. Our Gasthaus must have been well along in years when that momentous birth took place. Our room had a window that looked out on a graveyard, and our host assured us that this was the cemetery where Mozart was buried. I ventured the thought that Mozart was buried in a pauper's grave, exactly where no one knew. Our host dismissed that observation; he gave us his word that Mozart was right there outside our window.

He had to have some reason to charge us the outrageous price he had requested. His establishment, if that is the word, had no running water. The only toilet serving all his guests—and there were more than the place seemed equipped to accommodate—was in constant use. After one night we set out immediately in the morning to find another room, even if it meant giving up the proximity to "Mozart's grave."

It was hard to find. Finally we did. I still have in my mind's eye a picture of a young man from the next so-called hostelry—and I should not scorn it, for it had running water and more than one toilet—pushing a cart carrying our luggage and trundling down Getreidegasse, past Mozart's birthplace (I am certain of the authenticity of that proud claim), with us in pursuit, like immigrants from an unhappy land.

Salzburg, it must not be forgotten, had suddenly become *the* festival. After Hitler and the Nazis took over in Germany, Arturo Toscanini abandoned his commitment to Bayreuth and Wagner and agreed to conduct at Salzburg. Everyone who was anyone in the cultural and social worlds had to be in Salzburg. Reservations had been made a year in advance, as they are nowadays when so many festival-trotters are in motion.

In 1951, as I waited for my family to arrive by ship at Cannes, I was pleased with our reservation in Perpignan's beach suburb, Canet-Plage. I knew that the Casals Festival would draw people from all over Europe as well as from the United States. I had heard from friends planning to attend the Perpignan events that they had had to make do with rooms in towns a good distance from Perpignan, and I congratulated myself that we would be ensconced on a beautiful beach at the edge of a storied sea, only a short distance from the concerts.

The *Independence*, on its maiden voyage, arrived at Cannes a day and a half late after being delayed by a strike. It was well after noon when I gathered my family and their luggage into the small Simca I had rented, and we set out for what would be our pleasant home away from home, Le Tourbillon. It is a long, curving, spectacular drive—during daylight, that is—from Cannes to Perpignan, covering most of the southern coast of France. I had never been in that part of France, and at the rate we were going, I estimated that we would stop to have dinner and spend the night along the way. A glance at the map indicated that Montpelier, a sizable town, should be our objective. The trouble with Montpelier was that its only hotel was closed. We never found out why. Could it be that travelers always bypassed the town? We did find a decent restaurant; one would be hard put not to find one in France, I had believed, but I had yet to know Le Tourbillon.

It was twilight when we left Montpelier, and it was soon dark. Driving along an unfamiliar road in an unfamiliar region of France, I had all I could do to make out road warnings and other signs. Even if we were passing towns blessed with open hotels and available rooms, I would not have known where to look for them. My passengers were weary and nodding off. I decided that the only sensible thing to do was to push on toward Perpignan, where Le Tourbillon was waiting for us.

It was midnight when we pulled up in front of Le Tourbillon. I could see in the dark that the picture on the postcard was not merely flattering, it was a dreamlike invention. True, the white sand and the sea beyond glowed in the moonlight, but the only lights illuminating Le Tourbillon came from the bar, a thoroughly utilitarian room like the humbler establishments in the working-class districts of Paris. But it was bubbling with good cheer. There were more customers than one would expect after midnight in a place like Canet-Plage, and they did not look like people who had come to hear Casals and his colleagues make great music.

In my less than precise French, I called out, "Who is in charge here?"

A stocky man with a florid face who had a glass in hand approached me. *"Je suis Monsieur Habtiche, le patron."*

I mentioned my name, apologized for arriving so late and asked for the rooms we had reserved.

"Yes, yes," said M. Habtiche and resumed his conversation with his clients.

"My wife and children are outside," I said. "We would like our rooms."

M. Habtiche did not like being rushed. "Yes, yes," he said, while I waited.

I poked my head through the doorway, looking for something that resembled Reception. There was not even a desk to be discerned in the gloom.

"Ah, here we are," M. Habtiche said. A tired young woman who looked as though she had dragged herself out of bed shuffled into the bar. She took over sleepily as reception clerk, porter and bellboy. She helped us to unload our bags and carry them up to our rooms. At no time did M. Habtiche offer any help in installing his newly arrived guests.

Those rooms! They were spacious enough, and they each had two cots. But that was all. No closets, no wardrobes, no tables, no dressers. I must not be unfair: there were a couple of flimsy, straight-backed chairs in each room. It was too late and we were too exhausted to complain. The boys were instantly asleep. As I looked out a window facing the beach and the sea, I consoled myself, *It's a room with a view.*

The next morning as we took our place at a table on the terrace, we found that in one respect Le Tourbillon had prepared for us: there was milk. We discovered that the place held other guests. They waited to share the one W.C., situated on a landing halfway down the stairs. The breakfast was included in the fee for the room. For the boys, in addition to the milk there was one croissant each. For their parents there was coffee and one croissant each. The table was covered with a fly-specked paper cloth.

It was essential to deal with M. Habtiche. I began modestly enough. I complained about the paucity of furniture. "What do we do with things that we want to throw away?" I managed to convey.

"Don't worry," he replied, "throw them out the window."

"What?" I said in disbelief. "Onto the beach?"

M. Habtiche shrugged, "Why not?"

I tried another tack. "Could we have another croissant each for breakfast?"

No, the standard was one croissant per customer.

We had, of course, not unpacked. Our suitcases lay opened on the floor. The girl who had served as receptionist, porter and bellboy appeared with a couple of empty cartons. My appeal for wastebaskets had paid off. *Let's be patient and give it a try*, I thought. We took lunch on the terrace. The paper tablecloths were those we had had for breakfast. When the soup came, the flies attempted to share it, and a few drowned.

Clearly improvement was not to be expected from M. Habtiche, but I went looking for him anyhow. I found him at the side of his hostelry on a bit of lawn, playing what he carefully described as *la boule*. When I approached him, he waved me aside. One did not interrupt serious players of *la boule*. And M. Habtiche was serious about this French version of lawn bowling. That was all he seemed to do. His staff—I did not take a census count—seemed to consist of the young woman who had helped install us, another young woman, an indifferent waiter and, I suppose, someone who served as chef, though I never met him or her.

I looked for Sasha Schneider, did not know where he was staying and assumed rightly that if he had known of anything better than Le Tourbillon he would have grabbed it. We took a walk, looking for someone I knew. We even stopped strangers when we heard them speaking English to inquire whether they knew of any decent rooms to rent. The festival concerts began, and I met friends and acquaintances. Sasha was surprised to hear about Le Tourbillon's lack of amenities. I did not burden him with M. Habtiche's total absorption in *la boule*.

Before breakfast on our second morning as guests of Le Tourbillon, I got into the Simca and drove down the road toward the center of Perpignan, found a bake shop and acquired enough croissants to satisfy growing boys. For lunch we looked for a place we did not have to share with the flies. And encouraged by suggestions from friends, we began to cruise around the countryside, stopping at anything that looked like a hotel or guest house. At Molitg-les-Bains, a spa some distance from Perpignan, we seemed to have found what we sought— a fairly modern hotel with available rooms. I never learned whether it was actually a sanitarium, but I discovered that it was famous for housing and treating people suffering from serious skin diseases.

Though he seemed absorbed in the ongoing *boule*, M. Habtiche had noticed a few things. He had seen me take off in the morning and return with a supply of croissants. Indeed, I caught him staring at us one morning and shrugging as if to deplore the greedy habits of his American guests. Since we forewent the attractions of his fly-specked paper tablecloths at lunch and dinner time, he suggested irritably that it was expected that guests would take occasional meals at his establishment. All through the seven days we were confined to Le Tourbillon we lived out of our suitcases open on the floor. But we derived a modicum of virtuous satisfaction from the fact that we did not fling garbage onto the beach.

After seven days, deliverance. Thanks to Myra Hess, we were taken in by a delightful hotel in Argelès-sur-Mer. It meant quite a drive to the concerts in Perpignan, for Argelès-sur-Mer was a number of kilometers to the west, very near the Spanish border. Driving through and pausing in Collioure, a still unspoiled fishing village that had attracted leading artists, was a plus. So was the chance to visit Perthus, a village whose main street was the boundary between France and Spain. It was a thrill for the boys when we parked the Simca in France and walked across the street into a shop in Spain, where we bought delicious oranges.

The rooms in our Argelès-sur-Mer hostelry were not only spacious but actually furnished. The dining room had cloth table covers, and the food was fine bourgeois cuisine *sans mouches*. After our meals we would take coffee on a long veranda facing the main street, and we could watch village life go by. We missed the expanse of white sand of Canet-Plage, but the Mediterranean was not far away, while M. Habtiche and *la boule* happily were.

Our younger son, an uninhibited extrovert, struck up a warm friendship with Myra Hess. She and her friends dined at a table near ours, and the boy made a practice of standing by the great pianist and chatting with her about such topics of the day as the weather and the scenery. Oh no, this was not like a grandmother-grandson relationship, this was the palship of buddies. When she completed her festival appearances and prepared to return to London, Miss Hess made a special point of finding and bidding a firm farewell to her buddy.

With the festival over, we boarded our Simca and drove back over the length of the southern French coast by daylight, taking in views we had missed during the night drive west. We stopped for a lunch in a lovely restaurant overlooking the sea, called Le Lavandou. We spent a night in a fine hotel in Marseille. We were on our way to Bordighera on the Italian riviera, where we had reservations for the family in a modest but wonderfully comfortable hotel. There my wife and sons remained for six weeks while I circled Europe attending festivals, and managing to return for a weekend or two with the family. The food in Bordighera was first-rate, with the inevitable pasta at lunch and dinner. Our younger son, now three, mastered one phrase almost immediately. He did not like cheese with his pasta and learned to deal with the waiter when he stood over him prepared to sprinkle the Parmesan over his pasta. At the top of his voice he would shout, *"Senza formaggio!"*

Winding up that round of festivals, we were in Venice for the world premiere of Stravinsky's opera *The Rake's Progress*. We were also winding up a summer of

Nora (in dark shorts) with Bill, almost ten, and Philip, almost three, in Bordighera, 1951.

Bill and Philip on the Italian riviera, 1951.

The boys in Venice, 1951.

hotels at the Gritti Palace, a ravishingly luxurious antithesis to Le Tourbillon. On our first evening we took dinner on the romantic terrace overhanging the historic canal. The food was memorable, the service impeccable, and the silver looked as if it might have been created by Cellini. *What a life*, I thought, until I noticed to my horror that my preoccupied younger son was pushing a silver butter knife and teaspoon through an interstice between the wooden planks and into the canal. After that we had our meals in our rooms.

I recall with a sense of shame how we left those rooms. It was hot in Venice that September. The mosquitoes were hungry and relentless, and our windows had no screens. It was difficult for any of us to sleep through the night as they fed on us. As there were no fly swatters in sight, my only recourse was to soak towels and aim them at the bloodsuckers frozen on walls and ceilings when a light was suddenly turned on. I developed reasonably good marksmanship. When we checked out of the Gritti Palace, we left behind rooms with splotches of blood decorating the ceilings and walls.

Filled as we were with a sense of guilt, we took with us pleasant memories. Once we went for a ride on one of the vaporetti during the Venetian rush hour. The cabin was packed with cross-canal commuters. As sightseers we were pleased to be on the deck. But our endlessly curious younger son had to get a fix on what was going on in the cabin. Pushing open the door, he was startled by the density of the throng and the hubbub of Italian conversation. As if to establish that his was a presence to be reckoned with, he yelled at the top of his voice, *"Senza formaggio!"*

In Bayreuth that summer, where the Wagner Festival resumed after a hiatus caused by the war, I was again confronted by the problem of tight housing. I was alone. I had left my family happy in Bordighera. The festival's renewal had become, it seemed to me, more than a significant cultural occasion; it took on at times the proportions of an assertion of national pride. When *Die Meistersinger* ended with Hans Sachs hymning the enduring qualities of German art, the audience, mostly German and nearly all in eye-catching evening gowns or white tie and tails, rose to cheer with a sustained clamor that exceeded the deserts of the performance.

All the hotel space in Bayreuth had been locked up months before the festival, but since I was traveling alone, I could fend, I hoped, for myself. I had applied to the festival management for help before I left New York and had received word that a room had been reserved for me in a private home. After

Le Tourbillon I was wary of reservations made in my name. When I reached the address I had been provided with, I was warier still.

I stood in front of a small house on a side street with a main entrance at street level and another at the top of a stairway, leading to what? There were two different numbers; mine was for the stairway. I mounted, knocked, and the door was opened by an elderly couple. They bowed, they smiled, they led me into a small chamber filled with a large double bed. This was to be my room. Clearly I was in a tiny apartment. Was there another bedchamber somewhere off the combination kitchen–living room? There was not. The old couple slept somehow somewhere in that room. They had offered to let their one bedroom to earn a little money and to answer the appeal of city authorities to take in festival visitors.

My hosts were adorable. They fussed over me as if I were a returned prodigal son. They provided hearty German breakfasts and virtually stood over me to make sure my cup was never empty. In the evenings I tended to meet friends among the performers, notably George London, who was young and impressive as both Amfortas and Wotan, for supper. When I returned to my temporary abode, my concerned hosts were waiting up for me. The sweet old hostess actually insisted on coming into my—their—bedroom to tuck me in.

During the Festival of Britain in 1951, when that nation mustered all its cultural resources to demonstrate that it was recovering from the devastating wounds of the war, the hotel situation was also tight. During one stay I managed to find a room at Brown's Hotel. Years later there were extensive renovations, but in 1951 it was what one employee called with an excess of pride "an old-fashioned hotel." My room was in an attic where the floor had a marked incline, and when I lay in bed I had the illusion that I was in a tossing ship on an uneasy sea.

When Gian-Carlo Menotti founded the Spoleto Festival in 1958, I was there for the opening week. Again a rooming problem. There were no hotels in Spoleto. Friends and admirers of Menotti who trusted him to launch a festival that would have style and quality at its very inception had fortified themselves by renting villas in town and the neighboring Abruzzi hills. And Menotti had taken over a large edifice that had been a monastery to house his staff and close friends. When I arrived by train from Rome, I was met by one of Menotti's friends, who drove halfway up a mountain to the former monastery.

"Is this a hotel?" I asked incredulously.

"No," he said, "but it's where you're staying."

I was led into what had been—and still resembled—a monk's cell. There was a narrow iron cot with a minimum of other furnishings. No one to tuck me in. But how pleasant to be among friends and to share meals at the large refectory table with Menotti, his staff and guests. And when I wanted to write, I was ushered into a well-appointed office, created no doubt by a lay occupant of the former monastery, surely not by its abbot.

There was one problem. When I was ready to leave after a week's stay, I asked for the bill. "This is not a hotel," said a smiling young woman who was serving as a kind of executive secretary to Menotti, as if I didn't know. I told her that I would have difficulty explaining to *The Times* that I had accepted free board and meals from the director of a festival I was writing about. "But we are not ready to prepare bills," the young woman protested. At my insistence, however, she did a fine job of preparing one, charging me the going rates in places like Rome where there were hotels.

Gian-Carlo and I were old friends. Years earlier I had written about two of his first operas, *Amelia Goes to the Ball* and *The Telephone*. I had visited him and Samuel Barber when they shared a house called Capricorn in Mount Kisco, New York. The evening before my departure from Spoleto, Gian-Carlo and I were virtually alone. Everyone had gone down the mountainside to the lovely principal square to a performance in the attractive provincial opera house. I had seen and written about this production earlier in the week, and I wanted to relish for the last time the dazzling vistas from the terrace. Gian-Carlo just wanted

Gian-Carlo Menotti, 1978.

to rest. He was tired from this ambitious venture into impresarioship. I congratulated him on what he had achieved in so short a time. "But why," he murmured with a deep sigh, "why do I do it?"

I shall leave that answer to him. Although I have not been back to Spoleto in Italy, I have been to the festival he created in the United States, Spoleto in Charleston, South Carolina. For several years he organized and ran a festival in Australia, and at one time he talked about one in Edinburgh.

If I returned to Spoleto in Italy, I would not have to do with a monk's cell. There are now hotels. I have no doubt that hotels now exist wherever there are festivals to attract globe-trotting culture buffs. But I am sure that they still commute by car and bus from distant country inns as I did on several occasions from towns more than fifty kilometers from Bayreuth. And I hope that they do not have to deal with a *patron* with an addiction to *la boule*.

5

Bergman and Rossellini

H<small>OW DID</small> I happen to become a temporary historian of the romance between Ingrid Bergman and Roberto Rossellini, which had a large part of the world reading, gossiping and speculating in the early 1950s? Chance, just chance.

In the spring of 1951, at the end of a Tuesday luncheon of the Dutch Treat Club, George T. Bye, my literary agent, was chatting with Bruce Gould, co-editor with his wife, Beatrice Blackmar, of the *Ladies' Home Journal*. As I passed them on my way out, George stopped me. George was a mild-mannered, soft-spoken man who represented many successful writers, including such prominent, part-time ones as Eleanor Roosevelt. I was fortunate to be on his list; it meant easy entrée, at least for a first hearing or reading, into some of the best-paying editorial offices. Witness the encounter with Gould.

George knew that I was leaving in a few days for a four-month swing through Europe for *The Times*. Despite his low-pressure ways, he seldom lost an opportunity to get a remunerative commission for one of his writers. Having gone through the motions of introducing me to Gould, George wondered whether there was anything I could do in Europe for the *Ladies' Home Journal*. Aware that music was my beat, Gould said no. After an exchange of pleasantries, I started to go, when Gould had a second thought. He had been wishing, he said, that he could get someone to do a thorough, "objective" (*sic*) account of the true story of the Bergman-Rossellini affair, and the only way to manage that, he thought, was to have the full cooperation of the principals. Would I like to try?

I laughed; another pleasantry. "No," I said, "not my line." Furthermore, I had paid scant attention to the inflamed reports of the famous scandal and was not a bit interested in further investigation. I thanked Gould, told George that I appreciated his efforts and went on my way.

The evening before my departure for Europe I spent with friends who were involved in the film world, and to amuse them I related my conversation with Gould. "It's not as funny as you think," said my very good friend Jack Harrison, New York representative of the *Hollywood Reporter* and a man with a wide acquaintance in the film world. "You might be able to get the story."

"I don't want to," I protested.

"Don't be a fool," he replied. "You might not land the story but you could have fun trying for it."

But how? His particularly close friend Joseph Burstyn could be the honest broker. Burstyn was already in Europe and expected to be in Italy, and he, after all, was the American distributor of the two films, *The Open City* and *Paisan*, that had made Roberto Rossellini's name in the United States.

Burstyn was bound to be seeing Rossellini, and Jack promised to alert him that I would be coming and he must help me.

The odd thing about this plan is that Burstyn and I had become acquainted because of Rossellini's films. I had first heard of Rossellini in late August, 1945, shortly before my departure from Rome for demobilization from the U.S. Army. During my service on the staff of *Stars and Stripes*, I had written a piece about an effort to resume movie-making in Rome though the war was not over. The director of that effort was Alberto Lattuada. I visited him and his crew at work; I learned how they were making do with battered equipment and old film stock, and I sensed that the story they were shooting was not likely to deserve an adult's interest. At this very period, unknown to me, Rossellini was also struggling against the handicaps of a ravaged, depleted land to make *The Open City*.

Without guessing at the future, I got to know during my stay in Italy another Italian whose renown as a film director was to match Rossellini's—Vittorio De Sica, whose *Shoeshine* and *The Bicycle Thief* were also launched in the United States by Burstyn. In Naples in the late summer of 1944 I had gone to see a couple of plays in the recently revived theater to test the skimpy knowledge of Italian I was beginning to acquire. One of these was Claire Boothe's *The Women*, which I could follow because I had seen the original in New York, and the other was *Zazà*, a play that I thought would interest me because Leoncavallo had composed an opera for it, but unhappily I understood no more than scattered words.

The leading actor, however, was a tall, handsome man whose performance was so magnetic that it kept me in my seat to the end.

After the performance, another soldier and I took our time strolling to the station of the funicular that was to take us from the top of the Vomero, the hill that dominates Naples and its bay, down to sea level, where our working and living quarters were. We recognized De Sica, who was also waiting for the funicular, and by means of our minimal Italian, his halting English and our vestigial French, we talked. He was accompanied by a beautiful young woman, Maria Mercader, who had also had a role in *Zazà* and was later to be his wife. We invited them to stop at our billet for a drink. One of our buddies had acquired a cache of ordinary—very ordinary—red wine, and we persuaded him to let us have a jug. With a bit of bread and cheese—welcome, indeed, to hungry Italians, even to working actors—we sat and tried to make conversation. I met De Sica several times more in Naples, and when Burstyn obtained the rights to *Shoeshine* and *The Bicycle Thief*, I could give him some useful information about De Sica.

In another way I had some information about Rossellini when Burstyn came to distribute *The Open City* and *Paisan*. I had been one of the first persons to see the finished version of *The Open City*. Probably because I had written about Lattuada several months earlier, I received a phone call in late August, 1945, from a U.S. Army major whose name long ago escaped me. He had helped Rossellini with *The Open City* in some fashion and thought I might be of use in bringing the film to the attention of the United States.

I remember the film—and the particular evening—vividly. It had been oppressively hot all day, as Rome can be in August, and I drove to the site of the screening, a fair distance from the *Stars and Stripes* billet in the south part of Rome, in an open jeep. The film's fierce power and searing truth and the overwhelming intensity of Anna Magnani's performance shook me, and though my Italian was by then a lot better than the few phrases I had in Naples a year earlier, I did not need any language to be moved. I emerged from the screening room, almost too affected to speak, and murmured to the major who had invited me that he would hear from me.

During the time I was in the screening room, there had been a drastic change in the weather. A cold wind had raced through Rome, and the temperature had dropped at least 30 degrees Fahrenheit. I was wearing just a thin shirt and was drenched in sweat because the screening room had been as airless as a cell in

Anna Magnani rehearsing for a film in 1947.

solitary. By the time I reached the billet, I had a chill and knew I was going to be ill. In fact, it was the only cold I had while in the Army, even though I was exposed to rain and snow and heat and cold in Virginia, Alabama and Italy. Exalted by memories of *The Open City* and depressed by the sniffles I was beginning to experience, I crawled into bed, only to be summoned to see the commanding officer at once. Grumbling, I dressed, reported to the C.O. and was told to be packed and ready to depart early the next morning for Naples, a replacement depot and a troopship home. Several others in the unit were heading home, and we made the trip to Naples in an open truck. Under a scalding sun, I was miserable, sneezing and coughing and desperately dehydrated. Halfway to Naples, we made the equivalent of a pit stop, and there were Italian peasants bringing in a crop of plum tomatoes. I bought a few, and they were like nectar of the gods. At that moment I could have imagined a film devoted to Italian tomatoes as affecting as anything in *The Open City*.

I forgot about *The Open City* until I saw an advance screening at Jack Harrison's invitation. I made no secret of my enthusiasm, and Burstyn sought my advice. When he acquired the rights to *Paisan*, he again asked for advice. Since I had spent some weeks after the fighting in Italy ended traveling north to discover what role, if any, Italian partisans had played in the liberation of their country, I knew something about the people, place and spirit of *Paisan*.

When I met Burstyn in Paris in 1951, he informed me that he could arrange a meeting with Bergman and Rossellini. A slight, small man, Joe Burstyn seemed especially frail as we chatted in his room at the Hotel Majestic. He had a heart ailment which killed him while he was en route to Europe by air a couple of years later, and he lay on his bed as we chatted.

Joe had a quick, shrewd mind. He had had the wit to acquire the American rights to those fine, early postwar Italian films, and he had used all the skills he had learned in the movie business in years gone by to exploit them. He did not know whether Rossellini, with whom he was involved in ongoing film deals, would care to talk, and he could not guess how Ingrid Bergman, whom he knew only casually, would react. But it amused him, I think, to test them. If something extensive were to appear in the *Ladies' Home Journal*, it could be useful publicity for the next Rossellini film. I suppose such a thought occurred to Joe. In any event, we planned to be in Rome at the same time and arranged to stay at the same hotel.

The morning after our rendezvous in Rome, thanks to Joe's careful planning, we set out for a visit with the Rossellinis. Our chauffeur was a young writer who had collaborated with Rossellini on the scripts—such scripts as there were in the free, extemporaneous way of so much Italian movie-making of the time—of his films. He was a lively, witty, talkative chap named Federico Fellini, and his wife was the actress Giulietta Masina, who was little known beyond the small Italian movie community. Fellini's emergence as one of the great film directors of our time was yet to come, as was that of Masina as an actress in unforgettable performances in his movies—*La Strada, The Nights of Cabiria, Juliet of the Spirits*, and so on and on.

Fellini proved to be a jolly chauffeur and guide, while Masina, with her big eyes and shy smile, seemed to be as mousey and vulnerable as the characters I later saw her play in *Cabiria* and *La Strada*. The difference, of course, could have been that Fellini, who was full of curiosity as well as laughter, could communicate with Joe and me in English while Masina had very little.

We were on our way to Santa Marinella, a seaside village about forty miles northwest of Rome, where the Rossellinis lived. We drove through an iron gate, opened by a caretaker, and into a dreamlike—should one say film-fantasy—setting. Enclosed by a high fence was a generous strip of land embraced on one side by the Via Aurelia, the main west-coast highway to the north, and on the other by the gleaming Mediterranean. Rossellini had bought this property early in 1950 as a summer retreat and had poured large sums into rebuilding, creating flower and vegetable gardens and rearing up a high fence. There were three houses on the site. One near the gate was for the caretaker and family. The largest was being renovated while the Rossellinis lived in a smaller one fronting the sea. It had a stone veranda overlooking the rocky shore; viewed from the living room it looked like the deck of a ship on which we seemed to drift serenely on the calm June afternoon.

We were greeted warmly by Ingrid and Roberto. After all, I was the guest of friends and colleagues. I was not sure whether the Rossellinis were aware of the purpose of my visit. I had asked Joe whether he had explained it in advance, and his reply was, "In a way."

We were shown around the grounds by our hosts. Ingrid, looking even more attractive than when made up for a camera, was wearing a blue blouse, blue shorts and playshoes. Her skin was reddish brown and her blond hair was slightly bleached by the Mediterranean sun. She wore no makeup, and her hair, tossed by the wind, brushed occasionally across her sparkling eyes. Imagine a mischievous gamine flickering in and out of a cool, reserved demeanor, and you have an idea of Ingrid in this setting, on this June afternoon. Roberto, stocky, energetic, in slacks and open shirt, pointed to the disused tennis court he wanted restored so that he could resume playing; Ingrid whispered that he was good at it. They showed us the rectangular, boxed-in area for boccie (Italian bowling), at which Ingrid said she was becoming adept. She laughed when she came to the enormous outdoor fireplace. She had found an American magazine which had instructions with illustrations for easy construction of an outdoor barbecue and had turned them over to Italian masons, who had worked on the assignment for days. "It's a monument," she said. "It will stand for a hundred years." Robertino, born in February, 1950, before Roberto and Ingrid could be married, was wandering around the grounds under the supervision of a French nurse. A plump, blue-eyed, blond, gregarious little chap, he hated to be left alone for a moment. He had picked up his father's habit of tugging at strands of hair when absorbed and later toddled around the living room tugging at his hair in the same gesture.

Late in the afternoon Joe led Roberto and the Fellinis into the garden and left me with Ingrid in the living room. With half a smile Ingrid said that Joe had hinted at the reason for my visit, and she added quickly that she did not wish to talk for publication on any subject. I replied that I understood, that I would not pursue the matter and I merely wished to explain how I had gotten into it to begin with. I told her of my encounter with Bruce Gould and of the manner in which Joe had become involved. I added that I really was not qualified to do the story Gould wanted: I had read hardly anything about her affair with Rossellini, I was not interested in that kind of journalism, and I had gone along with the notion thus far simply for the pleasure of meeting her and Roberto.

She was amused by my disclaimer. Supposing that she and Roberto agreed to talk to me, she asked, how would I handle the subject? As unsensationally as one who had spent more than two decades writing for *The New York Times*. I should add that *The Times* in those years, unlike the new *New York Times* of recent years, often pretended that sex, liaisons, illegitimacy, divorce and remarriage scarcely existed among the people it wrote about.

As Roberto and the other guests returned to the living room, Ingrid said she would think about it, find occasion to discuss it with Roberto and let me know their reaction by evening's end. She went off to change her clothes. We then had a drink. We came out into the soft, translucent Mediterranean twilight; Rossellini insisted on entertaining at dinner at a favorite inn about ten miles away. I followed the Fellinis to their tiny Fiat, which could not seat more than four, and found that Joe and Ingrid were taking their places in the back seat. With a smirk I did not understand, Joe observed that I would have a nice ride with Roberto.

I did, I did. He led me to his open Ferrari. I climbed in beside him, and he handed me a crash helmet and advised me to fasten my seat belt securely. I had had no inkling that he had once been a racing driver; I had none that he still drove like one even on a curving, two-lane Italian country road where people and animals might be out for a promenade. I will say for Roberto that he had the foresight to activate his horn as he put the car in gear and to leave it in unrelenting raucous voice while he drove. I watched the speedometer with a horrified gaze as the needle went by the 100-, the 150-, the 200-kilometer mark, noticing with disbelief out of the corner of my eye men, women, children, dogs and cows scurrying wildly out of the way as we hurtled by them and trying at the same time to translate kilometers into miles in an effort to persuade myself that what I saw couldn't be true. During one short straightaway the speedometer needle shot up to 244. *That couldn't be 150 miles, could it?* I was still working at the arithmetic as we pulled up at the inn. I discovered later that Ingrid rode with Roberto in his Ferrari, but only when she had no alternative, and that Joe had made such a trip once.

Dinner was a delightful, expansive occasion, as Roberto liked such occasions to be. When it was over, Ingrid said she had had a brief discussion with Roberto—I couldn't figure out when—and she asked when I expected to be back in Italy for any length of time. I said I could manage a few free days in about a month, and she said she would let me know whether they were willing to see me then. We waved goodbye to the Rossellinis in the Ferrari, with Ingrid assuring me that Roberto would not be showing off on their ride home, and I gratefully followed the Fellinis and Joe into the Fiat for the trip back to Rome.

A week later in London I got word from Ingrid that I was welcome to return, and in several weeks I arrived in Rome. This time I met Roberto in their rented Rome apartment. Again he led me to the Ferrari, again I strapped myself in and put on the crash helmet, again he activated the horn and kept it blaring, and we sped through Rome, its outskirts and onto the Via Aurelia at speeds a film director should employ only in a wild chase scene. Ingrid had made arrangements for me to stay at a small family inn not far from the Rossellini place, and I was taken to it after she, Roberto and I had dined in their house and they had begun to tell me their story. I was shown to my room at the inn about midnight. The shutters were closed, and I thought, *What a dreary place compared to the Rossellini home*. In the morning I opened the shutters and stepped out on a balcony suspended over the sea. The view was so magical that it justified the return to Santa Marinella, no matter what else happened.

During that weekend Ingrid, Roberto and I talked through drinks and meals and walks and drinks again into the small hours of the night. This was the gist of their story.

During a New York visit in 1947 Ingrid dropped into a small theater on West Forty-ninth Street to see *The Open City* and was so stirred by it that she took a good look at the billboards to double-check the name of the director. Back home on the West Coast she talked about *The Open City* to friends and to her husband, Dr. Peter Lindstrom, who had undertaken to act as her agent as well as carrying on as a brain surgeon. In the early spring of 1948, back in New York, she went to see *Paisan*, and again the impression was shattering. That was how she would like to make films, she thought, without artifice and with an uncompromising commitment to truth. After consulting with her friend Irene M. Selznick, former wife of movie producer David Selznick and herself a successful Broadway producer, she decided to write to Rossellini. Her letter:

> Dear Mr. Rossellini,
>
> I saw your films, *Paisan* and *The Open City*, and enjoyed them very much. If you need a Swedish actress who speaks English well, who has forgotten her German, who is not very understandable in French, and who in Italian knows only *"t'amo,"* I am ready to come and make a film with you.
>
> > Best regards,
> >
> > Ingrid Bergman

The *"t'amo"* was a light touch, Ingrid said, so innocent that she asked her husband to read the letter before she sent it. On May 8, 1948, his forty-fourth birthday, Rossellini received the letter; he showed it to several friends, exclaiming, "What a birthday gift!" He sent her a long night cable and followed with a long letter with the outline of what was to become their first joint film, *Stromboli*. She liked the story idea, and she wrote to him that she would be in London for some time, making *Under Capricorn* with Alfred Hitchcock, and would he please send a script. He, of course, did nothing of the sort, since he never used a complete shooting script. Starting with a central idea, he shot scenes as he went along, with dialogue patched together the night before or even as the cameras were turning.

She was harassed by self-appointed "emissaries" from Rossellini, and finally she scribbled an angry note to him: "If we are to make a picture, I want to discuss it only with you." Shocked by the tone of her letter, Rossellini replied that he had only one authorized representative, Rudolph Solmsen. With the help of Solmsen and Ilya Lopert, a distributor of foreign films in America, who said he was prepared to finance a Bergman-Rossellini film, a meeting was arranged for late September in Paris. At this time Rossellini was shooting *The Miracle* around Amalfi. The film touched daringly, if indirectly, on the theme of the Virgin birth, and the star was Anna Magnani. When Rossellini described in Santa Marinella the pains he took to keep secret his planned Paris trip from Amalfi, he explained that it was necessary to avoid public discussion before something concrete had been agreed upon. He might have added that he was more than a little apprehensive about eruptions by the fiercely temperamental and jealous Magnani.

At noon on a Sunday Rossellini arrived with Solmsen and Lopert at the door of Ingrid's suite at the George V. It was one of the few occasions in his life, Ingrid recalled, when Roberto was punctual. Dr. Lindstrom had gone out before the visitors appeared, preferring not to meddle in her choice of film subjects but cautioning her against any premature commitment and promising to return at 1 P.M. With Solmsen and Lopert serving as interpreters, Ingrid asked questions and Roberto, addressing the interpreters, gave brief, diffident replies. No, he was not working on a script; never used one. He didn't know how long it would take to make the film—four weeks if she liked, or like Hollywood, he could require ten. Language? Any language; she could speak Swedish if she liked. Supporting cast? He'd find it as he went along. She found his casual attitude revelatory; the Hollywood way was not the only way.

At 1 P.M. Dr. Lindstrom appeared, and she told him quietly that she wanted to do the film. They all lunched in the suite, and there was a lot of business talk, with Roberto and Ingrid saying very little. As the visitors were preparing to depart, Roberto spoke directly to her for the first time, in heavily accented English: "Do we make the picture, yes or no?" Her response was "Yes."

Weeks went by as discussions about deals with potential partners took place, but without a script no one in Hollywood would consider negotiations. Though Ingrid kept reminding Roberto about the need for a script, none materialized.

In January, 1949, Rossellini arrived in New York to receive from the New York Film Critics Circle its award for the best foreign-language film of 1948, *Paisan*. Then he headed for California. While he was en route, Ingrid happened to be listening on Sunday night to the machine-gun delivery of Walter Winchell reporting on the radio that "Ingrid Bergman's one and only love is coming to Hollywood to see her." Her reaction, as she described it to me, was dismay. Had the possibility of falling in love with Roberto occurred to her by this time? She never mentioned it to me, but she did concede that she was always in an emotional flutter when a new, exciting film project was in the making.

Roberto alienated Hollywood during that visit by saying the wrong things and neglecting people who counted. He brought prints of two of his latest films, *Germany, Year Zero* and *The Miracle*, and they were shown at a small party in

Samuel Goldwyn's home to cool, indifferent responses. Goldwyn presently pulled out of a deal for a Rossellini-Bergman film, and Roberto broke with Lopert, who told him he would have to pay his own expenses. Roberto moved into the Lindstroms' guest house in Beverly Hills, and though Dr. Lindstrom was often there with them, Ingrid and Roberto spent considerable time together, and the intimacy grew. Meanwhile, Howard Hughes, who had just purchased a controlling interest in RKO, agreed to back the film. Roberto left for Italy, and Ingrid arrived in Rome a few weeks later, to be greeted by his light kiss on the cheeks and a whispered *"Je t'aime."*

By this time L'Affaire Bergman-Rossellini was a hot international subject. They were pursued everywhere by reporters and photographers, even when he drove with her in his newest Ferrari from Rome to Naples. Before they reached Stromboli, she wrote to her husband asking for a divorce. Dr. Lindstrom flew to Italy, and there were days and nights of tense, racking confrontations among the three. With *Stromboli* completed, Ingrid took an apartment in Rome alone. They never discussed the film with me, but I sensed that they were somewhat disappointed with it, as indeed the public proved to be. She was now pregnant, and no one could guess, until the pregnancy was well along, what her situation was. The child was born out of wedlock, and the storm of criticism achieved hurricane proportions. Finally she got a Mexican divorce, and he, who had had the marriage to his first wife, Marcella De Marchis, annulled in Austria in 1949, now had that annulment confirmed by an Italian court. A proxy marriage took place in Juarez, Mexico, on the morning of May 24, 1950, with Marcello Girosi, a close friend of Roberto's, there to see that everything went as scheduled. At the same hour in the evening, Ingrid and Roberto went alone to the Chiesa della Navicella, an old church near the Colosseum, where they knelt and exchanged rings.

After the long weekend with the Rossellinis, I left to resume my newspaper chores. With the multiplicity of details the Rossellinis had provided in their candid talks, I began to work on a first draft of their story in my spare time. In the meantime I had written to George Bye, telling him of the time I had spent with the Rossellinis, and he had notified Bruce Gould, who flew to Rome to confer with me, so eager was he for the story. We dined at Tre Scalini on the Piazza Navona, and I filled him in on what I had heard. He urged me to get a manuscript to him as soon as possible, and I told him that I had promised Ingrid

Bergman and Rossellini in Stromboli, *c.* 1950. Courtesy of the Academy of Motion Picture Arts and Sciences.

and Roberto I would let them see it first to make sure that I had all the facts right.

In September my wife and sons joined me in Rome, and we spent a day in Santa Marinella. Ingrid and Roberto were charming hosts, and even Robertino fell into the spirit of the occasion, allowing Philip, our three-year-old, to ride alone on his child-sized car.

Ingrid and Roberto read the manuscript, corrected several facts but did not tamper with it in any way. During my trip back to the United States—a lovely, long sea voyage from Genoa to New York aboard the Italian liner S.S. *Conte Biancamano*—I revised the story. George Bye sent it to Bruce Gould, and eventually the word came from the *Ladies' Home Journal* that it did not want the article after all. As Gould wrote to Ingrid, in what she described in a letter to me as "an unpleasant tone," too many of his editors were "violently against printing my love and marriage to Mr. R."

Bye sent the article to *Look*, which paid well for it and ran it as a two-part series. When the first of these articles appeared, Lester Markel, Sunday editor of *The New York Times*, hauled me up to his office and berated me for not offering it first to him. I explained that I could not see any possibility that *The Times Magazine* would accommodate an article of this nature, and I was, of course, right. Nowadays, even the most decorous publications would not only retail all the phases of so famous a romance but would expect a lot more lurid detail than I was prepared to provide.

I had a note from Ingrid dated February 22, 1952, that she had received many letters from America praising the *Look* articles, and she added that she hoped it would "teach a lesson to *Ladies' Home Journal* and its thirteen editors who were so 'violently' against the story!" Only one letter, she added, "came saying the article was awful and that I have no conscience . . . that letter came from my daughter!"

I was pleased to read a news item in 1958 that Ingrid had joined her daughter at a family reunion that Christmas in the United States.

6

Shostakovich

I MET DIMITRI SHOSTAKOVICH only twice, yet he and his music are a thin but strong connecting thread that binds together my impressions of Soviet art and artists accumulated intermittently in more than five decades.

I encountered the music long before I met the man. The First Symphony, which appeared in 1926 when the composer was nineteen, proclaimed the arrival of a greatly gifted composer. The opera *Lady Macbeth of Mtsensk* had its premiere in Leningrad in early 1934. Based on a story by Leskov, it told a tale of adultery, murder and suicide in raw colors made rawer by music of shocking rhythms and harmonies and savage instrumental outcries. It was reviled by *Pravda*, the party newspaper, in a furious editorial, as verismo with a vengeance and ordered off the boards. The symphony, written as a graduation piece with a brash impudence and sense of fun, delighted me. The opera, which reached New York only a few months after its Soviet premiere in a special production conducted powerfully by Artur Rodzinski, left me with ambivalent feelings: awe at the composer's command of parody, satire, violence and old-fashioned sentiment as well as unease that amid so much creative abundance there was a lack of discrimination.

On my first visit to the Soviet Union in 1935 I looked forward to a possible meeting with the young firebrand. I was told that as a young writer on music at *The Times* I might get to see him. It did not work out that way; he was not in Moscow. But I was granted an opportunity to talk with three Soviet musicians: Dimitri Kabalevsky and Aram Khatchaturian, composers, and Grigori

Aram Khatchaturian, Soviet composer, in 1960.

Shneerson, musicologist. Shneerson spoke English well, and we had no need of
an official interpreter. They came to my room at the National Hotel, responded
without apparent concern to searching questions and expressed satisfaction that
The Times would be interested in further information about Soviet musical life.
Would I care to have a large sampling of Soviet scores to take back to the United
States? Indeed I would! Would I like an occasional letter telling of new developments? Certainly.

   Shneerson and I did correspond for a time. Then, after the crackdown by
Stalin and his culture hatchet-man, Zhdanov, on Shostakovich, Prokofiev and

other so-called formalists and cosmopolites, the correspondence ended. I did not see Shneerson again until 1958 during my second visit to the Soviet Union. He was with a group led by Tikhon Khrennikov, the domineering secretary of the Union of Soviet Composers and a perfect model of a hardline apparatchik, and the poor fellow was at great pains to seem not to know English or me.

After the 1935 session at the National Hotel, two large bundles of scores arrived. There were symphonies, sonatas, occasional pieces by Kabalevsky, Khatchaturian and other leading composers. The prize, in view of the world-wide commotion that *Lady Macbeth of Mtsensk* had stirred, was a piano and vocal reduction of the opera. I retied the bundles with the rough wrapping paper in which they had come and managed to find a stout cord with which to hold the scores safely together.

I left Moscow by train on my way to Warsaw, where I planned to spend a night on the way to Vienna, then Salzburg and its festival. At the Polish border all passengers were debarked with their luggage to change to a far more modern and comfortable Wagon-Lits train. The Polish government was intensely anti-Communist and regarded anyone and anything emerging from the Soviet Union with unremitting suspicion. Its customs officials went through all luggage as if any piece might contain a bomb. In those days of travel by train and ship, no one traveled light, and there was a lot to examine. Nothing threatening was found, and the little labels denoting clearance were pasted on my valises. A customs official then turned to my two bulky packages.

He began to undo the knots as he asked in Polish, of which I had not a word, what I presumed was "What's this?" In a mixture of English, French and German, none of which he understood, I explained that the packages contained music. He picked up a score; the printed legend in Cyrillic was enough. He shook his head emphatically. He glanced at other scores. More Cyrillic lettering, more Russian names. He opened the bound volume of *Lady Macbeth*, turned the pages and saw that they contained a Russian text. Now his head-shaking was almost furious. This score and all the others could not enter Poland—they reeked of subversion. I argued vehemently.

A superior officer approached. We must hurry, the train must leave. He spoke a little French, and I explained that I was spending just one night in Warsaw, not enough to be a carrier of Communist propaganda. Sorry, Soviet scores were not welcome in Poland. I argued, how could black notes on white paper infect his country? He just shook his head.

I now resorted to the only tactic left to a desperate traveler—a calculated tantrum. I ranted in English, threw my hat to the ground, literally jumped up and down. The customs officials looked at each other in dismay; I must be a lunatic. The station master came by to say that the train must go. At this point the senior customs official offered a compromise: the Shostakovich score could not under any circumstances enter Poland; if I gave it up, the other scores would be granted clemency. "But the Shostakovich," I shouted, "is the one I want most!" The official offered another compromise: wrap it and mail it direct to the United States. While the train lingered, I made a separate package of the score, with the official's help, paid the postage and left it with him, while I triumphantly though wearily carried the other scores onto the train.

To my total disbelief, the Shostakovich score, which I had given up as gone for good, was waiting for me at *The Times* when I returned to New York. At that time it was a rare document, for it was the version that Stalin's government had suppressed. I daresay that under Gorbachev's glasnost, other copies have surfaced in the Soviet Union. If anyone is disposed to examine what was so heinous to Soviet and Polish authorities in the 1930s, my copy is now in the Cornell University archives.

In 1958 I spent almost a month in the Soviet Union. My objective was to investigate the place of the arts under the more benign leadership of Nikita Khrushchev. I spent some time in Leningrad, Kiev and Tbilisi as well as in Moscow.

I had a long, formal meeting at the Union of Soviet Composers with a delegation led by Khrennikov. Unfortunately, the man I wanted most to meet, Shostakovich, was not there. When I regretted his absence, Khrennikov assured me that a meeting would be arranged. The group discussion was amicable. Khrennikov made the introductory remarks and more often than not replied to questions, even though I tried to address them to others. With the experience of Shostakovich and Prokofiev, whose lives had been darkened by government and party ukases, in mind, I asked about judgments from on high. "Oh no," Khrennikov insisted, "it was not party leaders who criticized but other musicians." If a score strayed from the path of Socialist realism, it was composers who pointed the proper direction. What could be more democratic? As to music of consequence being created in other lands, Soviet musicians, he explained, had access to any scores and recordings they wished to examine. As to the Soviet public, Khrennikov contended with the assurance of one who

In Moscow in 1958 with Tikhon Khrennikov (right), general secretary of the Union of Soviet Composers. Igor Alexandrov, the interpreter, is at left

could fathom the minds of millions that it wanted music that was clear, melodic, optimistic, realistic, joyous, affirmative. *Like Tchaikovsky's Sixth Symphony*, I thought, *with its black despair*—then and now a program staple in the Soviet Union.

Could the public always be depended upon to be right in its response to a first or second hearing? Had it always been right about Shostakovich and Prokofiev? Khrennikov alluded to Prokofiev's *War and Peace*. The initial production was misconceived and ineffective. A better production turned the opera into a success. Ergo, producers and performers, not the public, had been wrong.

In the days that followed, I asked repeatedly through my interpreter and a chap in the Ministry of Culture who spoke English and had been designated as my contact man, "What about an interview with Shostakovich?"

"Not to worry. We'll be back in town soon; it will be arranged."

I made my scheduled visits to the other cities. The farther one got from Moscow, the more relaxed artists seemed to be about talking to an American. The party line on the arts was not referred to as ultimate wisdom. These artists were ready for glasnost decades ago.

Tbilisi was an unforgettable experience. The Union of Georgian Composers, apprised of my forthcoming visit, sent a message inviting me to lunch. The setting was a pavilion atop St. David's Hill to be reached either by funicular or a drive up a steep, twisting road. On a long table were heaping plates of caviar, sturgeon, fresh vegetables, delicious flat Georgian bread and a staggering collection of wine bottles, all full, representing every vintage of the Soviet Union's principal wine-producing area.

No mention of Socialist realism here; only sly comment about cultural bureaucrats in Moscow. The party lasted from noon to 6 P.M. It comprised five Georgian composers, the southern republic's most important; a representative of Georgia's Ministry of Culture; my interpreter, who had flown down with me from Moscow; and since she did not know Georgian, a local interpreter.

A long, gracious toast from the *tamada*—the Georgian word for the man at the head of the table—and a glass of wine, tradition requiring that it must be drained. It was my obligation to respond; my toast was a lot briefer and less flowery. A tall, exuberantly mustachioed composer rose and launched into a lovely Georgian folk song, beginning with a melismatic phrase that reminded me of the music of the Middle East, and the others joined in three-part polyphony with pinpoint accuracy. A handsome, gallant man named Otar Taktakishvili delivered a toast to America's writers beginning with Steinbeck, sat down happily flushed as we brought our glasses to our lips, then jumped up to apologize for the unpardonable omission of Hemingway. Toasts followed toasts; songs became livelier and, I guessed, bawdier. At one point I made a ghastly booboo: I offered a toast to the *tamada*, without realizing that such a toast in Georgia signifies the party's end. I wriggled out of it by insisting that I was toasting Alexei Machavariani in his role as composer and not *tamada*. He was, I had learned, a Lenin Prize winner, and I was to hear his music that evening for a long ballet based on *Othello* (alas, I dozed more than I heard or saw).

At 6 P.M. we wove—at least I wove—our way to the cars, carrying, as ordered by the *tamada*, wine glasses. Halfway down the mountain, we pulled up at the side of the road, wine bottles were produced, and we drank—this time without toasts—presumably just for the road.

Back in Moscow, before coping with the problems of getting to see people I wanted to see, like Shostakovich, I wrote what was a faithful and, I hope, amusing account of the six-hour lunch, which *The Times* ran on page one. Several years later there was a dividend. Paul Hofmann, Rome correspondent of *The*

Lunch at Tbilisi in 1958. Alexei Machavariani, Georgian composer, the *tamada*, heads the table.

Otar Taktakishvili, Georgian composer, at Tbilisi.

Machavariani, a Lenin Prize winner.

Times, was tracking down an important story about the Vatican and approached Cardinal Agaganian of the Curia for help. Did Hofmann know the man who had written about a lunch in Tbilisi? Hofmann did; the cardinal helped him in his quest, asking him to tell that writer that for him, who came from that part of the world, it was most agreeable for once to read the truth about "the kind of people we are."

Finally I was told that an appointment had been made for me with Shostakovich. When my interpreter arrived at my hotel on the given morning, she was unhappy. Shostakovich was ill. Maybe he was; maybe not. A replacement was offered, Nikolai Pogodin, a Stalin Prize winner and author of the long-running play *Kremlin Chimes.* I accepted, even if he was, as I assumed, trustworthy by party standards. Not that Shostakovich had failed to behave after being abused and humiliated publicly. At least he gave me the appearance of toeing the line. The Fifth Symphony, which he wrote after the official excoriation in the thirties, was thoroughly conservative in style, and the Seventh, known as the "Leningrad," written passionately to honor that city and its heroic defenders who held out against the besieging Germans for many months, was similarly accessible. But in many of his works there were eruptions—clashing rhythms and sonorities, anguished themes that expressed his bitterness and dissent, passages that seem to me to sing of rebellion.

My interpreter and I drove to Peredelkino, the Moscow suburb where leading artists had their dachas. Pogodin, a small man with a glint in his eye and a cynical twist of the lips, received me correctly enough, though he was probably irritated to have this visit foisted on him. And I who did not believe that Shostakovich was ill, vented my annoyance by asking tough, undiplomatic questions. His answers were curt, deliberately insolent and provocative.

We had arrived at the dacha at 11 A.M., and just before noon, feeling that I was getting nowhere, I said it was time to go. With a weary air Pogodin replied, "So our American friend will not accept our hospitality?"

I was startled: what hospitality?

"He expects you to stay for lunch," my interpreter explained. "His wife and daughter are preparing it."

We stayed for lunch. His wife and daughter, a bright, intelligent chemist, joined us. The conversation became animated. He showed me his state-of-the-art American shortwave receiving equipment. I asked whether it had been a problem to acquire.

"No," he said, "not if you have the money, and if you mean black market, no again." He showed me shelves of boxed tapes. "I like your jazz," he went on, "and I have a better library here than some of you Americans."

We talked about music, writing, the stage. My interpreter was struggling to keep up with question and answer, thrust and retort. Soon we were ignoring her. Pogodin evidently knew more English than he had admitted to and seemed to understand me, and I who knew no Russian but grasped words and phrases that belonged to the lingua franca of the arts understood much of what he was saying. There was absolutely no mistake: he was deploring the limits that the party and its Socialist realism were imposing on artists. Shostakovich, if permitted to see me and speak candidly, could not have been, if I may use an oxymoron, more indirectly forthright.

Nikolai Pogodin, distinguished Soviet playwright, in the large study at his dacha.

I finally did meet Shostakovich the following year. I had no opportunity to talk to him alone, not even with an interpreter. He was a member of a distinguished group of Soviet musicians who came to the United States in 1959 as a phase of the cultural exchanges then in full flower between our country and the Soviet Union. In 1958 four of our composers—Roger Sessions, Roy Harris, Peter Mennin and Ulysses Kay—had toured the Soviet Union. The reciprocal delegation included Shostakovich, Kabalevsky, Khrennikov, Fikret Amirov and Konstantin Denkevich, composers, and Boris Yarustovsky, a critic.

The pattern for these exchanges was relatively formalized, with the host country fixing itineraries and arranging meetings. In the Soviet Union our composers visited a number of cities, heard performances, met with musicians, discussed mutual problems, rarely got into individual homes. Here the situation was not much different, thanks to Soviet insistence that the delegation must make all appearances en masse. CBS invited Shostakovich and Kabalevsky to be guests on the Sunday program "Face the Nation," but the reply was that all six must be invited or none would appear. CBS decided that a half-hour program with six guests would be too unwieldy to be useful.

One meeting with the visitors turned out to be less formal, more flexible and franker than most of the others with their routine politesse and obligatory toasts to peace and friendship. It took place in the New York City home of Norman Dello Joio, and the other Americans were Aaron Copland, William Schuman, Samuel Barber, Mennin, Kay, Nicolas Slonimsky, Russian-born musicologist who served as interpreter, and I.

Shostakovich asked the first question. How many opera houses did the United States have? Touché! Very few three decades ago, compared with what we have now, and very few indeed compared with the many in the Soviet Union. An American countered. How many orchestras in the Soviet Union? Touché for us! Only a few compared with the multitude in the United States. The discussion turned to the duty and right of composers to be their own person, to be bold in pursuing their own creative inclinations. The visitors understood that this was the key issue. Khrennikov, who often arrogated to himself the privilege of answering and speaking for the others, argued that the greatest boldness lay in being simple and direct. Kabalevsky denied that the Soviet composer was restricted and contended that there were stylistic differences, for example, between Prokofiev and Glière, between Shostakovich and Khatchaturian.

I directed hard questions at Shostakovich. Why had his *Lady Macbeth* been suppressed after one performance? He replied that he had decided to revise the opera to "remove impurities and crudities." What had happened when he and Prokofiev were castigated by the party leadership for the sins of formalism and cosmopolitanism? I knew I was being ungallant and putting him on the spot. He flushed and labored to give an answer that, I surmised, would pass muster with Khrennikov, who with his apparatchik's zeal was undoubtedly the delegation's monitor. The answer was painfully lame. It followed the Khrennikov, that is, the party, line about the need for simplicity and directness. With his myopic eyes and an almost defensive posture, Shostakovich was so palpably uncomfortable that I regretted my questions. When the meeting ended Shostakovich accorded me the coolest of goodbyes.

Years before I had written an article for the Sunday music pages in which I argued that Shostakovich needed the freedom to write as he pleased, and he responded with an article in a Soviet publication asserting that he had complete freedom. We were antagonists at a distance of thousands of miles.

At least so I felt, rather sadly, until an encounter in Washington months later, when I was there on a mission for *The Times*. I was staying at the Statler Hilton,

Dimitri Shostakovich in New York, 1959.

and having arisen early, I was at the elevator bank, heading for breakfast and a newspaper at an hour when hardly anyone else was stirring. The door of the lift slid open. Inside was one passenger—Shostakovich. I learned later that the Soviet delegation, which had visited Washington, San Francisco, Los Angeles, Louisville and Boston as well as New York, had returned to the capital for a final debriefing. Shostakovich, like me, was evidently an early bird.

Automatically I reached out to shake his hand, wondering whether he would respect it. He grasped mine warmly. We did not have time in the lift's swift descent to try for a language we both spoke. We just stood there and looked at each other. At the lobby level, as the door opened, Shostakovich impulsively rushed at me, embraced me, kissed me on both cheeks and plunged out into the lobby. I did not try to follow him. I never saw him again, but we both understood.

Poor, unhappy man! How he must have suffered in those years when he was made a whipping boy by tyrannous ignoramuses! There is some indication of how he felt in the book that Simon Volkov produced and that purported to be Shostakovich's testament.

What about his music? As time passes we are able to achieve a perspective on it. It is no longer good enough to have a knee-jerk reaction like that of some American critics, who have tended to dismiss most of the music as the inevitable banal product of an imposed rigid doctrine like Socialist realism.

One thinks of the way Mahler was dismissed a couple of generations ago as being too inflated for his own good. It took the commitment of a Leonard Bernstein to make a strong, fresh case for Mahler by playing all the major symphonic works in a coherent succession and then recording them for television.

Shostakovich's music is being played increasingly not only in the Soviet Union but in other countries, including the United States. During one week his Eighth Symphony was offered in New York by two different orchestras. In a visit to the Soviet Union in 1986, I heard the Leningrad Philharmonic play the Sixth Symphony in that lovely Hall of the Nobles which the composer, a native of the city, might have had in mind when he imagined the sound and movement of his symphonic works.

Nor is it only the symphonic works that should commend Shostakovich to us. He wrote fine, lively music for films. His stage music for dance and opera is too little known. And there is in his chamber music, particularly that of his final years, the sorrow and the pity and the occasional exaltation of a man who has endured and survived much.

One wonders at times what Shostakovich would have produced and what paths he would have pursued if he had lived his entire life in a free atmosphere. One might as well wonder what Mozart would have achieved if he had lived beyond his thirty-sixth year. It is enough to be grateful for what Shostakovich, a composer of true genius, did manage to reveal of himself and his heritage in an abundance of music in many forms.

7

Irish Patriot—and Racing Mentor

I F RAY KELLY, sports editor of *The New York Times*, had not become an opera buff, I would never have known Emmet Dalton, and that would have been a loss for both of us, that is, for Kelly and me.

It all began when Ray, who, knowing of my occasional interest in baseball, football and thoroughbred racing, would feed me tickets for attractive sports events, accepted a pair for the Metropolitan Opera in a reciprocal gesture. I do not know any longer what the opera was; I do know it had Lily Pons in a leading role. The exposure to Miss Pons wrought an extraordinary change in Ray's life. He wanted more of Miss Pons. He tried other operas in which she appeared. He heard her again and again in all her roles and began to analyze subtle differences in each performance. An orderly man, accustomed to sports writers' penchant for statistics, he kept a diary of each Pons performance he attended—date, role, rest of cast. I cannot believe that the petite, charming coloratura soprano had a more faithful fan.

The time came when Miss Pons sang less and less at the Met—and finally no longer. *Faute de mieux*, Ray thought he would try other singers in operas that had not been in the Pons repertory, beginning with Italian works that did not have showy coloratura leads. He liked them, too. He would come around to chat with me about this wonderful world that was giving him so much pleasure. Fascinated by the way his tastes were broadening as were his personal opera stats, I led him on. I introduced him to Wagner; that also took. His adventurousness grew on what it fed. He ranged out into the concert hall to hear orches-

Lily Pons as Lucia in
Donizetti's *Lucia di
Lammermoor,* 1931.

Ray Kelly, sports editor of *The Times,* in 1947.

tras, pianists, violinists. His stats became formidable as did his record library.
In his retirement he was seeing a lot of his old friend and Fordham University
contemporary Frank Frisch, the former major league baseball player and manager *par excellence,* who had also become a fine-music buff, and they were constantly vying for superior opera house, concert hall and record collections stats.

Ray was not responsible for my fondness for the racetrack. I owe that initi-
ation to my former colleague Sam Zolotow, *The Times'* redoubtable theater news
hound. Sam, as everyone in the theater knew for half a century, was relentless
in tracking down items about the Broadway stage but managed to keep abreast
of the racetrack.

Some weeks after my son William was born, Sam bustled into the Music
Department from his clangorous niche in the Drama Department and
announced that a horse named Bright Willie was running in New York that
afternoon.

"You have to bet him," he ordered in a voice that intimidated producers,
writers, actors, directors and backers into revealing all.

"Why?" I said meekly. After all, I had never bet on a horse.

"Because your son is called Willie, isn't he?"

When I resisted this irrefutable logic, he said impatiently, "Come on, I'll split a $2 bet with you."

I gave in, and Sam went out to place the bet with the office bookie, who, mind you, was not employed to serve as a handy bookie but simply plied his profitable trade as a sideline with full knowledge of the crusty Edwin L. James, the managing editor, who liked to back his fancy in thoroughbreds and was one of his customers. After I returned from war service abroad, the *Times* employee-cum-bookie told me that while I was away a horse named Taubman was entered in a race and that James, in a touching, sentimental gesture, had bet on him— and, sad to say, had lost.

Late in the afternoon of my maiden venture into playing the ponies, Sam rushed into my office and handed me $9; Bright Willie had come in 8 to 1.

Several weeks later Sam was at me again: Bright Willie was running that afternoon and didn't I intend to bet on him?

Sam Zolotow, *Times* theater reporter and racing enthusiast, in 1950.

"Will you split a $2 bet?"

He declined. "But you have to follow him!" An order was an order. I gambled the full $2 myself, and of course Bright Willie won, paying 7 to 1.

Now it was incumbent on me, Sam thundered, to go out to the racetrack the next time Bright Willie ran, and I had no choice but to do as I was told. Even though Bright Willie did not win, that visit to Jamaica or Aqueduct or Belmont—I don't remember which—affected me in a way like Ray's exposure to Pons: I went often to the racetrack though, unlike Ray, I kept no comprehensive record of what I saw and heard.

In the spring of 1951 I was planning a four-month assignment in Europe: to cover the Festival of Britain, the resumption of the Bayreuth Festival after a long hiatus, the Casals Festival in Perpignan, the Holland Festival, the Salzburg Festival and the premiere of Stravinsky's and Auden's *The Rake's Progress* in Venice. Ray came by and suggested that I might like to report the Derby at Epsom Downs when I was in England. I thought it would be fun to investigate the British racing scene, and I accepted his offer. That was how I came to know Emmet Dalton.

Emmet lived in London, where he worked for Samuel Goldwyn managing British distribution of Goldwyn films. Two close friends of mine, Alfred Crown and David Golding, the former in charge of international sales and the latter in charge of public relations, were also Goldwyn executives. Alfred, other friends and I had made a ritual of attending the big races in New York on Saturday afternoons, and with David, based in Hollywood, I would share a visit to the racetrack when we were together on the West and East Coasts. Like honest, devoted horse players, we were proud of my Derby assignment, and they saw to it that I would meet Emmet as soon as I reached London.

Emmet had an office on Jermyn Street, and when I phoned him, he asked me to come right over. I found a slim, wiry, forceful man who exuded a sense of authority. "Let's have lunch," he said, and led me down the street to Fortnum and Mason. "So you want to write about British racing." I had ordered a drink at his invitation. He no longer drank; he had learned, after a difficult and necessary struggle, to abstain.

I explained that I had no ambition to write about British racing, I merely intended to cover the Derby for *The New York Times*—and for personal kicks. To understand British racing, he told me severely, I must do a lot more than go to the Derby. I must visit other courses, Newmarket, Ascot and less renowned and smaller venues, and if I really cared about the sport, the place to find it in its purest form was Ireland, and especially at the Curragh. Unhappily, I never made it to the Curragh with or without Emmet. Nor did I get to Ireland until years later, after Emmet's death, when I spent some time with members of his family and filled in details of Emmet's career that he had chosen not to mention.

Emmet had earned the right to be called a true Irish patriot. As a very young man and a native of Ireland, he had volunteered to fight with the English in World War I. Not that he loved the English, but he believed strongly in their causes. His gallantry in action earned him the Victoria Cross, Britain's highest award for heroism in battle. He never would describe the events on the battlefield, but he relished telling about the presentation of the award. The ceremony took place in the presence of George V at Buckingham Palace. Winston Churchill, then Lord of the Admiralty, approached him to place the riband with the cross around his neck, and it was expected that he would bow from the waist in deference to the King. He remained standing ramrod straight in defiance of the court etiquette he had been instructed to observe. And the moment the last presentation had been made, he bolted the room and the palace. "I suddenly swelled with rage," he recalled more than thirty years later, "at the memory of the Easter Rebellion not too many months earlier." In the early 1920s he was, in his twenties, the youngest major general in the Irish Republican Army. He was deeply involved in Ireland's internal and external struggles but was reluctant to discuss that exhilarating and troubled period in his life. An occasional word would indicate how he grieved about the partition and the problems of Northern Ireland.

"The first thing," Emmet said at lunch, "is to begin immediately. We shall go to Hurst Park on Saturday." On Saturday morning he arrived at my hotel with a tall, pink, sandy-haired friend whom I shall call Colonel Dickie. He and Emmet were co-owners of several horses who were in the care of Noel Murless, the Queen's trainer, and who were ridden by Gordon Richards, Murless's favorite jockey. Colonel Dickie, Emmet whispered as he led me out of the hotel, had been a daredevil in the Royal Air Force during the war. One would never have known. Colonel Dickie was not a man for small talk, indeed for any talk at all. As we drove to Hurst Park, Emmet and I sat in front while Dickie occupied the rear seat. Emmet and I chatted, and occasionally I addressed a remark to Dickie, who smiled and made no reply.

Emmet and Alice Dalton, *c.* 1950. Photograph courtesy of Nuala Cuddy.

I don't know how things are arranged at English racetracks these days; it is almost three decades since I visited one. The last time was to Ascot with, of course, Emmet. But his heart was no longer in it, nor, I would guess, his means. At Hurst Park the stands described literally their use. There were no seats; you stood. Emmet and Dickie bet with bookies passing by at the foot of the stands. Hand gestures were all that was necessary. The amounts they risked were large. As a $2 bettor I was shamed into venturing as high as £5, apparently an embarrassingly paltry wager that caused Emmet to factor it into his bet. There was a flurry of excitement when a horse wearing Churchill's colors won a race, and Emmet pointed with pride as the old warrior, whom he evidently had forgiven, stomped to the winner's circle. Our little group had a larger *frisson* when Dickie won a huge sum and invited us to the bar for champagne. "Now," he said, and they were almost the only words he spoke to me, "you are one of us."

On the drive back to London, again I sat with Emmet in front, where we chatted while Dickie, silent as before, seemed lost in deep contemplation. The conversation in front ran down, and we rode in silence for some moments. Clearing his throat, Dickie at last spoke.

"The Duke of Northumberland is a proper duke," he said, and after a long pause, "the Duke of Roxburghe is not a proper duke."

Unsmiling, Emmet kept his eye on the road. Silence. I thought happily that Dickie was now ready to converse, and to encourage him to expand on this weighty pronouncement, I turned to him. "Why is the Duke of Northumberland a proper duke?"

He gave me a compassionate look as if to suggest that one must be patient with dim Americans, and replied with a finality meant to avoid further chitchat, "Because he does the proper things."

Some days later Emmet took me to Newmarket, the next and more important step in my introduction into English racing. As we drove north Emmet told me that Newmarket was the heart of English racing, the home of the all-powerful Jockey Club. Despite his intense Irish patriotism, he had great respect for English civility and adherence to tradition. As we neared Newmarket, he explained that he would have to leave me in the car in a parking area because I would not be admitted into the members' enclosure with him unless he had an invitation for me countersigned by a member of the Jockey Club.

"Don't laugh," he said when I laughed. "It's not a formality."

I sat for a while in the parked car while he went off, perhaps with a touch of concern about a guest with something less than blue blood, to seek a member to approve my application. When he returned some minutes later, he wore an odd smile.

"The first member I ran into," he said, "was a gentleman who served in the British Embassy several years ago, and when I asked him whether he would sign for my guest, he examined the card carefully, nodded and said, 'I recognize that name. Good chap. Used to read him about music in *The Times* when I was in America.'"

In Emmet's mind my prepping for the Derby had become at least tolerable. On to Epsom Downs. For this trip Emmet had two old friends from Dublin in the car, and lively companions these Irishmen were. I had studied the entries, more than twenty of them, and had noticed that there were three Irish horses in the field. I asked my Irish fellow travelers whether they fancied any of them. I was not about to watch the Derby without a flutter on something. Unanimously they warned me against backing any of the Irish steeds: they were remote prospects.

The winner of that Derby was Arctic Prince, owned by a man named McGrath, whose principal occupation was running the famous Irish Sweepstakes. In the car with us was the owner's brother.

I thought it would be only right, if not perhaps tactful, to commiserate with my Irish friends.

"Too bad we didn't have Arctic Prince," I observed sympathetically.

Emmet and his compatriots roared with laughter. "Who says we didn't have him?"

One said, "What kind of Irishmen do you take us for? We bet big on all three Irish horses. Wouldn't you if you were Irish?"

Emmet admitted that he had put down a large wager at 50 to 1 months earlier.

In my swings through Europe that summer I returned to London several times and always arranged to see Emmet, though to his regret I could not spare the time to pursue further instruction in English racing. I visited him and his family in their pleasant, spacious maisonette in Plane Tree House on the edge of Holland Park. I took his eldest, Emmet Jr., a physician, to the Paladium, where Danny Kaye was appearing, and provided a riotously good time. Thanks to my friendship with Danny's manager, we watched him carry on from the wings. I invited one of Emmet's daughters, Audrey, to be my guest at the Sadler's Wells Ballet. She was a beautiful seventeen-year-old, and Emmet, I thought, hesitated before permitting her to go with an older man, even one with a taste for racing. Audrey some years later was signed to a Hollywood film contract and had leading roles in several films.

After that summer I did not see Emmet again until June, 1960. Before taking over as drama critic of *The Times* in succession to Brooks Atkinson, I wanted to spend a month in England, seeing plays and meeting people, and I thought it would be agreeable to rent a flat rather than stay in a hotel. What could be more natural than to write to Emmet to ask whether he knew of such a flat?

"Yes," he replied laconically, "mine."

An enticing answer, I replied, but what would he do? I did not want to drive him out of his own home. I knew that Alice, his warmhearted wife, had died, and so, alas, had Emmet Jr.

"Not to worry," he wrote, "the place is yours." No mention of terms. Later I had to argue with him to accept an adequate rental.

It was a good, happy month at Plane Tree House. There was one surprise: we—my wife and sons, who had not met Emmet before, and I—found that we were sharing the place with our landlord. He did not have to move out of his own quarters in the large duplex apartment, and he refused to take meals with us, though he had arranged that the cheerful, buxom Irishwoman who cleaned for him would be available to cook delicious lunches for us.

Emmet kept out of our way almost too scrupulously. I chided him for excessive self-effacement, but he was subdued for other reasons. The loss of wife and son had hit him hard. He was no longer working for Goldwyn, and though he seemed to be involved in other film ventures, he was not as energetic as he had been. His devotion to Ireland remained unchanged. He thought it was time for Ireland to have a film industry of its own, which would not only enable it to deal with material that spoke best for the country but would also be a stimulus to the economy. He was more reticent than ever, and he did not leave Plane Tree House very often. What meant a great deal to him was his friendship with Madeleine C., who occupied the maisonette opposite. She had been—apparently still was—connected with one of the government's secret services. Most evenings we went off to the theater, and as far as we knew, Emmet would walk across the hall to take his evening meal with Madeleine. When we returned, we would invariably find him ensconced in front of the television set. I offered to get tickets for him and Madeleine for some of the plays we were to see, but he always declined—emphatically.

Two years later, expecting to spend another month in London, I wrote to Emmet asking about the availability of his flat and stressing that we would take it only if it meant not cramping his freedom of movement in his own home. In a carefully written letter he intimated that he might be staying with one of his daughters, Sybil, who now lived in Dublin, or he might take a trip to California to be with Audrey. In any event, the place was ours. When we reached Plane Tree House, Emmet, of course, was in residence, even more reclusively than in 1960. Once we were invited to dinner with him and Madeleine in her flat, and she confided to Nora that he was becoming more tightlipped and stubborn than ever. Occasionally the ancient Irish heat would flare up, but when he relaxed once or twice after our return from the theater, the old personality compounded of passion and irony was there for our enjoyment.

We saw Emmet only once more. We were briefly in London about seven years later. Madeleine had kept in touch with my wife, largely by exchanging

Christmas greetings. Emmet had long since given in to the entreaties and cash offers of the developer who intended to tear down Plane Tree House and replace it with a large apartment block, and he had moved in with Madeleine. She had held out more determinedly and had ended with a settlement large enough to pay for a lovely house in Radlett outside of London. We traveled up to Radlett to have dinner with them. Relations between them clearly were strained. I do not know what had gone wrong, but there was the faintest intimation in great confidence from Madeleine to my wife about a difference over a possible marriage. I do not know the facts, but having learned how fiercely Emmet held to his convictions, whether his patriotism or his Catholicism, I guessed that she felt it was time for them to marry and that he refused because she had once been married and divorced, and it was strictly against his faith to marry a divorced woman.

Not long after that we heard from Madeleine that Emmet had moved to Dublin, where he lived with one of his daughters. Before he died Irish television made a TV program recalling his services to Ireland. I found occasion some time later to visit Dublin for the first and only time, and his daughters played the tape for me. There was much, much more about his heroism and dedication to the cause of Irish independence and freedom. Impressive as that was, even more affecting was the story told by one of his daughters. A few days before he died, he had walked out to take a bus on the way to see his doctor, and an unheeding driver seemed ready to leave without him. He strode out into the street, stood in front of the bus and, in his most imperious way, waved his cane and ordered the driver to wait and take him aboard. The man who would not defer to George V was not yet willing to yield to a mere bus.

8

Horowitz and Television

I FIRST HEARD Vladimir Horowitz in 1929 in his second season in the United States. In his mid-twenties he was the fabled virtuoso incarnate. There is no need to expatiate on the control, the subtlety and variety of sonorities, the sense of rhythm, the headlong accuracy of the playing of the young firebrand of six decades ago, nor to remind ourselves of the extraordinary longevity of this remarkable career.

I became acquainted with Horowitz more than half a century ago through his wife, Wanda, Toscanini's daughter, whose honesty and forthrightness I always admired. In those days I wrote frequent profiles of musicians for *The New York Times Magazine* as well as other magazines. As the twentieth anniversary of his fantastically successful American debut in Carnegie Hall was approaching, Wanda suggested that Horowitz would not mind cooperating, though he normally refused such cooperation, if I were to do a commemorative piece for *The Times Magazine*.

I was invited to come to their town house in the East Nineties at an unexpectedly late hour. The Horowitzes, as I came to know in the ensuing years, dined late. It was his unvarying habit to lie down for a half-hour or more before dinner, come down at 8 P.M. or a bit later, dine and then return to his bedroom for another half-hour of bed rest. It was up to Wanda to entertain guests during pre-dinner drinks and post-dinner conversation. When Volodya, as I came to address him, returned to the living room, he was as fresh as most of us are in the morning and was brimming with eagerness for gossip or the piano.

Vladimir Horowitz in 1929 at age twenty-five.

We began our interview about 10 P.M. We sat in the large room dominated by his Steinway grand—he at one side of the room, I at the opposite side. As he was not in the habit of granting interviews in those days, he translated his hesitancy into maintaining his distance from the interviewer. Wanda occupied a position in the middle of the room as if to establish the role of impartial mediator. I had trained myself not to take notes when dealing with a diffident interviewee, trusting to my memory to retain what I would need. Accordingly, we chatted casually, and I led the conversation in a low-pressure way to points on which I sought information and opinions. As this polite dialogue drifted along with an occasional comment from Wanda meant to give the talk direction,

The Horowitzes in 1943.

Horowitz began to show signs of nervousness. He kept pushing his chair back until it was against the far wall and he shifted restlessly in it. It was well past midnight when he erupted. "When," he demanded, "are you going to begin the interview?" I replied that it was finished and I was ready to depart.

He was so astonished that the piece in *The Times Magazine* quoted him accurately that as an interviewer I became distinctly *persona grata*. Indeed, as a way of covering ground we had not touched on for the twentieth anniversary of his debut, he was delighted to cooperate for another long article to signalize the twenty-fifth anniversary. By 1967, with the fortieth anniversary still a year away, he began discussing how to celebrate that occasion.

By then I had become a frequent visitor and dinner guest. In the mid-fifties and early sixties he had withdrawn from the wearing concert routine. Undoubtedly he was the victim of recurring periods of depression. I saw him in another, later depressed interval when his spirits were low, and he would invite me to sit with him and watch television—any dumb, boring show on the tube—and his listlessness was painful to observe. But such behavior was rare when I saw him during the twelve-year layoff from public appearances in the fifties and sixties.

After the postprandial obligatory sacking out, he would almost prance into the living room, curl himself up on the large divan and begin talking. He read the newspapers, listened to the radio and was *au courant* with the affairs of the world. He liked to talk politics. And he loved gossip, especially about musicians. He would probe for any fresh morsel and would retail what he had picked up from other sources, including visits by other musicians.

From time to time he would bring up the subject of his alleged retirement as a pianist and would scoff angrily at the rumors that he was washed up as a performer. He would leap to the piano and begin playing. He might dash off a taxing piece by Chopin with the flair and brilliance that knew no difficulties, then turn to me with a big grin and say, "Not so bad?"

No, not so bad at all. Nor was the way he played what he decided to do next. He would sit at the keyboard for a couple of hours, and I, weary at the end of a long working day, would be refreshed by the private performance. Was this his way of practicing? A man of enthusiasm, he would concentrate at each visit on a composer he had decided to explore anew. One night it might be Scriabin

Horowitz at home in 1948.

into the early hours; another, Medtner; another, Clementi. He was constantly discovering remarkable similarities, like the presaging of a theme in Beethoven's *Eroica* in a piano sonata by Clementi.

At one period he was into bel canto singing, and I remember a delightful evening when he insisted on playing snatches of recordings of such great exponents as Mattia Battistini, Giuseppe Anselmi and Leonid Sobinov. He lingered on Sobinov, a name new to me, because long, long ago while still a youngster in Russia, he had once played piano accompaniments for this Russian tenor. The way that Sobinov and other singers of another age phrased in melting, unbroken lines was to Horowitz a lesson in music-making, and his enchantment reminded me of his father-in-law Toscanini's exhortation to his orchestra players to "sing, just sing."

Horowitz was able to contemplate something special for the fortieth anniversary of his American debut because in 1965 he had made a triumphant return to public performance, and in 1967 his career was back in full incandescence. It was after a pleasant dinner and the usual half-hour of lying down to let the gastric juices do their comforting salutary duty that Volodya, in his favorite corner on the sofa, broached the 1968 anniversary as if it were imminent, rather than more than a year away.

Horowitz at a Carnegie Hall recital in 1965.

Did I have a suggestion? I had not even remembered that 1968 was a round-numbered anniversary and did not realize that it loomed so large to him. It chanced that for some months I had been serving, with the permission of *The Times*, as an occasional consultant to the CBS television network. After I ceased being drama critic of *The Times* and, in early 1966, became critic-at-large, succeeding Brooks Atkinson once more, it seemed a challenging opportunity, and *The Times* agreed, to do what I could to encourage superior programs on the air. Michael Dann, vice-president for programming (who later moved to ABC), had invited me to be available and started by asking me to look at some potential theater projects. Having carried out several brief assignments for Dann, I had fallen into the habit of thinking about television.

My reply to Horowitz was spontaneous: "What about television? Why not appear on television and let the whole world see and hear you?"

The Horowitzes responded almost as one: "Never!"

"In the concert hall," I said, "you sell out every time, it is true, but the audience is in the thousands, and on television it would be in the millions."

They were adamant, as if I was proposing some species of moral turpitude. I shrugged. "Well, it's just an idea, think about it."

In fact, it was just an idea. I had not thought of it before and had obviously not mentioned it to anyone who might bring such a proposal to reality. At a meeting with Dann some days later, I asked him what he would think of presenting Horowitz on television for the first time. Mike was and is a quick study, with an excellent showman's instinct for exciting and fresh approaches. The idea appealed to him. He promised to look into it. Among his achievements as vice-president for programming had been the introduction of a hugely successful series, "Beverly Hillbillies," which was greeted by the more intelligent spectrum of the viewing public as a sort of nadir. Perhaps Mike thought that a Horowitz program would be a respectful antidote to the critical flack for "Beverly Hillbillies." I suspect that when he presented the prospect of a Horowitz broadcast to his superiors, William S. Paley, the chairman, and Frank Stanton, the president of the corporation, were hospitable.

The next time I dined at the Horowitzes, I reported as much. The notion was brushed aside, but not with the abrupt explosiveness of the first reaction. In the next few months it gradually grew into a subject that could be discussed seriously. Questions cropped up repeatedly. Where would he play? What would he play? Who would be there? What would he be paid? How could he find out how he looked and sounded on television?

The Horowitzes in 1966 on a bench along Fifth Avenue. Photograph by Sam Falk.

In response to the last question, Mike Dann made a remarkable offer: CBS would rent Carnegie Hall, bring in a crew and tape a program as a trial run. If the Horowitzes liked what they saw, there would be a full recital before an invited audience, and the taping would eventually be shown on television.

That did it. Horowitz accepted, provided, of course, that a contract fixing the terms for the telecast was in place. I shall pass over the details of what seemed to be a continuing negotiation between CBS and Horowitz's lawyer. I was not privy to the backing and filling that went on. I do remember that late one evening just before the trial taping, I had an agitated call from a CBS negotiator to help settle a trivial point holding up the contract's completion.

Horowitz had established over the years a well-earned reputation for being a tough, demanding bargainer. He was supposed to scrutinize his manager's financial statements with a searching eye, monitoring even the most modest expenses promoting his appearances. Perhaps he was reacting to his painful experience in his first years in the United States. After his debut in 1928 he became an instant box-office draw, and he suddenly found himself in possession of a lot of money. Upon the advice of people around him, he invested most of his earnings in the stock market. Like a host of other optimistic investors, he sustained heavy losses in the crash of 1929. He never told me how much went down the drain, but if ever a man was traumatized by a shocking experience, it was Horowitz in his attitude toward his earnings. He never again considered stocks. He did purchase a few paintings, in the forties, I think, by Picasso, Manet, Degas, Modigliani and Rouault, and though they graced the living room for many years, they were to him investments that would not dissolve away in a numbers game. Some of the paintings he sold during the long layoff in the fifties and sixties. But there had been a lot of income when he was on the concert trail, and there were earnings from his many recordings. What did he do with his money? I never asked, but one day when the talk turned to preserving assets, he left the living room and returned with a huge bundle of savings bank books, issued by what seemed scores of different banks. Each of these, he observed cheerfully, was insured up to $100,000.

With the permission of *The Times*, whose executives agreed that I was making a valuable public contribution by getting a Horowitz on television, I made an agreement with CBS to serve as executive producer. The contract with Horowitz was signed. The date for the trial taping was set for the beginning of 1968. Late in the preceding evening I had a frantic call from a CBS executive. Just as the electronic equipment was to be moved into Carnegie Hall and set up for the morrow's taping, a quarrel between a couple of unions had broken out. The taping would have to be postponed for a few days, perhaps for weeks.

Like some characters in Russian novels, Horowitz had a tendency to assume that things would go wrong. After the union squabble and the deferment of the trial taping, he predicted that nothing would ever happen. A new date was set, and on the preceding evening I dined with the Horowitzes. I had been assured that there were no further obstacles to moving the equipment into Carnegie Hall and setting up. But Horowitz found other reasons for pessimism.

When we sat down to dinner, he announced in a lugubrious voice, "Ninety percent."

"Ninety percent what?" I asked.

"Ninety percent no. Ninety percent, there will be no television."

As he ate, his mien remained somber. "Will you make a bet?"

"What kind of bet?"

"Will you bet that the performance will not be repeated?"

"How much?"

A thoughtful interval. "A hundred dollars?"

Done. His contract stipulated a fee of $150,000 plus another $75,000 if the performance were telecast a second time.

There was another long pause. "Would you make another bet?"
"On what?"
"Whether I will ever be asked to make another program. I say no."
"How much?"
"A hundred and fifty."
Done.

For Horowitz, betting against prospects was probably a talisman against disappointment. Horowitz was wrong on both wagers, and no doubt pleased that making them had helped to secure what he wished. As I write I realize that he never paid up. Oh well, his performances were more than adequate payment.

There had been problems leading up to the trial taping. What, for example, to play? Horowitz wondered whether it would not be advisable to offer a program of short, familiar pieces since he was reaching out to a vast audience that might be inexperienced musically and would turn off anything demanding. I insisted that he must play some of Chopin's greatest music. He reluctantly agreed to include the Ballade in G minor and Polonaise in F-sharp, grimly warning that they would be too difficult for the television public.

Wanda demanded that the entire program must be shot from the point of view of an audience in Carnegie Hall. I argued that to do so would be to deprive the broadcast and the public of some of television's special possibilities. Close-ups of a pianist and his fingers on the keyboard, I argued, add to the impact of a performance. Volodya joined Wanda in contending that such close-ups would tend to become visual stunts and would detract from the music. I had no choice, in the face of their obdurateness, but to say that I would try to have their wishes respected. When I conveyed them to Roger Englander, our director, he looked at me as if I were mad. I proposed a small compromise: since it was a trial taping, I told him, include a few close-ups and even some shots head-on, though these shots were also to be interdicted.

During the taping a television monitor was set up for Wanda in a Carnegie Hall dressing room. I shuttled between the truck parked outside the hall, where Englander and his assistants were working, and the room in which Wanda was watching. When Roger moved his cameras in for head-on shots and a close-up of the Horowitz fingers in their dazzling traversal of the keyboard, she objected strenuously. She bawled out Englander so angrily that he offered his resignation. Later she apologized and he relented.

When the Horowitzes watched the trial taping in a CBS studio some weeks later, they were pleased. He looked fine, he sounded great, the impact of the close-ups was exciting. All his gloomy predictions that after seeing himself on television he would never consent to making such a sight public were proved wrong.

On, then, with the real show. A date was set. A large public—friends of the Horowitzes, friends of mine, friends of everyone at CBS, friends and clients of his management agency—was invited. A stand-in had been retained to sit at the piano for a morning run-through. I remember that a CBS official watching on a monitor objected to giving Steinway—the name was, of course, imprinted on the piano above the keyboard—free advertising. What did he propose? "Cover it or paint it out," he suggested. Even, I asked, if it was Horowitz's favorite piano? He walked away, shaking his head.

The taping enhanced my respect for Horowitz as a thoroughly disciplined professional. I do not refer to the caliber of his performance, which was magisterial. He was uncomfortable in the intense lighting needed for television, but he did not complain. He did not let the cameras disturb him, though their movement forward and backward, down and up, could have been unsettling. During breaks he chatted cheerfully with the cameramen. When the taping of the scheduled program was finished and the audience left the hall, Roger and I felt that a retake of the coda of the Ballade was essential because the sequence was not right visually. I went into the dressing room to tell Horowitz what we wanted. Though he was tired, he came out on the stage and without grumbling went through most of the Ballade again. Once more the pictures were not satisfactory, and it was my unpleasant task to bring the bad news to him and to bid him to repeat. If at that moment he had exploded in irritation and refused, I would not have been surprised. He raised not the slightest objection, went out quietly, sat down at the piano and played much of the Ballade unforgettably. You can hear for yourself if you listen to the audio disk "Horowitz on Television," released some months after the broadcast.

The CBS broadcast, sponsored by General Telephone, was set for a Sunday evening in September, which turned out to be Yom Kippur eve. The ratings were good but would have been better in some areas if it had not been the most solemn of all Jewish holidays. To make up for this oversight in scheduling, CBS aired the show again in late December, once more with General Telephone as the sponsor.

To celebrate the success of the telecast there was a dinner party early in 1969 at the Horowitzes' for Leslie H. Warner, chief executive of GTE, and Mrs. Warner. Unexpectedly the conversation veered from music to baseball. In his years of absence from the concert stage, Horowitz's habit of killing time by sitting in front of a television set had grown, and he had become interested in baseball. Fascinated by the way the St. Louis team, whom he called almost fondly the Cardeenahls, had made a late run for the pennant, he had become their devoted fan, and his eyes lit up when baseball and the Cardeenahls became the topic of conversation.

"Have you ever been to a baseball game?" Warner asked.

"No."

"Would you like to go?"

"Why not?"

"We'll arrange it," Warner promised.

Within a few days I had a call from the vice-president for public affairs inquiring whether a date in mid-June would be convenient for a visit to Shea Stadium. "Tell Mr. Horowitz," he said, "that the Cardeenahls"—he relished pronouncing it à la Horowitz—"will be playing the Mets."

"Yes," I said, "I will tell him," not believing for an instant that Volodya would violate his almost inflexible routine for an event as insignificant as a baseball game. After all, this was to be a night game. Forget about this need to lie down before and after dinner; what about dinner itself? He brushed my doubts aside and insisted that we must accept the invitation.

Warner and his party gave us ample notice that on that June date they would pick us up at the Horowitz residence at 6 P.M. I had arrived a few minutes ahead of time, and Horowitz urged me to phone Warner immediately to say that the whole thing was off. But why?

"It's a warm, muggy evening, and it will be uncomfortable at the ball park."

I said it was too late to reach Warner. I was not stalling; undoubtedly his limo was on the way.

Horowitz sighed with the air of a man who had committed himself to a fearful enterprise. The doorbell rang; it was Warner. "Tell him I'll be right out," and he hurried in the direction of the kitchen. He emerged with a small package wrapped in tinfoil, which he jammed into his pocket.

Through the Doyle, Dane, Bernbach agency, Warner had laid on a program that must be ranked as Super VIP. We were driven into a special parking place at Shea and then ushered into the office of Gil Hodges, the Mets manager, who, to Horowitz's surprise and delight, said that he and his wife had actually heard him in the concert hall. He had a gift for Horowitz—a toy concert grand.

"Would you like to meet some of our players?" Hodges said.

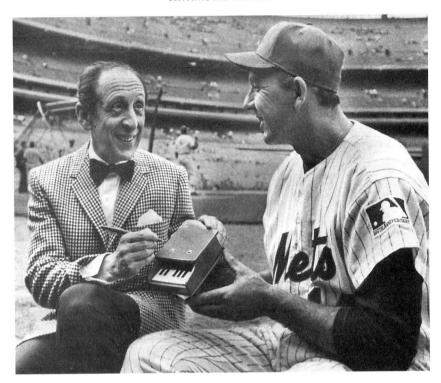

Horowitz with Gil Hodges in 1969. Photograph by Barton Silverman.

Happy as only a fan, even of the Cardeenahls, could be, Horowitz nodded eagerly. In came Tom Seaver, Jerry Koosman, Tommy Agee and Ron Swoboda. A playful lot, they had, I am sure, planned a little fun. As they were introduced, each shook Horowitz's hand, with Swoboda bringing up the rear. That brawny young man, one of the strongest of the Mets, had been coached by his buddies, I suspect, to make his handshake especially vigorous. Coached or not, that is what he did, only to jump when Horowitz squeezed back. Someone in that gang must have guessed that a pianist would have a steel-like grip.

We were next led out on the playing field where the Cardeenahls were taking batting practice. To my amazement it developed that Volodya had been reading about the Cardeenahls not only in *The New York Times* but also in *Sporting News*. Introduced to Lou Brock, he asked about the player's off-season florist business.

"Isn't your wife's name Wanda?" Horowitz asked.

"Uh-huh."

"How did that happen?" I wondered as I listened to the exchange whether Horowitz hoped that she had been named after his wife.

Brock's response: "How should I know?"

Our guide led us to a mound where Bob Gibson was warming up, but that dominant pitcher refused to be interrupted, even to meet a famous piano virtuoso.

Horowitz was sympathetic. "He's an artist. We shouldn't bother him when he's working. Did you know that he's also a singer?"

To my shame I did not know.

That season, of course, was the year of the Mets miracle—the glory year when the Mets won the Eastern division, the National League playoffs and the World Series. On that hot June evening a young Nolan Ryan outpitched the veteran Gibson, much to Horowitz's dismay. It was a tight game, but the scoreboard took time to flash the glad tidings that the great pianist, Vladimir Horowitz, was in attendance. Back at the town house, I learned later, Wanda loyally had tuned in on the game and had seen the announcement on the scoreboard as well as a shot of her husband in his seat in one of the boxes.

At a ball game it is almost mandatory for fans to fortify themselves with a hot dog and a beer, and that was what we in the Warner-Horowitz party did. Volodya, who was notoriously fussy about his diet, declined these goodies. As the moment approached when he would normally descend from his upstairs seclusion to dine, he whispered that it was time to start home. I said it would be embarrassing, but he insisted. I was about to offer his apologies to Warner, but the game became even more exciting. As I leaned toward Warner, Volodya pulled my arm and murmured, "We can't go now." Then came the evening's biggest surprise. Volodya pulled the package covered in tinfoil out of his pocket, unwrapped it and produced a cold hamburger sandwich, which he proceeded to eat as if he had spent years as a fast-food addict.

As for television, Horowitz became a kind of veteran of the airwaves. My stint as his executive producer ended with that first show. But he went on to play at one of the White House programs. He appeared with orchestra. He allowed the cameras into his home and took part, speaking and playing, with Wanda at his side as a casual, often wry commentator, in a couple of hour shows. Most memorable was the telecast of the Moscow concert marking his return to the Soviet Union after an absence of sixty years, with emotion overflowing on both sides of the stage. You will note that this moving event was another commemoration of a round-numbered anniversary.

9

My "Feud" with David Merrick

A "FEUD"—that's how the brouhahas that flared up after David Merrick, the busy and noisy producer, opened a play or a musical that I did not review to his satisfaction were characterized in many quarters. But it takes two to make a feud. Whatever the provocation, and there was a good deal, I avoided personal controversy. To have responded to his baiting would have been like doing the tango his way; I would not dance with him or to his tune. I declined to become his accomplice in getting him or his enterprises further public attention. Despite the commotion stirred up by his blatant or indirect attacks on me, he seemed a paper tiger I found easy to ignore.

I was frequently urged to write about my "feud" with David Merrick. I could have done so while I was still at *The Times*. After I retired, I was invited to do so by other publications. I do so now, not out of rancor, but to contribute to what may be the understanding of a man who cut a wide swath in the theater world.

For a time—certainly in the period between September, 1960, and the end of 1965, when I was *The Times'* senior theater critic—Merrick was Broadway's most conspicuous producer. If one judged by the stir that accompanied many of his undertakings, one would have thought that no other producer risked so much and so often. But an examination of the records establishes that Roger L. Stevens, alone and in partnership with others, was a more prolific Broadway producer. Merrick, however, did bring in four, five and six shows a season, many of them imports and quite a few created under his aegis. Stevens, like virtually all producers, had backers as well as partners who were identified. Merrick did

David Merrick on Broadway, 1970. Photograph by Neil Boenzi.

not make a habit of naming his backers publicly, and he did not choose to give his biggest investors billing as co- or associate producers, as is the custom nowadays. Byron Goldman, listed as one of the producers of the huge success *Jerome Robbins' Broadway*, was, with Max Brown, a constant and important financial supporter of Merrick productions. Much as he would have liked a program credit, he had to wait until the production of Gian-Carlo Menotti's opera *Maria Golovin*. As Byron wrote to me in 1969, "The first time I had my name up there was with 'David Merrick, in association with Byron Goldman, presents *Maria Golovin* by Menotti.'" For the pleasure of that credit Goldman put up most of the money to bring the piece to Broadway. He has insisted that he did not resent Merrick's failure to put his name there before; after all, he shared in some of Merrick's huge winners.

The bottom line for all producers and investors, even those who present and support a work out of a deep commitment to what it has to say, is whether it runs and makes money or closes quickly and loses its investment. And a key factor is whether it gets what the trade calls money reviews. Such reviews were always crucial and have grown increasingly so. Brooks Atkinson, for thirty-five years drama critic of *The Times*, used to recall that when he started on the job in the twenties, there were eleven newspapers, and the theater notices in *The Times* were nowhere near so vital as they became as he approached his retirement in 1960.

When I took over in 1960, there were seven newspapers as well as reviews on radio, television and in magazines. Nevertheless, even with a Walter Kerr on the *Herald Tribune*, *The Times* was regarded as most influential in the impact of its reviews on the box office. I had proof of that from Robert Fryer, one of the producers of *Advise and Consent*, the dramatization of Allen Drury's immensely popular novel. It arrived on Broadway in my first months as drama critic. Where my six colleagues on the dailies wrote about it enthusiastically, I made no bones about my distaste. What Allen Drury had done in the novel and Loring Man-

After-theater Broadway throng, 1964.

del in the dramatization was to turn a rabid, unprincipled, destructive U.S. senator, modeled presumably in part on Joseph McCarthy, into a wildly demagogic liberal. I ended a Sunday follow-up article by describing the play as an ignoble way of turning history on its head. I was hardly prescient about the 1988 presidential campaign when the Republicans, led by George Bush, sought to convert "liberal" into one of the dirtiest words in the political lexicon.

In their efforts to overcome whatever harm my comments had done to their play, the producers of *Advise and Consent* ran a series of large ads in *The Times*, reprinting in full one day at a time the reviews of my colleagues with an explanation at the top of the number of years each reviewer had held his post. The message, of course, was that I was too new and green to be heeded. Fair enough to fight for the life of one's production. When Fryer came in to see me in the spring, he told me that though *Advise and Consent* had run for months, it had not done well financially. If it had had a good sendoff in *The Times*, he said, it might have run profitably for several years. What he wanted to explore was how I would react if the play were rewritten to make the demagogic senator a reactionary, more in fact like McCarthy. I replied that I could not and would not comment in advance. I would, I said, consider reviewing a revised production.

The all-important money review! Its absence in *The Times* had prompted what Fryer must have realized and what I knew was contemplation of a strange reversal. Not that I scoff at the power of the money review. Nor do I think that its influence prevails only on Broadway. An unreservedly enthusiastic review, particularly in *The Times*, will do wonders for presentations Off Broadway, Off Off Broadway and in regional theaters. Such a review will bring unexpected returns at the box office in movie houses, opera houses and concert halls. Such reviews will crowd museums and sell enormous quantities of books.

But whoever lives by the review may die by it. Too many people go to hits and not theater. Some of the hits may well be rewarding theater; some of the flops may be at least as rewarding. I remember getting a call for help from Hal Prince for his 1964 production of Anouilh's *Poor Bitos*. It was an angry play, intelligent and sardonic, deserving a life on Broadway. Prince said that *Poor Bitos* needed immediate support or it would expire, and with it another chance for serious drama. The favorable review I had written indicated unmistakably that it deserved an audience. But it was not a money review.

Merrick, of course, was hell bent for money reviews. Anything less was to him an affront to nature. With his flair for exploiting his wares in his advertis-

Hal (Harold) Prince in 1967.

ing and publicity stunts, he could make money even with shows that received less than raves. According to a story in *Time* on March 25, 1966, he had produced thirty-seven shows, beginning in 1954, of which twenty-two were profitable and eleven were smash hits. "On an investment of $7 million," wrote *Time*, "Merrick had grossed $115 million and shown a net projected profit of $14 million." Of that thirty-seven I dealt with twenty-nine. Obviously, neither I nor my colleagues did him irreparable damage.

In my first season he was involved in six productions: *Vintage, 60*, a mild, forgettable little revue; *Irma La Douce*, a musical from France via London, which sought cheerfully to make vice as innocent as a bedtime story; *A Taste of Honey*, a touching play by Shelagh Delaney, a nineteen-year-old British girl who never realized on the promise implicit in this piece, which had a glowing performance by Joan Plowright; Anouilh's *Becket*, with Laurence Olivier and Anthony Quinn; *Do-Re-Mi*, a musical by Garson Kanin, Betty Comden, Adolph Green and Jule Styne, with Phil Silvers; and *Carnival*, a musical based on the film success *Lili*. My reviews of all but *Vintage, 60* and *Do-Re-Mi* were largely favorable. But they were not reviews that called for dancing in the streets. They were not money reviews that would lead to enormous successes like *Forty-second Street*, but they were reviews that contributed to bringing in customers and money for the profitable productions.

Early in my second season Merrick brought in Terence Rattigan's *Ross*, a play based on the life of T. E. Lawrence, which had a searching, dazzling performance by Alec Guinness, and I wrote approvingly of it. I did not really pan a Merrick production until *Subways Are for Sleeping*. There was no malice in the review; there never was, I hope, in anything I wrote about Merrick. It just struck me as an awful show, and I kissed it off in my opening paragraph: "If it weren't for disturbances on the stage and in the pit, *Subways Are for Sleeping* would be."

I guess the review stung him. The day it appeared I received a wire: "DEAR MR. TAUBMAN AT LAST YOU WERE DEFINITE AND I CONGRATULATE YOU DAVID MERRICK."

A week after this musical opened, with unfavorable reviews from all my colleagues, Merrick ran a full-page ad in which the seven New York newspaper critics' names were printed in large letters beside photographs of seven unknowns who happened to have the same names—no one ever bothered to check whether the truth about those names hadn't been stretched a little—and who were quoted in unreservedly laudatory approval of *Subways Are for Sleeping*. It was a cheeky and amusing, if futile, thrust; apparently Merrick didn't mind spending his and his backers' money to have a little fun.

Since he seldom lost an opportunity to attack the critics, I naturally was a favorite target. Once he published a quote from one of my reviews, translated into Greek, and suggested that I needed vocational guidance. But none of his needles, however ingeniously applied, drew blood from me. Perhaps that is what drove him to what certainly was an extreme. On Wednesday night, April 17, 1963, he opened a London import, *Rattle of a Simple Man*, by Charles Dyer, with Tammy Grimes, Edward Woodward and George Segal, then a young actor in a bit role. Of the reviews that appeared on April 18, mine was the least favorable.

On the morning of April 19 there appeared a full-page ad in *The Times*. Its message in big, black type was that "tonight David Merrick reviews Howard Taubman on the Johnny Carson show." Throughout the paper were scattered small, two-column ads referring readers to the full-page splash. I did not watch Merrick's performance. I was at the opening of an unfortunate musical called *Hot Spot*, in which a valiant Judy Holliday made one of her last appearances.

My wife and sons watched that night, and when I got home, Nora observed that they did not know whether to laugh or cry. They had made an audio tape of the performance, and I listened to it.

It was not necessary for me to comment then; it is not necessary to comment now. I prefer to quote from three publications. Robert Lewis Shayon, writing in the *Saturday Review* of May 11, said in part:

> During "The Tonight Show," Johnny Carson, the host, asked Mr. Merrick, "Do you and Mr. Taubman ever speak at all?" The producer answered, "I'm afraid not. He was invited to come over here tonight but refused." Phil Foster, a comedian who was also a guest on the show, added: "Howard the coward." The studio audience laughed. Perhaps the vast television audience found the gag amusing, too. Unfortunately, Mr. Merrick's statement that Taubman had been invited but refused to appear was false.
>
> Mr. Taubman had never been asked by NBC or anyone else to appear on "The Tonight Show." Johnny Carson was NBC's only representative on camera. Someone at the network either knew or should have known that Mr. Merrick was speaking falsely on a matter of no small significance. A journalist's thirty-four-year career was being denigrated on a publicly owned channel. The license of the station is a trustee for the public; his independent judgment in operating his privileged enterprise is subject to limitations of the letter and spirit of FCC regulations with respect to fair play and the public good.
>
> The program had been videotaped at NBC from 7:30 to 9:30 P.M., Mr. Merrick told me in a telephone conversation afterward. The tape was not scheduled to be put on the air until 11:30 P.M. The producer said that network lawyers screened the tape and cleared it without change. Was not the action culpable, whether the false statement was permitted to stand in ignorance or in knowledge?
>
> Mr. Merrick made serious charges about Mr. Taubman on the program, in an atmosphere charged with antagonism and obvious malice. I did not see the show, but I have carefully examined the relevant portions of the transcript, read reviews and talked with people who saw the program. The mood was not one of serious discussion about esthetic issues, but rather that of a mock trial, the object of which seemed to be to fascinate viewers with a spectacle of abuse. Impressions of Mr. Taubman as a man and as a drama critic were conveyed to a great number of people, many of whom were probably learning of him for the first time. He was held up to public ridicule, and whatever balance was possible under the circumstances rested in the hands of the program host and the visiting comedian, who were

hardly capable of lifting the conversation from its pervasive level of comic saturnalia. The producer said that Taubman "hates Broadway." He offered a tasteless, irreverent public prayer to *The Times* to remove Mr. Taubman. He was allowed to display an advertisement showing a diapered baby with the legend "Time for a Change," which he described as a picture of the critic. Mr. Merrick cruelly caricatured the manner in which Mr. Taubman spends his day. The people I talked with about the show are far from prim moralists; they relish sophisticated satirical repartee. Nevertheless, they all agreed that this particular spectacle revolted them.

Harriet Van Horne, writing in the *New York World-Telegram and Sun* of April 23, said in part:

> I watched last Friday night and the fun was reminiscent of a seventeenth-century hanging at Old Tyburn. The mood was ugly, the spirit nasty. And not one minute of this vilification should have been permitted into America's living room.
>
> One cannot say, of course, that Carson himself is an offender. In him you will find none of the vengeful spite nor childish bad temper of Jack Paar. But he can be rightly criticized for sitting by with a foolish grin on his face while a mountebank Broadway producer savagely attacked, on Friday last, the character, integrity and sanity of a New York drama critic.
>
> Why the attack? Why, because the critic dared to write an unfavorable review of the producer's latest play.
>
> Mind you, the critic . . . had in no sense questioned the honor or sanity of the producer. He simply didn't like the play.
>
> To be sure, the producer . . . had every right to differ with the critic's point of view.
>
> But to bustle onstage with disgusting little charts and drawings, to characterize his adversary as "an incompetent hack . . . a blind idiot . . . a man who feeds poison nuts to squirrels"—this is a vicious form of buffoonery. And it passed all understanding how NBC's legal department—to say nothing of those busy, pious little men who are forever fussing over offense to the Bible Belt and the Veterans of Foreign Wars—could sanction the airing of a bitter personal feud.

At about the same time, *Variety* ran a long account of the broadcast with a sidebar headlined "GOOD" NOTICES, YES! which read in full:

> Display ads being run by David Merrick to announce that Arlene Francis and Jack Klugman are now co-starring in his Broadway production of *Tchin-Tchin* in the

roles originated by Margaret Leighton and Anthony Quinn, carry the following single comment about the play:

"Weaves an enchanting spell," Taubman, *Times*

My phone rang all weekend and early the next week. One message was from a distinguished lawyer, whom at this time I knew only by reputation and who offered to represent me, without fee, contingent or otherwise, in a suit for slander against Merrick, Carson and NBC. When I arrived at *The Times* on Monday, there was word that Turner Catledge, the executive editor, wished to see me. His first question was "Do you intend to do anything?"

"Nothing," I said.

"Good decision," he replied.

Two days later there was word that a messenger had arrived with an envelope that he was authorized to hand over only to me. I went out and got the envelope. It was from Merrick. It contained a letter from him that I showed only to Orvil Dryfoos, then publisher of *The Times*, Catledge and my family. It is time, I think, to publish it. Dated April 24, 1963, it said:

Dear Mr. Taubman:

What was intended to be a bit of satirical ribbing last Friday on television turned out to be ugly and strident. I want to apologize—it seems clear to me that I must confine my activities to producing plays, which I think I do well, and give up being a controversial figure, which I don't do well.

Again, I'm sorry about Friday night's undignified doings, although I suspect you were easily the winner and now probably the best-known drama critic ever.

Sincerely,

David Merrick

I replied with a one-sentence acknowledgment that I had received his letter. I did not remind him that a private apology for an attack on a national network did not amount to adequate contrition.

I judge from the mail I received that NBC had been the recipient of outraged protests. Two weeks after the broadcast, a letter from Art Stark, producer of "The Tonight Show," extended "an open invitation to appear as a guest on our program." My reply: "This is to acknowledge your letter of May 3, inviting me to appear on 'The Tonight Show.' Your invitation is two weeks late." Later in May I received from a reader who was unknown to me a copy of a letter he had sent to NBC, which had informed him in reply to an earlier letter of protest that the network had invited me to appear on "The Tonight Show" and that I had declined. "I consider your letter as a weasel," this correspondent wrote to NBC. "It is immaterial if Merrick does or does not apologize. The apology to Mr. Taubman should come from NBC. And on the same show." It never came.

Months after, Merrick had opened *Hello, Dolly* to begin one of Broadway's longest runs—he had no complaints about my review then—and I happened to be lunching in the Oak Room at the Plaza with Howard Teichmann, the playwright who was serving as an advisor to the Shubert Organization (the foundation that owns most of the Broadway theaters and sometimes produces shows). Merrick was at another table, and he kept staring at us. Teichmann wanted to know why; I had no idea. We chanced to remain at our table after most other lunch patrons had gone. Merrick had departed, but we noticed that

Carol Channing in *Hello, Dolly*, 1964.

he kept walking up and down the corridor and pausing to stare at us through the glass door.

"What's got into him?" Teichmann wondered.

"Do you know," I said, "Merrick and I have never met face to face, have never been formally introduced and have never spoken a word to each other."

"That gives me an idea," Teichmann said. "I'll bet he'd like to meet you. Would you be willing, if I told him I could get you to have lunch with him if he'd contribute some seats to *Hello, Dolly* for our school's program?"

I said I could stand it if Merrick could.

A few days later we had lunch—Merrick, Teichmann and I. The conversation was correct and civil. The broadcast was never mentioned. Teichmann got his tickets.

In the summer of 1965 I spent a few days in San Francisco, and one day I had the pleasure of being a lunch guest of Louis E. Lurie, who owned the city's two major theaters and enough real estate to make him a millionaire many times over. Lurie held forth every day at lunch at Jack's, where he presided over a round table with an assortment of lively guests from business, law, the arts and other fields. Somehow the conversation turned to Merrick, and Lurie wrote him about it. Merrick replied to Lurie, who was good enough to send me a copy of the 1965 letter. Here is part of it:

> Poor Mr. Taubman, to get mixed up with all the David Merrick friends!
>
> I'm glad to hear he spoke well of me. I had a very pleasant luncheon with him a few months ago, and I was impressed with his clear-cut affection for the theater. I suppose our difference of opinion in the past might be summed in a little anecdote. Remember the famous baseball umpire Bill Klem, who late in his life after forty years of umpiring said, "I never called one wrong in my life"? My philosophy is exactly the same: I have never produced a bad show in my life. I daresay Mr. Taubman's feeling is, conversely, that he has never called one wrong. Therein lies the difference. But Howard always has the last word.

My last review as *The Times* drama critic was of a Merrick import from London—Peter Weiss's play *The Persecution and Assassination of Marat as Performed by the Inmates of the Asylum of Charenton under the Direction of the Marquis de Sade*, known more simply as *Marat/Sade*. It opened on December 27, 1965, and my review the next morning was full of praise for the intelligence of the play and the imagination of the production, directed by Peter Brook. It was, I guess, a money review. That afternoon or the next, there was a farewell party for me in Sardi's Belasco Room, with the Shubert Organization as host. Among the guests was Merrick. He found occasion to speak to me alone. "I thought of deferring the opening until after New Year," he said, "when you'd be gone, but I gambled and won. Thank you."

I encountered Merrick a final time late in 1968. Friends of Lyndon and Lady Bird Johnson threw a wingding of a farewell party at the Plaza Hotel. Although the President was about to leave the White House under the bloody, shameful Vietnam cloud, the mood was festive. The guests were not only associates of the President but also friends who understood that despite the failure of the enormously costly policy in Vietnam, the Johnson Administration's successes in domestic affairs were among the most admirable in the nation's history.

As the evening was ending, I happened to stroll down the side of the ballroom, and at a small table seated alone, while everywhere else people in pairs and groups were dancing or conversing animatedly, was Merrick. He stood up as he saw me and offered his hand. I extended mine.

"Why don't we have lunch again?" he asked eagerly.

"That would be nice," I replied.

He promised to call but didn't.

I did not really expect him to. But then and later I wondered about the strange psychology of a man who could be ruthless in the pursuit of his business and personal goals and who at the same time would seek the good opinion of someone he had knowingly sought to injure. Was it guilt or insensitivity or both with a mixture of addled pride?

10

Fred Loewe and the Real McCoy

Mention Frederick Loewe and the other name that comes immediately to the mind of anyone who has a passing acquaintance with the history of the American musical theater would inevitably be Alan Jay Lerner. Not for me. I think of George McCoy.

How could my memory be so errant? How could it permit the intrusion of an outsider like George McCoy into the unforgettable bracketing of Lerner and Loewe, the team that created such joyous musicals as *Brigadoon, My Fair Lady* and *Camelot?*

The answer is simple. I knew George McCoy. I got to know him well when we were both on the staff of *Mediterranean Stars and Stripes*, based in Rome. I can tell you what I did on the U.S. Army newspaper: I wrote and edited. I cannot tell you what George's assignment was. My guess was that his most important duty was to keep out of sight.

The truth was that George had no skill or experience that suited him for a newspaper or, for that matter, for the Army. Before being drafted in his late thirties, he had established a reputation for quickness and humor with a radio program in which he interviewed out-of-towners under the marquee of the late lamented Astor Hotel on Broadway and Forty-fifth Street. I don't know to which branch of the service he was assigned. Whichever it was, he was miserable in it, and landing in Italy did not cheer him up until our first sergeant, a bluff, warmhearted man named Irving Levinson, ran into him and contrived to have him shifted to *Stars and Stripes*.

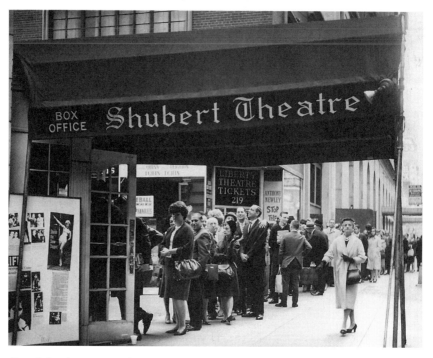

Crowds lined up on Broadway to buy theater tickets, 1960.

Now that I think hard about George and *Stars and Stripes*, I find I cannot recall his ever being in the large fifth-floor room of the plant of the Italian paper *Il Messaggero*, which the Army had requisitioned, where we pounded typewriters, edited copy and wrote headlines from 1944 to 1946. George could be found from time to time in the store fronting on the Via del Tritone, where copies of *Stars and Stripes* as well as the Army magazine *Yank* were on sale. I suppose he was listed as a member of the circulation crew, but he rarely sold papers. However, he did circulate.

With the permission of *Stars and Stripes*, he began to do programs for our armed forces radio. Standing under the balcony of the Palazzo Venezia, from which Mussolini had harangued thousands of Italians packing the Piazza Venezia, George would assemble a group of GIs to interview. His opening line was "Anyone here from out of town?"

The program was ad-lib, often amusing, occasionally touching. It did not, however, consume a lot of George's time. He developed an enormous acquaintanceship among Romans of all sorts. I recall that at one time he was courting an attractive woman who had been a dancer and was attempting to create a dancing school. He persuaded me to come and visit her, explaining quite candidly that producing a friend who was a music critic for *The New York Times* in peacetime would raise his standing in her eyes. At other times he introduced me to several inmates of a posh bordello not far from our headquarters, and one day I found him taking care of the child of one of the women in the bordello. It seemed that she had an urgent, important customer and no one to take charge of her child. Like the good samaritan he was, George came to her rescue. He had the child seated on one of the counters near an unsold pile of *Stars and Stripes* and was cooing at it with a semblance of expertise.

After the war George had some difficulty getting back into radio and attempted press agenting. That was how he came back into my life. I had returned to my post on *The Times* as music editor, and one day in 1947 I had a call from George.

"Have you seen *Brigadoon?*" he asked.

"Not yet. Why?"

Brigadoon had recently opened to great acclaim. I was pleased that George, whom I had not heard from in several years, cared, though I was not so innocent as to imagine that he had no purpose but my well-being.

"Well," said George, "I'd like you to see it."

"It's a nice idea, George, and I'd like to, but why do you ask?"

George could spout blarney at will, but with an old friend he came straight to the point: "I need a favor. I'm working for Fred Loewe, and I want a piece about him in *The Times*."

"That should be easy, George. His show is a big hit. Get in touch with the Drama Department."

"That's not what I want. Fred would like someone who knows about music to write about the score of *Brigadoon*."

"Let me think about it, George, and call me back in a few days."

When he called, his pleading was more urgent. I had made some inquiries and had learned that George was truly hard up and could use some help. I might have considered writing about Loewe and the *Brigadoon* score for the music pages, but George wanted it badly in the drama section, preferably on the front page of the Sunday section. If he succeeded in landing a piece on the front page of the Sunday arts section, he might hope to attract other clients, perhaps build a new career.

An article on Loewe, even before I saw *Brigadoon*, had possibilities, and I proposed it to my friend Lewis Funke, then drama editor as he remained when I succeeded Brooks Atkinson as senior drama critic. Lewis said he would be glad to consider it, and I let George know that I was ready to see *Brigadoon*.

"Fred would like you to have dinner with him," George said. When Nora and I arrived at the restaurant, George was at the door and led us to the table where Loewe waited. The composer was tense and jittery. George, even more up-tight, pleaded another obligation, said he would be back well before curtain time and shuffled away. I suspect that he could not bear to be there if the meeting did not go well.

It went pleasantly and well. Loewe, small and delicately made, relaxed as we chatted. He told of his background. The son of a Viennese operetta tenor who had been a star in Oscar Straus's *The Chocolate Soldier*, Fred was proud of his musical training. He had studied with Ferruccio Busoni and Eugen d'Albert, both virtuoso pianists and distinguished composers. He had done his own choral arrangements for *Brigadoon* and could have made his own orchestrations. In his teens he had drifted into popular song–writing. At fifteen he wrote a song called "Katrina" which sold more than two million copies, but all he earned from the hit tune was about $12. He did not explain why; there must have been some shifty publishers in his native Vienna. He came to the United States seeking a career in music, appeared as a pianist at Town Hall with little success and tried other professions, such as busboy in a cafeteria, flyweight boxer and riding instructor in New Hampshire, with even less success. In 1943 he met Lerner. They began to collaborate, and their musical *The Day Before Spring* was a *succès d'estime*. What they wanted to do next was a musical based on Barrie's *Little Minister*, but they could not get the rights. Determined to fashion a musical with a Scottish setting, they cooked up their fantasy of a Scottish town, *Brigadoon*.

What Loewe wanted to talk about most was his music. He was sure that I, a music critic, would understand what he had accomplished. He did not say plainly that he had brought the subtlety and sophistication of a trained, serious composer to his score, but he implied that I would recognize them when I heard his music. It would have been the obvious thing to use bagpipes frequently to evoke the spirit of Scotland, but he used them only once in a death scene to create an eerie effect. He was proud too that he had employed the chord of the open fifth played by the strings to convey another Scottish effect despite the fact that, like music students for generations, he had had it drummed into him that he must avoid that banal musical interval like the plague. He was proudest of his music for the extended dance sequence that opened the second act.

George returned to get us into the theater on time. Our seats were in the front row, almost on top of the percussion. George and Fred sat with us, and I could not believe that Fred did not think we were too close for comfort. Surely it was George, in his anxiety, who had arranged for these seats. There were moments when the orchestra, playing at full tilt and volume, seemed to be assaulting us. At intermission time when the pounding ceased, I found myself muttering, "for this relief, much thanks."

George led us to a tavern near the theater where he had reserved a table. We had a drink, and Fred resumed talking about the structure and intricacy of the music for the ballet, interrupting himself to assert, "We must not miss the ballet." George repeated, "We must not miss the ballet." Then Fred ordered a second round, saying there was time enough before the ballet.

You have guessed it. When we got to the theater, the lights were down and the ballet was over. Fred glared at George. George looked at me miserably. When I wrote about Loewe and *Brigadoon* I could not, of course, mention, let alone discuss, the music for the ballet.

I did not get around to writing about Loewe and his music for many weeks. I was preoccupied with a multitude of obligations in my department as well as with commissions for other writing. At least once a week George would call, insinuating gently and mournfully that if an article did not appear soon, he would be out of a job. He appealed so poignantly that I finally wrote the piece. Using *Brigadoon* and two other fine musicals running on Broadway—*Oklahoma!* (Richard Rodgers) and *Finian's Rainbow* (Burton Lane)—I developed the theme that solidly trained musicians, as in the days decades ago when a Victor Herbert was frequently represented, were contributing to successful musical shows. Kern and Gershwin had done so somewhat later. Rodgers and Porter were current exemplars, and if Irving Berlin had had a minimal sophisticated musical education, he was the example beyond others of the need for a great natural gift beyond all else.

New delays ensued. More urgent subjects evidently required space on the drama pages. George resumed his piteous calls, and I promised a big push to get the piece into the paper. I pressed hard, and one Sunday morning it appeared on the front page of the drama section with a carryover to page three. At last, I thought, I have discharged my promise to George. I expected a happy, grateful call, at least a written message. But not a word.

Weeks later, walking up Broadway, I ran into George. We shook hands, and I waited for him to say something. He looked at me with a woebegone expression. For a man as talkative as George, he was singularly quiet. I reproved him for not calling or writing to say thank you.

"I didn't have the heart for it," he groaned. "How did I know that the minute your piece made it into the paper I would be fired!"

11

Noblesse Oblige

WHAT A FORTUNATE coincidence! During a two-month tour of nine Asian countries in 1968, I came to Bali hoping to rediscover the marvelous dancing I had seen when a company from that Indonesian island toured the United States in 1952. But it was the off-season, nothing was happening, and I was disappointed. However, a ray of hope appeared. Something special was being organized for Haile Selassie, Emperor of Ethiopia. Perhaps a representative of *The New York Times* could be invited to this private performance if he promised to behave and keep his distance from the royal visitor and his party. I gave my solemn pledge.

It was a magical performance. A group of dancers had been assembled for this occasion, led by the woman who at the age of eleven had enchanted New York in 1952. Apparently an ancient rule that a girl must stop dancing in public when she reaches puberty, the marriageable age, had been waived in honor of His Majesty. At twenty-seven, now the mother of three, the woman still moved with exquisite grace and authority. Something disarmingly ingenuous and pure that had been so magical in 1952 was gone. Nevertheless it was an unexpected privilege to see her and the young dancers who appeared with her.

But what is a delicate, shimmering performance to an imperial guest and his eager hosts? In the midst of a lovely, elaborate dance by the entire company, a troupe of servants marched down the aisles of the open-air theater bearing trays of coffee and sweets. The little Emperor, who had been stroking his tiny dog on his lap, handed the pet to an aide and between sips began an animated

Haile Selassie, Emperor of Ethiopia 1930–74.

conversation. I felt like shouting to the dancers, "Don't perform unless they pay attention!"

Diplomats, like nobility, sometimes behave as if the old attitude toward artists is still in effect: they are little more than servants to be patronized. In New Delhi I was graciously invited to the British Embassy for an evening of performances by one of India's great exponents of *bharata natyam*, a highly regarded form of the country's classic art. A performing space was set up at the edge of an attractive garden. The invited guests sat in chairs ranging in a semi-circle around the temporary stage. The front rows were empty when the performance began. The dancer was well into her program when a line of men and women marched out of the embassy and took the empty chairs, seemingly unperturbed by the fact that the dancer was dancing. Was this an example of refined diplomatic protocol?

If only the dancer had had the temerity to behave as Arturo Toscanini had once done in Salzburg. It was 1935 when the maestro, out of revulsion for Hitler

Performers in a dance drama from the Indian epic the Ramayana.

and Nazism, had shifted his summer activity from Bayreuth to Salzburg. The week I spent at the Salzburg Festival that year is still luminous in my memory. Toscanini conducted *Fidelio* with Lotte Lehmann in the title role and *Falstaff* with Dusolina Giannini and Mariano Stabile. Bruno Walter conducted Mozart—*The Marriage of Figaro* and *Don Giovanni*—with Ezio Pinza and Elisabeth Rethberg among his singers. And one morning Toscanini led the Vienna Philharmonic in a choice orchestral program. After the intermission he resumed his place on the podium and gave the downbeat for the beginning of a Mozart symphony. At that moment a "very important personage, no less than a maharajah," I was told later, marched down the aisle with his party to his seats in a front row. Toscanini stopped the music, turned around and glared. Would he resume the concert? It must have seemed to the maharajah like an eternity, or had he done what came naturally to one of his lofty position? When Toscanini

Lotte Lehmann as Fidelio at Salzburg, 1935.

turned to face the orchestra, the public saluted him with a burst of applause. This was one time when true noblesse—the artist—prevailed.

I do not equate myself with the artist. As a writer for *The Times* I did not expect special consideration. I wanted to do my job. In 1958 I was assigned to spend the better part of four months in Brussels covering Expo '58 and the Festival Mondial that was its remarkable and continuing highlight. But covering was not easy. It became a source of recurrent problems, largely because of the old chaste notion that journalism belonged to a lower estate than nobility and diplomacy.

Before getting to the way I dealt with my problems, let me summarize the history of Expo '58. World Fairs in the past had been designed to catch the attention of people attracted to gadgets, technical wonders and projections of imagined new worlds. If they included some cultural events, it was to give them a bit of class. Expo '58 had an impressive representation of the normal run of exhibits leaning to scientific and business interests, but its great distinction was the immense emphasis on the arts, where it set a standard that later World Fairs in Montreal, Seattle and Osaka sought to match. So great was the commitment to the arts in Brussels that Expo '58 became the most ambitious, extended worldwide festival ever assembled, a magnet for an unparalleled constellation of performance.

The Festival Mondial, as it was called, was not the achievement of any vision or planning by the Belgian government or the people it put in charge of the fair. It was the conception of private entrepreneurs, and it grew in scope and diversity as governments engaged in what came to be a happy cultural competition.

Maurice Huisman was one of the instigators behind the scenes. He managed the Royal Opera at the Théâtre de la Monnaie as well as a private concert business. I do not know whether he approached Soviet authorities or they him, but I suspect that he persuaded them that Expo '58 would be an excellent forum for their performing forces. It should be remembered that after the end of World War II, few Soviet artists were seen or heard in the West. There was a breakthrough in 1951 when a group of musicians appeared at the Maggio Musicale in Florence. I chanced to be there and heard for the first time Emil Gilels, Mstislav Rostropovich and his wife, Galina Vishnevskaya. By the mid-fifties there was further cultural exchange. With the imminence of Expo '58, the Soviets saw an opportunity to make a grand cultural splash.

When Huisman and his friends suggested to the fair's principal planners that the Festival Mondial would be an exciting addition to the exposition, they held back. They declined to be designated patrons of the festival. Belgium's feisty Dowager Queen Elisabeth did not hesitate. Always appreciative of the arts, especially music—she gave her name to the earliest of prestigious competitions for violinists, pianists and singers—she gladly consented to be a supporter and patron of the Festival Mondial.

Participation in this aspect of Expo '58 evolved, to everyone's surprise, into a matter of national pride and honor. Once the Soviet Union had made a weighty commitment to Festival Mondial, the United States found it had no option except to compete. Great Britain, France, Italy, Argentina, small countries from all over the globe, registered their determination to be represented. Clearly the Théâtre de la Monnaie and other venues in Brussels would be inadequate to accommodate all the visiting artists. Expo '58 authorized construction of an auditorium to be built on the fairgrounds. The Grand Auditorium was a mess; it had inadequate backstage facilities, no pit and miserable acoustics. But it did have magnificent boxes on each side—one for royalty and the other for official magnificoes of various degrees of social and political importance. In a triumph of one-upmanship the United States built a modern theater of its own near its handsome pavilion. Constructed at a cost of $1 million, it seated eleven hundred and was too large for some attractions, too small for others. It had no parking facilities and was difficult to get to. The Grand Auditorium had better provisions for parking, but they were limited and, naturally, only for the use of nobility and diplomats. Since it rained nearly all the time in Brussels, it was a common sight to see elegantly dressed people splashing their way to the auditorium or the U.S. theater.

Rain or no rain, the attractions were irresistible. From Austria there was the Vienna State Opera in *Figaro* conducted by Herbert von Karajan and *Salome* conducted by Karl Böhm. From Italy came La Scala in Cimarosa's *Matrimonio segreto*, staged by Giorgio Strehler, and *Tosca* with Renata Tebaldi and Giuseppe Di Stefano. From Czechoslovakia the Prague Opera in *The Bartered Bride.* From China the enchanting Peking Opera before it was undermined by the Cultural Revolution. From the Soviet Union the Bolshoi Ballet with Galina Ulanova, a woman in her fifties dancing an incredibly radiant and youthful Juliet; the Moscow Circus, with its superb clown, Oleg Popov; and the Moscow State Orchestra. From Great Britain, the Royal Vic. From the United States, in its own theater managed by Jean Dalrymple, the premiere of Gian-Carlo Menotti's *Maria Golovin,* Jerome Robbins' *Ballets U.S.A.*, the musicals *Carousel* and *Wonderful Town,* and a host of other performances.

In a sense the Festival Mondial overflowed into the other parts of Belgium. Visiting performers appeared in other cities. Special attractions were created. In Antwerp at the house Rubens had lived in, there was a pageant that sought to re-enact the marriage of the painter to Hélène Fourment. An audience of about fifty, all that could be accommodated in the limited space, assembled in the garden, which had been preserved with its statuary to look as Rubens had painted it. Performers in the costumes that the painter had immortalized on his canvases went through a formal ceremony with the accompaniment of appropriate music. Treated as guests at the momentous occasion, we in the audience were served wine by costumed servitors, and we joined in a toast to the happy couple.

The fair and its Festival Mondial became an exercise in the conduct of international relations. There was not only competition but also constant social contact among leading figures in governments. The social, political, diplomatic and royal games were played to the hilt. The players, persons of one sort of rank or another, had the highest priority. They were honored at endless successions of lunches, dinners and soirées. They occupied the best seats at performances. And of course they had the run of the vast, sprawling fairgrounds by car while the rest of us walked.

That was how I came to lose patience. As a representative of *The Times* I was there to write about the fair and especially about the remarkable diversity of Festival Mondial. To my amazement fair authorities seemed indifferent to my needs and those of other press representatives. I could not always get tickets to events I wished to cover, either by purchase or invitation. Huisman came to my assistance a number of times by wangling tickets from officials of other countries. The diplomatic and social elite were granted parking privileges near the Grand Auditorium while working stiffs like me had to park our cars at the edge of the fairgrounds and walk long distances, usually in the rain.

I complained about the difficulties I was encountering to the people in charge of the press office, but nothing changed. Indignantly I wrote a letter to Baron Moëns de Fernig, the Belgian King's representative as chief executive of the fair. I listed the difficulties I had to face in covering the fair and the Festival Mondial. I explained that I had requested some ameliorative action but had gotten nowhere. I pointed out that thousands of Americans were attending the fair and that it was probable that many of them were stimulated to do so by my reports in *The Times*. I ended by saying that if Expo '58 would not help me to do my job properly, I would recommend to *The Times* that I be called home.

I had an immediate response from an aide of the Baron. Would Nora and I be the guests of the Baron and his wife at the Belvedere Palace, his official residence for the duration of the fair? We went to lunch. There were two great round tables, the Baron presiding at one and the Baroness at the other. My wife was asked to sit at the Baron's right, I at the Baroness's right. We were virtually the only non-official, untitled guests. The lunch was splendid; it is only fair to record that Brussels cuisine compares favorably with that of Paris, and it was at its best at the Baron's table. After lunch the gentlemen withdrew for coffee and cigars, and the Baron, in an expansive mood, approached me and asked, "What do you think of us now?"

"I enjoyed the lunch and the company," I replied, "but will my situation change?" He smiled. I became a kind of V.I.P. I received permission to park near the Grand Auditorium. I had no further difficulty in gaining admittance to all events. Now I became, temporarily at least, a member of the noblesse. Did I, as a result, have obligations to my colleagues of the Belgian and world press? I believe they thought that I ought to fight for them, and I fear they had a point. In any event they began to avoid me as if I had ratted and gone over to the enemy. Was I guilty of violating the standard of noblesse oblige?

Here I must admit that not every problem I faced in Brussels could be traced to the fourth estate. Naturally, we took shortcuts to achieve speed and save money. Each day I would hurry back from a festival event to my rented house in the south of Brussels, type my review, phone the London bureau of *The Times* and dictate it, to be recorded and transcribed by a member of the London staff and cabled to New York.

I began one article with the line "Folk art is rarely great art." To my horror, back in New York, I found that the sentence read, "Folk art is really great art." Clearly to an Englishman my "rarely" meant "really." So much for the slip-ups due to international differences. My fault. If you deal with words that might involve different pronunciations, spell them out.

A few years later when I was drama critic at *The Times*, I ran into difficulties of another sort with a producer who seemed to have delusions of authoritarian grandeur—noblesse *sans* oblige. Lawrence Langner had undertaken to organize a company headed by Helen Hayes, which would prepare a couple of plays—*The Skin of Our Teeth* and *Our Town*—for a government-sponsored tour of countries in Latin America and Europe. Before their foreign appearances, these plays would be presented in Washington. I informed a Langner press representative that I would like to come down to the Capital to see the productions. Word came back—Langner forbade me to do so. I asked, "On what grounds?"

"They will not be ready for review," I was told, "but we'll present them in New York after the foreign tour."

Is the tour, I wondered, *a tryout for Broadway?* It seemed to me of some consequence to have an idea of what foreign audiences would see. I phoned our Washington bureau and requested that tickets be purchased for the productions that were going abroad. I wore no disguise but felt like an interloper when I took my seat in the Washington theater. Would I be recognized? Would Langner or one of his associates try to have me evicted? I sat through the performances and wrote about them with a reasonable appreciation of their merits and an awareness of deficiencies.

Langner was furious. He wrote a letter of protest to Arthur Hays Sulzberger, publisher of *The Times*, who sent it to me with an amused comment. Months later I accepted an invitation to lunch with Langner, who had forgiven me a little for my failure to obey orders.

There was another encounter in 1951 where I tangled with the noblesse of the conductors' guild. That was when I was in Florence to hear the unexpected group of outstanding Soviet musicians. It chanced that I would have an opportunity to hear the soprano who had become the talk of Europe. She was, of course, Maria Callas, the American, who was being hailed as the brightest new luminary of the opera. She was singing two roles at the Florence festival—in Verdi's *I Vespri siciliani* and Haydn's *Orfeo ed Euridice.* There was no problem about the Verdi opera; there was a performance during my week in Florence. Callas sang beautifully. Her voice as pure voice never sounded as well in later years; it was clear, unforced and even throughout the scale, perfectly controlled above the scale where later it could take on a reedy buzz, and it was used with high musical intelligence. She was, to put it plainly, fat, like prima donnas of the other generations, but she could be enormously persuasive in her use of song as a vital dramatic element.

The Haydn opera, however, would not be available to the public until after I left, and I begged the Maggio Musicale management to let me sit through a dress rehearsal. Erich Kleiber, the conductor, had given strict orders that no one must be allowed into the rehearsal. What to do? The management decided to take a risk—with proper precautions. It slipped me into a dark corner of a rear box with a nervous injunction not to make even the smallest sound. I have rarely sat anywhere so quietly, not daring to cross a leg or change my position in my chair. As for anything like coughing, what would his highness the conductor think? I felt I was lucky to be permitted to breathe.

Just as the first act was ending, Kleiber whirled around and shouted, "Get out! Get out! Whoever is up there, out!" I skulked out. How did he know? Could he hear me breathing even though orchestra and singers were busy at work? Such furious noblesse had darn well to be obliged!

A few months later in the same year I was at Bayreuth when the Wagner Festival was resuming after the war. The two conductors that year were Hans Knappertsbusch, the sixty-three-year-old distinguished veteran, and Herbert von Karajan, the forty-four-year-old brilliant new star of the podium. Knappertsbusch conducted the opening performance, Wagner's *Parsifal,* which the composer's grandson Wieland turned into an unforgettably compelling dramatic tour de force by depending almost entirely on lighting and the musical

Herbert von Karajan in rehearsal at Bayreuth, 1967. Photograph by Sam Falk.

eloquence of the conductor and his performers. Ernest Newman, the English music critic, wrote of this *Parsifal* and its conductor, "Knappertsbusch does not beat time, he beats eternity."

Knappertsbusch was to conduct the first *Ring* cycle at Bayreuth that year and Karajan the second. One afternoon I was at the Festspielhaus to pick up some photographs to be used in *The Times*, and I saw Knappertsbusch sitting at a table in one of the restaurants on the festival grounds, sipping a beer. I was astonished to find him there when I knew that rehearsals for the first *Ring* cycle were under way. I greeted him and asked how he happened not to be directing the rehearsal. The big, ruddy face broke into a wide grin. "I'm letting Karajan conduct the rehearsal," he said. "The young fellow needs the practice."

Noblesse oblige; indeed!

12

This Was the Army, Too

I T TOOK THREE men to see me off. I was leaving Camp Lee, where I had survived six weeks of basic training, and was destined for Camp Sibert for something called special training. I felt like a one-man troop movement in a mad
farce. In a letter home the next day I described the scene:

> A corporal from Co. F led me to Battalion Headquarters. And I mean led me. I
> left my company area at 10 P.M. on Tuesday and at that moment the camp had an
> air raid alert and blackout. It was so black you could hardly see your nose in front
> of you. Then we stumbled into a building—Battalion Headquarters—and we
> couldn't see a thing; the sound of voices assured us that people were around. A first
> lieutenant took me in charge at 10:30 P.M. He had a truck and driver with him and
> they transported me to the railroad station. My train didn't come in until mid-
> night, but the lieutenant sat around waiting to deposit me on the train. We each
> bought some reading matter. The lieutenant sat around reading comic books, and
> his charge, who couldn't be trusted to get on a train by himself, read Walter Lipp-
> man's *U.S. Foreign Policy* in a Pocket Books edition.

I had only a vague idea of why I was headed for Camp Sibert. All I had been
able to find out about this installation not far from Gadsden, Alabama, was that
it was rumored to be a training center for chemical warfare, and apparently it
had recently become headquarters for some sort of specialized outfit as remote
from chemical warfare as a vaudeville circuit house. I guessed that this outfit
might have some distant connection to music. I had been music editor of *The*

New York Times when I was drafted in 1944, and my good friend Harold Spivacke, chief of the Music Division of the Library of Congress, had suggested to friends at the Pentagon that at the age of thirty-six I might be more useful at a desk than toting a rifle in the infantry.

Apparently Harold had been influential. I was scheduled for eleven weeks of "technical training" before being assigned to Captain Howard Bronson, the Army's music officer, at the Pentagon. As it turned out, I never met Captain Bronson, and as for the "technical training"—you shall hear.

I became a member in good standing, as if I had a choice, of an outfit called Special Services Training Group. Eventually it numbered three hundred men. We learned, almost by rote, to explain ourselves by reciting this catechism: "There's nothing special about us, we provide no service, we got training and we are as far from being a group as three hundred wildly different individualists could be."

In this haphazard assemblage of individualists there were musicians—jazz, country and classical; actors—screen, stage and radio; hoofers; professional athletes; and, I swear, animal trainers. There was a movie projectionist. There was a man who had bought and supervised radio offerings for a big New York ad agency, and there was a director of radio drama. The chap with the oddest mixture of skills was an expert at trick whistling, jiujitsu and knife throwing.

I began to get acquainted with my new buddies. There was Cecil from "Indianny," a shrewd character who played at being the stereotypical hayseed complete with high-pitched, twangy voice. "Well, sir," he told me right off the bat, "this here arthuritis I've got," and he demonstrated his difficulty in walking, one of a dozen ailments that plagued him. No matter what the doctors said, he just "cain't" walk. But he sure could talk—about farming, working in a quarry, carpentering. I never discovered what his specialty was. Did he get the medical discharge he was bucking for? I don't know. One day he was gone.

There was Lambert, who played a mean clarinet. Soon after his arrival, he was taken to task for not cleaning his rifle. His explanation was that he didn't know how. He had been through six weeks of basic training, and it seemed that he had been paying his neighbors in the barracks to clean it for him. When the furious sergeant fired away at him with a particularly vivid verbal salvo, Lambert, his face unruffled, responded appraisingly, "Good script. Who wrote it?"

There was a sharp-faced bird of a man, bald, mustached, weighing less than a hundred pounds, who liked to chew away at a fat cigar. He was a bullfiddler by profession, barely visible when he stood beside the huge soundbox of his instrument looking like a worldly Mickey Mouse. By avocation he was a barber, and as far as I could make out, his special service during the time I knew him was cutting our hair for a fee. I can testify that his handiwork was satisfactory and his rates were competitive.

Another bullfiddler, another avocation: tailoring. This chap canvassed the mess hall hawking his wares, offering to shorten, lengthen or widen suntans soon to be obligatory for dress wear. Somehow he had managed to bring to camp with the rest of his gear a sewing machine, and he was meticulous about keeping his account book up to date. His customers unfortunately were not as scrupulous about paying. One payday he positioned himself outside the paymaster's shed with his account book in one hand and a baseball bat in the other. "Pay up or else!" he shouted, and pay they did.

The musicians had a variety of skills. There was a guitar player who would strum away for sing-alongs in the barracks just before lights were supposed to be out—and sometimes beyond. There were two saxophone players who would start by working away like companions in a band and then go off in different directions, ending in a contest of speed, volume and dexterity. A jam session? Yes, of an excruciating sort.

There was Jimmy Troutman, a topnotch trumpeter, who had most recently been with the Glenn Miller band. There was an excellent French horn player who had also been in the big bands. He was fiercely dedicated to keeping his lip in trim. Whenever there was a break, he would get out his horn and play "Embraceable You." We figured he knew more than that pleasant Gershwin tune, but it was the one he constantly warmed up on. After a while the barracks joined in demanding surcease from "Embraceable You." By popular request he sought and found another place to practice—in a boiler room down the company street. In a way it became a kind of comforting touch of stability, to go by the boiler room and to hear in counterpoint the hum of the boiler and the yearning strains of "Embraceable You."

There were longhair musicians, too. Roland Gundry, who had begun an impressive career as a solo violinist before being drafted at the age of twenty-one, would practice from time to time. I remember in particular one soft, southern moonlit evening when Roland and another kid, a good fiddler whose name escapes me, sitting on their footlockers, played Mozart and Viotti together.

Boris Matusevitch became a good friend. And why not? The first thing he said when he met me was that he had read my book *Music as a Profession*, published some years earlier. Boris played the concertina brilliantly, and his repertory was enormous. I would kid him, demanding to know how a serious, talented musician could devote his life to a squeeze-box. He laughed off my remarks, but in exasperation offered to play the Bach Chaconne—all of it. I didn't think I could endure the Chaconne in these surroundings, especially from a concertina. Boris argued; I demurred. One very warm day after lunch, I lay down in my bunk and dozed off contentedly. I was awakened by the Chaconne. There stood Boris, grinning mischievously and pumping away with intensity. As I roused myself to reach for a pillow to fling at him, I found that he had planned carefully! So-called friends gripped me by the arms and legs, and there I remained pinned down until the last notes of the Chaconne. Boris knew it all and played it remarkably well. I did not get to see Boris after the war was over. He died some years ago, and I never learned whether he had entertained other Army buddies with a complete rendition of the Chaconne.

The actors included Lester Damon, who had developed a large following as Nick Charles in the radio series based on the hugely successful film *The Thin Man;* Laurence Hugo, whose last Broadway appearance had been a play, *Decision;* Guy Kingsford, Sam Wanamaker, Bobbie Breen and Dickie Moore—all shapes, sizes, backgrounds and experience.

Someone in authority decided to get the camp some attention and arranged for a radio station in Birmingham to agree to broadcast a program to be called "Sibert Sounds Off." Damon, Kingsford, Ed Fleming, who had been a CBS announcer, and I were assigned to prepare the program. I suppose this was to be regarded as a phase of the "technical training" we were assumed to be getting.

As far as I could make out, I was officially classified as the only writer in the unit. Later I learned that a man who had invented gags for Red Skelton was in camp; Skelton himself appeared for training at Sibert after I left.

I no longer recall how we shared responsibilities in preparing "Sibert Sounds Off." I do remember that it became an excuse for evading other duties, most of them unpleasant. Obviously we had to do an endless amount of conferring and consulting. I know that I contributed a five-minute sketch because I have a letter I sent home saying that I did. I even heard the program while I was in Birmingham on a weekend pass, and I reported that it went very well. And why not, with pros like my pals? I even turned out a lyric for a song, but it was rejected by higher authority as being too off-color for an Army offering. I might add that it deserved to be rejected because the accent in "morass" belongs on the second syllable:

> In good old Burma
> The terra firma
> Is covered by a morass.
> It's best to fly there
> For in the sky there
> You won't ride on a sore ass.

We were suddenly in demand. Besides the radio programs, we were asked to prepare a live show for a bond-raising rally in Birmingham. We drew on the talents of other "technical trainees." There was a barracks-mate, Paul Parks, a big, gangling chap with a warm, whimsical sense of humor. He wrote the words and music of one of our brightest songs, "How'm I Going to Jump in These GI Shoes?" It was as witty and bouncy as Paul himself. One evening some of us went into Gadsden to see a movie called *Christmas Holiday,* not especially because it starred Deanna Durbin but because our Paul was in it, accompanying her at the piano in one of her songs.

Our "technical training" encompassed regularly scheduled classes in enclosed areas that were called classrooms. I can do no better than quote from a letter I sent home to convey the flavor of the space and the class:

> The classroom we work in is a large barnlike room. What goes on is worthy of a scene in a madhouse play. In one corner several of us sit, talking about a variety show to be done ten weeks from now. In another corner some guys sit and write letters, as I'm doing this morning. At one side three hillbilly performers stand with guitars and practice hillbilly songs. To the left a couple of tap dancers practice a routine. Beyond them a couple of acrobats who had never seen each other are beginning to work out an act. A loud-voiced baritone practices songs. A couple of comedians are working out a routine. There are always a few, including the instructors, who just bull. The only frustrated soldier is a man with a dog act. Unhappily, his dog is stored somewhere in the north. But he is happier today. He received permission from the commanding officer to keep his dog in the company area and has sent for it. When the dog arrives, that should be something.

It was. With permission from the brass, a kennel was prepared for Snooksie, and it stood next to her owner's bunk. The day Snooksie arrived, transported from the north by owner Omar's wife, Omar wore a beatific look. One of my letters reported,

> The little dog is with him all day. When we're out in the morning for calisthenics and games, the dog sits on the sidelines waiting patiently. When the master, an acrobat in an act here, practices his routine in the gym, the little black and white spotted mongrel sits on a bench and watches. Finally Omar begins to rehearse with the mutt, the dog romps around wildly and the master's eyes glow with a father's pride. The dog sleeps near her master, and in the morning at reveille she is on hand to help wake everyone up.

For one of the shows we did in a town some distance from Sibert, a group of us plus Snooksie made the trip in an Army truck. Snooksie, curled up near Omar, dozed without a worry in the world. When called upon to perform before a large outdoor audience, Snooksie carried on like the pro she was, doing spectacular somersaults and spinning with dazzling speed while based on Omar's palm. On the long truck ride back to camp, Snooksie curled up on Omar's lap, and when we traversed a rough stretch of road, Omar cradled her in his arms.

We had another animal trainer at Sibert. Even with the best will in the world, the Army was not prepared to help this chap with his act. His métier was training lions. He was a Hindu who worked in a circus somewhere out of Chicago. When his drafting became imminent, the British consul wrote to him urging him to join the British army and offered free transportation—minus lion, of course—to England. A fierce patriot of his native India, he said he knew Nehru a bit, and when I told him I had read Nehru's *Toward Freedom*, he regarded me with admiring wonder, as if such an animal at Sibert was as rare as his lion would be. As for accepting the British consul's offer, he would rather go before a firing squad, he expostulated, than fight for the raj.

One morning the unit's top officers looked in on classrooms. We had been tipped off by a non-com that they were coming and were implored to make the session look not only credible but snappy. I was drafted to act as the instructor, and the subject for the day was script writing. I proposed a specific problem and invited my students, who included not only knowing characters who had dealt with radio scripts professionally, but also hillbilly musicians, acrobats and an ice skater from a famous ice show—what he was to do with his skates and skills on ice in a southern camp where there was no ice to practice on, no one ever figured out—and other non-intellectual types. It was fascinating to observe how this heterogeneous group got involved in the problem. When the new commander of the unit, a major, walked in with his sidekicks, a captain and a lieutenant, the class was thoroughly absorbed in plotting the script. I ended the session by delivering a solo dissertation, glib and learned enough to impress officers who knew even less than I did.

The performance of all so impressed our commanding officer that he announced he would like to bring a general due in a couple of weeks for an inspection to another of our classes. Again I was asked to play the role of teacher and leader, and we decided—my professional-act friends and I—that we would not attempt to wing it. We prepared carefully what bits they would do if called upon with apparent unexpectedness. The session was under way and had the required military pizazz when the general and his retinue walked in and seated themselves at the back of the classroom. I asked questions and proposed demonstrations as if I were just thinking them up, and my good buddies stood up, paused reflectively as if they were creating silently and launched into a monologue or a scene for two or more that they seemed to be improvising. If I had been writing a criticism of this performance—theirs, not mine—I would have composed what is known in the trade as a rave. The hour ended and the class started to file out, walking by the general and his retinue. As I reached the door, the general stepped behind me and tapped me on the shoulder. Puffed up with pride at how well we had done, I anticipated a word of praise, or at least satisfaction. "Soldier," the general said in crisp, general-like tones, "you need a haircut."

I don't mean to give the Army—or this part of it—a bad name for mismanagement. I was chosen to lead classes merely to demonstrate how well our "technical training" was progressing. We actually had instructors, non-coms who had had extensive experience in civilian life. There was Jim Worden, tall, lean, mustachioed and restless. He was an instructor in theater classes who never instructed. He professed to have had a gaudy past as a Broadway hoofer and road tour company manager. He was the most ambivalent instructor I ever encountered: on the one hand he wanted to be sure that we would look thoroughly occupied if an inspecting officer came by, and on the other hand he hated to remain in the classroom. He would keep hunting for pretexts to pop out for several minutes. All morning his angular frame would be shooting in and out of the door.

Worden was full of stories, delivered in an inimitable hybrid of Broadway jive and GI lingo. If they were not faithful to the truth, they ought to have been. This one I know really happened. About sixty of us had traveled down to Birmingham in five trucks to do a big radio show, and it went so well that our major purred. We were entertained royally by Birmingham business interests and fed drinks and dinner during intervals in the double show. Afterwards a few of us repaired to rooms in the good old Tutwiler Hotel, but some of the boys had to make do with sleeping on sofas in the lobby. One of them was Worden. At 3 A.M. he was awakened by a little man who introduced himself as Nathan something. Nathan said he was a salesman for a New York dress factory and did not like to see soldiers sleeping in lobbies. He invited Worden to use his room upstairs, where he had scores of dresses on display on racks for local buyers, and suggested that he take along another soldier. Worden woke up a pal of his named Hylbert Hams who was also listed as a "theater instructor" and who seemed never to have had any kind of experience in the theater. Nathan shared a large room and a large bed with another salesman, whom he awoke, and he and his roommate slept on the floor while the bed was turned over to Worden and Hams.

It was not really astonishing that radio and war bond shows were prepared and performed effectively. After all, the performers were experts in the milieu. What was constantly mystifying was that officers who knew little or nothing about show-business professionalism insisted on asserting their authority as if performance problems could be solved by military discipline. One lieutenant whom we called "the Brain" went about sounding off about "his musicians" and "his actors" as if he was one of the Shuberts. We had one innocent officer who asked, I swear, "What are cymbals?" I quote from a letter I wrote in class:

> A futile discussion is under way about the war bond show we're to put on. There are a lot of specialty acts in the group, and each one is a prima donna. The soldier-actors and the lieutenant-producer got into a temperamental row. The lieutenant is GI, used to ordering men around. The actors are used to being stars, even if they appeared in second-rate joints. Naturally, when the discussion concerned a revue, their civilian business, they spoke out honestly, and their views differed sharply from the lieutenant's. Result, the lieutenant went off pouting to complain that he was not getting cooperation. And some of the men went off sulking that they had

been insulted as artists. It's nice to be a writer at a time like that. At the moment a compromise is being worked out because the privates cannot afford to ride the lieutenant without end, and at the same time the lieutenant cannot afford to badger the men since they could easily give a bad show.

But a writer could have problems, too. Another lieutenant, who had once had something to do with a summer theater and happened to be fond of Gilbert and Sullivan, gave me a writing assignment: to do a sketch for those two former kid movie stars—Bobbie Breen and Dickie Moore. As a prelude to getting on with this task, I was invited to attend an audition this lieutenant was holding. What a farce! Here was an amateur, despite his alleged experience, telling professional entertainers how to do their jobs. As for the sketch I was to write, the lieutenant wanted a patter song à la G & S. Mercifully, the lieutenant was reassigned, and my writing job was not mentioned again.

Meanwhile my future was being determined in Washington or New York or North Africa or somewhere. I had learned through newspaper friends who were still civilians that Colonel Egbert White, commanding officer of *Stars and Stripes*, the Army newspaper being published in Britain and North Africa, had put in a request for me. How would it fare when evaluated beside the one from Bronson in the Pentagon? I had no way of knowing, even when a sergeant friend at headquarters tipped me off that new assignments for many at Special Services Training Group were being processed and that he had asked an officer whether he knew what mine would be, and the only answer was, "It's good." Obviously, either one would be good. A desk job in Washington would mean not getting shot at and being near my family in New York. An assignment to *Stars and Stripes* would mean traveling—something I liked—and, with luck, not being shot at.

Clearly a decision had been made, and I became at Sibert a kind of dangling man. The word was that I must remain close to my barracks in case orders came through. I was relieved of classwork, such as it was when there was no crap or poker game in progress. I was freed of such things as physical efficiency tests, which meant pull-ups, push-ups, sit-ups, squat jumps, the 100-yard dash carrying a man your own weight piggyback and the 300-yard run. I had managed a couple of them with the help of a little cheating, like the second time I did the obstacle course at Camp Lee and, like a lot of other shortcutters, got lost in the woods and timed my return at the finish line to be back with the others and breathing just as hard.

I did not feel guilty. Evasion and downright dishonesty were endemic. I remembered my clumsiness on the rifle range at Camp Lee, how I had driven my platoon sergeant to rage and despair because my legs would not heed his instructions to be properly flexible so that I might assume the required prone position while firing at the target. My record for accuracy was deplorable. I wondered wistfully whether the Army would treat me the way some colleges deal with hopelessly ungifted freshmen—bust me out. When I completed basic training I was awarded, to my utter bewilderment, a certificate declaring that I had qualified as a "marksman." Obviously the sergeant was not about to have his abilities impugned. Indeed, I heard him declaring proudly, with a straight face, that all his charges had made "marksman."

Once it became clear at unit headquarters at Sibert that my assignment had come through, I chose to become even less of a soldier and more of a goldbrick than I had been in earlier weeks, if that were possible. No one, of course, told me officially where I was headed next, but there were hints I would soon be on my way overseas. I formed the conviction that in this period of waiting to move on, I had no further obligations to Special Services Training Group. I persuaded a new acting first lieutenant that I was not to be taxed with further responsibilities. My subtle campaign succeeded because this sergeant, who had a bad shot at major league baseball and hoped to keep his name green in the baseball world, dreamed that I might be of use. I had some weeks earlier managed to write and have published in *The New York Times'* Sunday radio pages a small article describing how we GIs had put together "Sibert Sounds Off" and other shows, and the sergeant, I suspected, imagined that I would write something about him that would reach *The Times'* sports pages. Alas, I could do nothing for him. After the war, I looked for his name in the sports pages. Evidently he had not been able to do much for himself.

He became my confidant, however. When something really unusual happened—bear in mind that the unusual was usual at Special Services Training Group—he would tell me about it. Even he was astounded by the fellow who asked for permission to visit the medical staff and was told there was no doctor. Finally, he confessed that the symptoms he complained of were being experienced by his wife some thousand miles away, and he was trying to achieve a diagnosis by remote control.

In this period of semi-limbo, I took care of personal interests for which I had not had the time or energy since my induction. I arranged for a short-term subscription to *The Times*, which I shared with some buddies. One fellow wanted only the page with the racing results. A young man from Boston who hoped to build a career as a composer came around and asked whether I would be kind enough to listen to him play some original piano pieces. I went with him to an empty classroom and sat while he played. I have no recollection of what they were like nor what I told him. I hope I was encouraging.

I resumed reading *Moby Dick* where I had left off a dozen years earlier and managed to finish it.

Being on what was called "alert," I had advantages and disadvantages. Of the latter, the worst was that I could not send my clothes to the laundry, and twice a week I had to be my own laundry man. I could not bring myself to the ultimate resort of one chap who showered in his socks on the assumption that he was cleaning them. I took my shirts and trousers to the dry cleaner on the post, but he was about as efficient as some of the people running the camp. Spots and stains were never eradicated.

Among the pleasantest advantages was a long afternoon and evening I spent in the hills twenty miles from Birmingham. As I was typing weekend passes, one of the chores I deigned to accept because that was one way to be certain that nothing would go amiss with mine, the company clerk, a Corporal Glenn Nichols, came over and whispered an invitation to accompany him to a picnic supper. Nichols lived in Birmingham, was a musician and knew something of my civilian career. We hitched a ride into Birmingham, where a friend of his picked us up at the hotel and drove us to a magnificent estate owned by a man named Dorsey Whittington. He had been a pianist of parts in the 1920s and had moved to Birmingham, bought a conservatory and built it up. The setting was something that a man who had spent weeks on the arid, dusty grounds of Sibert could appreciate, an immense house with pine-paneled rooms looking down a large, private lake that lay beyond manicured lawns and walks bordered by a riot of flowers. A number of music teachers were there, including an elderly gentleman who had recently taught himself Russian so that he could translate a book on counterpoint by Sergei I. Taneyev, a nephew of Alexander Taneyev. The conversation was good, adult and civilized, and the food, to a Sibert inmate, was a true indulgence.

Finally, movement of a sort. The day came when I was equipped for further travel. I received a new duffel bag, really a large barracks bag that had a handle and could be carried like a suitcase, a mattress cover, three pairs of woolen socks to replace three cotton pairs and a dust respirator. I guessed that the last item could only be for someone headed for North Africa, perhaps the Sahara desert for all I was told or knew. I hastened to do another laundry, and as I was hanging the wet things on an outside line, a friend came by and asked sweetly, "How is Mrs. Taubman today?" I returned to my bunk, and another smart alec poked his head in and called out, "Hey, Tawbman, do you think jazz is here to stay?" Another well-wisher shouted, "Ain't you gone yet?" I went to Special Services headquarters in the evening to type a letter, but a slew of soldiers, junior officers, non-coms and plain GIs were intent on the same errand, and the talk and horseplay were incessant, topped off by Jim Worden, who walked in, stared in disbelief at the busy typists and cried out, "Well, knock my jock off, who are these people?"

These people, the men with whom I entered Special Services Training Group, were ending their eleven weeks of "technical training," and as a parting reminder that they were still in the Army, they were taken out on a ten-mile hike. When they returned, they were drooping and beat. I marveled at their restraint when they found me on my bunk reading a fine book, Victor Weiskopf's *The Firing Squad*, which Wanamaker, who always had good reading on hand, had lent me. If they were not so exhausted, they might have been tempted to wreak some sort of vengeance on me.

At last my orders to leave arrived. I was to travel, alone once again, to Camp Patrick Henry in Virginia, the port of embarkation for my assignment to *Stars and Stripes*. I said fond farewells to a number of good companions, like Eddie Bartell, who had been in the raffish Broadway hit *Hellzapoppin*, had been a member of the Radio Rogues and had retained his sense of proportion about serving in an Army in which he had a son who was a sergeant.

I did not learn what happened to these men. I do know that many were formed into small units and were sent out on missions to entertain their fellow servicemen. I have no doubt that many of them did a wonderful job. Evidently Special Services Training Group, despite all the irreverent reaction it inspired in us, did in time provide some valuable, cheerful special services.

I have often wondered what happened to my Hindu friend, the lion-tamer. With his dark skin, he was a reminder to some of us that there were no blacks in Special Services Training Group. Hard to believe, isn't it, that in an Army that included hundreds of thousands of black soldiers—and in Special Services Training Group, to which all sorts of entertainers were assigned—there were no black musicians, actors, dancers or athletes.

13

Still in the Army and Exploring Italy

W̶E WERE a party of three when we boarded the good ship *Santa Paula* in 1944—Lyle Dowling, Hugh Conway and I destined for *Mediterranean Stars and Stripes*—the minutest consignment on a troopship that carried two thousand. Lyle had been the managing editor of the *Brooklyn Eagle* and Hugh had been a reporter on the *New York World-Telegram*, newspapers now long defunct. An unlikely trio of fighting men, we had learned the Army art of getting an edge. After the first day at sea, we persuaded an officer to let us produce a news bulletin, to be disseminated via the loudspeaker system and a daily mimeographed sheet.

The reward was a number of pleasant perks. We had access to the quarters of the civilian skipper, a thoughtful man who arranged to have such goodies as doughnuts and coffee for us, a welcome snack on a packed vessel that could serve only two meals a day, a hearty breakfast and an ample early supper. Because of our duties we were permitted to go to the head of the endless chow lines and were excused from K.P. But our sleeping quarters—mine was a middle hammock in a tier of three in an airless, fetid hold—were like those of the common folk. Like most of them, we slept on the deck, happy to do so even if it meant being a sardine in a tightly packed can.

It was a sixteen-day voyage. We were on our way to North Africa, we thought, and on the southern route the sea was kind. We were in a large convoy and could travel only as fast as the slowest vessel. It was whispered that because of a submarine threat we turned south off-course for several days, but even though we served in the lofty role of the ship's news purveyors, the skipper did not confide in us.

I was content to share the deck as a bedroom because I badly needed my hammock for another purpose. Having been warned that there would be no soap where we were going, I took the precaution of providing myself with a box of soap flakes at the last minute and deposited it at the top of the duffel bag in which I had all my clothes. It was pouring when we marched down the Virginia dock to board the *Santa Paula*, and not only was I drenched but everything in my duffel bag was now saturated with soap bubbles because the paper box containing the flakes had dissolved. I rinsed my clothes as best I could without additional water and spread them on the hammock to dry.

Our landfall was Naples, not quite the magnificent harbor of song and story because the Allied bombers had done a job on it. There were ships on their sides, others almost entirely submerged and still others in various stages of ruin. One section of the port was smashed to rubble, with buildings nearby showing gaping holes. In preparing to disembark, I made a lucky mistake. I had been entrusted with the papers for our consignment of three, and as a responsible leader even if only momentarily, I asked the landing officer for guidance. He told me to look for a certain sergeant and I fortunately went to the wrong one, who led us to a replacement depot on the outskirts of Naples. Had I found the right sergeant we would have been taken to Caserta, where Allied headquarters had been set up and where we would have languished for days until we were sent back to Naples and *Stars and Stripes*. Thanks to my gaffe, we were installed at *Stars and Stripes* in Naples within a day.

Our office was in that of the requisitioned daily *Il Mattina*, on the Via Roma, and our living quarters a few steps away were two apartments on the top floor of an immense building, part of the Galleria Umberto, its glass dome now smashed. From the moment we joined *Stars and Stripes*, Army life was almost at an end: no discipline, no reveille, no chow lines, no disagreeable duties. The members of our staff each contributed $3 a month—the best investment I ever made—and with the money in this kitty, Italians were hired to cook, wait on table, launder for us, clean up.

Our new colleagues led us into the kitchen and introduced us to Mamma Mia—I never did learn her name—a round, cheerful, bustling, expansive *chef de ménage*. She had a large staff of daughters, nieces and cousins who buzzed around her like chicks with a mother hen. When she saw me, she ran to me, squeezed my hands and screamed, *"Mio fratello!"* Then she embraced me and wept. I wondered what sort of madhouse this was. I did not understand what she was saying. It seemed I resembled a brother who had been sent off to fight by the Fascists and had not returned, and for a few minutes she refused to believe that I was not he. Mamma Mia was warm and responsive to all the Americans, but it is possible that she favored me from time to time when many of us were clamoring for attention.

Many months later when the war was over, I was back in Naples waiting for shipment home, and I paid a visit to the old billet. When Mamma Mia saw me, she shouted excitedly and rushed to embrace me. Her apron was covered with flour, and when she released me, so was my uniform. By now I spoke Italian fluently if not correctly. I had begun picking up some Italian in the few weeks I remained in Naples, though not from the serious old lady Lyle and I hired for a couple of days, who began our lessons with the Italian equivalent of "What does the cat do? The cat meows." In Rome and in other parts of Italy, I had even learned something more cultivated than earthy Neapolitan phrases. As Mamma Mia and I chatted, she stopped me to call her abundant family to her side. Once they were assembled, she urged me to talk some more. Then she stopped me again and turned to our audience. "See," she said proudly, "how they educated him in Rome."

It was a pleasure to become a newspaperman again—to write, to edit, to go out on a story, to descend to the catacombs where the presses were and where we made up our eight-page tabloid. But getting a good night's sleep was a problem. The enemy was bedbugs. When I first strolled along Via Roma, I noticed that the women all had welts on their stockingless legs, and I wondered what Neapolitan plague affected only females. It did not occur to me that the men were wearing trousers that covered their legs until I woke up to find my body covered with a host of angry red splotches.

I got rid of an infested mattress and found that the replacement also harbored the enemy. I tried sleeping on an Army cot. The bugs found the path to share my bed. I did something that horrifies me retroactively in these days of concern about the environment and pesticides: I lined the edges of my cot, all four sides, with DDT powder. It was a procedure that worked, but not against another menace, which could mount an assault by air—the mosquitoes.

My room, which, of course, I shared with other *S & S* staff, was a companionable place. On the top floor it had French doors facing onto a balcony. All around were other balconies of apartments in which Neapolitans lived. On one nearby was a court of hens and the reigning rooster, who serenaded the dawn and woke me early if the mosquitoes didn't. On another were a couple of sheep.

My work was not demanding and time-consuming as it became in Rome, where I was transferred after a few weeks. I had time to attend performances at the ornate San Carlo opera house, which was not far from our abode. On my first visit my buddies and I were escorted to the royal box in return for a tip of cigarettes. The next time, I attended a ballet performance danced by a sad, inept, clumsy company. I wrote what I hoped was a humorous piece describing with scrupulous literalness what passed for dancing. Since our British allies had assumed the responsibility of getting the San Carlo back into action, an English officer called to reprimand me. "After all," he said, "the ballet is being put on only for the troops."

A colleague and I managed to wangle a ride on a fireboat into the gorgeous Bay of Naples for a picnic on Capri. We hired a rowboat to take us into the Blue Grotto. Our boatman, an old fellow, wielded a huge pair of homemade oars with incredible skill while my pal and I stretched out on the bottom to avoid getting conked. Capri rises sheer as a wall most of the way around, and in its shadow the blue waters of the bay turn a rich dark blue. Our oarsman slid us under the passageway into the Blue Grotto, and for the first time I understood the sense of mystery that the grotto scene in Debussy's opera *Pelléas et Mélisande* should convey.

One day a friend, Ted O'Gorman, who had been a music critic on the New York *Post*, turned up. My signed pieces in *Stars and Stripes* were useful as a calling card throughout my stay abroad, and Ted came around to say hello. He was in the merchant marine, serving as the captain of a huge ocean-going tug. Ted had dinner with me, and the next evening I ate with him in his comfortable quarters on the tug. Some days later I accompanied him on a mission—to steam across the bay to bring in a floating drydock from a small port. A simple job, Ted said, and his men were adept at making the tow secure.

The fun began when the tow approached port and two small Italian tugs took over. The Italians were excitable and voluble and paid scant attention to Ted, who, I found to my delight, was an impressive mariner as well as a reliable music critic but not exactly at home with Neapolitan dialect. Three men in Ted's crew who had gone aboard the drydock to throw off the steel cable lashed to the big tug were left high and dry on the drydock. Every time Ted circled his vessel to get near the drydock, the Italian tugs carried out maneuvers that were the opposite of what Ted thought he was requesting. The only way the three on the drydock could be brought back to their home tug was to signal a small motorboat to do the job. Hurrah for our side, if not for our ability to communicate in Italian.

My duties at *Stars and Stripes* in Naples were not onerous—the main task of gathering and assembling the news was done in recently liberated Rome, where our principal edition was published. I had ample time for relaxation and the good luck to encounter a man named Trowbridge who headed a team of American Red Cross workers. He had taught at Andover and Rollins College and was supervising religious work. We had at least two things in common: he was also a Cornell graduate, some years ahead of me, and he too had engaged in the losing fight against bedbugs. He was rather boastful about one of his losses: he had been bitten while he sat in the royal box at the San Carlo.

When we discovered that we were both tennis players, we decided we must play. Trowbridge commandeered what he insisted was the only court in Naples, found he had three ancient balls that barely bounced (new ones were unobtainable) and knew where he could borrow a racquet for me. The trouble was I had no sneakers, but ever-resourceful Trowbridge dug up a pair two sizes too large and lent me bathing trunks meant for a man twice my size. We played a couple of times, if one cared to call it tennis.

I did not play tennis again for more than a year. By then I was in Rome and the war in Europe was over. I had acquired presentable gear, even though the tennis clothes and shoes I had asked my wife to send me from home never reached me. I can't believe that anyone would have appropriated them; perhaps they went down at sea. I had also begged for tennis balls.

In Rome I had received a letter from Dorle Jarmel Soria, who was press representative for the New York Philharmonic and for a host of famous musicians, wondering whether I could visit an uncle and aunt of her husband, Dario Soria. The elderly Sorias had been hidden by the Vatican when Jews in Mussolini's Italy were suddenly at mortal risk, like Jews in the rest of Europe terrorized by Hitler, and now they were back in their large, comfortable apartment across the Tiber not far from the Vatican. Dario had heard from them but would appreciate an objective report.

I arranged to visit the Sorias. I had undertaken similar missions for friends in the United States and had learned that one did not go empty-handed. I had gone to see the Luigi Colonnas—Luigi was a promising conductor—for my friends Nikolai and Nora Lopatnikoff. Kolya Lopatnikoff was a composer who had escaped from the Soviet Union via Estonia before the war, and his wife and Rosie Colonna had grown up together in Finland. I had been informed that the Colonnas had a two-year-old daughter, and I took along a couple of cans of condensed milk. The little girl, her parents told me, had had virtually no milk since birth, and their gratitude was indescribable.

I carried a bag of chocolate bars, cookies and cake to the Sorias. Uncle Soria, frail and drawn, was in bed. I do not know what ailed him besides age and weariness and no doubt hunger. Aunt Soria, a bright, sweet old lady who attempted a few phrases of English, drew up a chair near the bed. We exchanged messages in her fractured English and my catch-as-catch-can Italian, then I presented the bag. Aunt Soria insisted that Uncle Soria deal with it. He poured the contents onto the bed, and the two wept. With tears streaming down her face, Aunt Soria held mine in her hands and kissed me. Uncle Soria reached out to embrace me. I was, of course, deeply touched, but I also felt thoroughly uncomfortable, as if I were trapped in a lachrymose movie scene.

I wrote to the Dario Sorias in New York, and so apparently did Uncle and Aunt Soria. Dorle phoned my wife; she and Dario were so, so grateful, and what could they send Howard? Nora made a suggestion. If the Dario Sorias wondered what sort of war I was fighting, who could blame them?

In due course a package arrived from the Sorias. I took for granted that it contained food supplies for the uncle and aunt. After all, I had written that I sensed they lived on very short rations, as did other Italians I had encountered in Naples and Rome. I could have delivered the package myself but, coward that I was, wanted to avoid another teary, emotional meeting. I asked Mario, an Italian employed by *S & S*, to be the messenger.

Several hours later the telephone rang in the editorial room of *Il Messaggero*, whose plant we used to put out *S & S*, and a colleague who answered it called out, "Hey, Howard, there's a babe here, crying. What you been up to, buddy?" It was Aunt Soria, and she was saying something about *sbaglio*. Finally I understood that the package was for me. Clearly I would have to do the manly thing, retrieve it myself, even if it meant an emotional scene. When I arrived, Uncle and Aunt were laughing as they held out the package for examination. It contained a dozen tennis balls, brand new and full of bounce.

I had brought some coffee. Uncle Soria was out of bed, and we sat and chatted over a hot cup, I in my uninhibited, inaccurate Italian and Aunt Soria in elegant Italian threaded with an occasional English phrase. They wanted to know all about my family and insisted that I show them a photograph of my three-year-old son. Uncle Soria just beamed; his only repeated comment was *"Mi piace,"* in uncritical admiration of anything I said.

I do not wish to pose as a unique good samaritan. My colleagues at *S & S* were generous to Italians in need, and so were countless American servicemen and servicewomen. Poverty and hunger, especially in Naples, were everywhere. I don't deny that some of the sharing of extras acquired at the PX or in one's billet was barter rather than generosity—trade for companionship, including the most intimate sort, and for such precious objects as paintings and prints or a chance to hear music.

Several of us with a hankering for good music splendidly played wished we had a decent record collection. We remembered that someone had reported the Principessa Pignatelli had the best record collection in Naples. We telephoned her without knowing her, and with the gall of an occupying army invited ourselves to hear her records. Probably she was unhappy to say yes and fearful to say no. We drove down a drab street and stopped in front of tall iron gates, which were opened for our jeep after some palaver and a bit of bargaining with cigarettes. Behold, gardens, a gracious park and a magnificent villa tucked away on the other side.

The Principessa, a porcelain-like little lady of a certain age, who must have been a belle and a *grande dame* in her time, was hospitality itself. She played records for us, and though she protested that they were old, she had choice things not readily available in the United States in those days. I was especially delighted to hear Mattia Battistini, one of the great Italian baritones of bel canto, who never sang in the United States. She showed us around the impressively decorated villa, pointing out where the Germans had jimmied open handsomely wrought cabinets and stolen her silver and linen. There were paintings on the walls by Van Dyke, Velázquez, Guido Reni and Andrea del Sarto. I wondered why the Germans had not carried off any of these.

We offered the Principessa no payment in barter for her hospitality, but when she graciously invited us back for another visit, we accepted gladly, listened to more music and brought her some goodies to eat and drink that even she, probably one of the richest persons in Naples, had not been able to obtain. All we wished to do was say thanks.

While I was in Naples, Katherine Cornell and Brian Aherne began their tour of European war zones in *The Barretts of Wimpole Street* with performances in the lovely court theater in Caserta, the Versailles-like complex created by the kings of Naples. I attended the first performance and recall it as one of my rarest experiences in a lifetime in concert halls, opera houses and theaters. I expected that Rudolf Besier's play would be a problem for some of the GIs who packed the theater: its language, period and atmosphere had to be remote from their usual movie-house fare. For many of them, "round actors," as they called live ones, were a novelty. But the play and the performance worked their magic even though whistles and guffaws erupted in unanticipated places at the outset and from a top gallery rang one loud, startled expostulation of "Oh my aching back!" One soldier became so immersed in the drama that he shouted angrily as McKay Morris, who had played the somber, unyielding Edward Moulton-Barrett, took a curtain call, "Kick him in the ass!"

Guthrie McClintic, Miss Cornell's husband and the director of the play, and Miss Cornell told me that they had never played to such audiences: everyone seated before the lights went down, no one needing to be pushed to be back after intermissions and hundreds sweating it out each show as standees—and it was hot in that theater without air conditioning. "They bring," Miss Cornell said, "that most precious of gifts to the theater—a refreshing eagerness to be moved."

And once again note the generosity of the GI. Out of gratitude many came backstage to offer gifts of food. One soldier insisted on presenting McClintic with a cigarette lighter, hard to find in the war zone. Another brought a bottle of Scotch—surely greater gratitude hath no man.

If one had to be away from one's family and in uniform, interrupting one's career at a lowly enlisted man's pay (a subvention of $100 a month from *The Times* to my family was mighty helpful), Rome was one of the most agreeable places to be. A spacious pensione on the Via 16 Settembre served as our billet, and it was a delightful walk past the Fontana di Trevi to the Via del Tritone, where we worked in the *Messaggero* building. If time allowed, we tossed pennies into the famous fountain (we all knew the song "Three Coins in the Fountain") to make sure we would eventually return to Rome. If we were in a hurry, we used a kind of bus service that tooled between Settembre and Tritone. In our free time, we had the glory that remained Rome to explore.

But we worked hard on *Stars and Stripes*, some of us who had more journalistic experience and know-how harder than others. And we turned out an eight-page paper six days a week (later we added a Sunday edition with feature supplements), of remarkable quality, I thought, judging it by standards I was accustomed to at *The Times*. We carried no advertising, and we kept articles short. Censorship rarely interfered with a truthful presentation of the news about the war, the home front and the rest of the world, and there was space enough to cater to the interests of the men and women serving in our zone.

Of course, there were shortcomings. But what impressed me most was what this eight-page tabloid meant to the men at the front. I remember sitting with several tank men down briefly from the area where they had been trading fire with the Germans across the Arno, and listening to them thanking us for the paper. They read it, they said, from cover to cover. Next to letters from home, it was what they looked forward to most eagerly. They remembered stories that had appeared weeks and months earlier. They talked about *S & S* as if it were an old and loyal friend. How many newspapers, I wonder, have had such a passionately devoted public?

Accustomed as I was to the pressure of daily deadlines on *The Times*, I found it exhilarating to work hard. To prove that the decades have not inflated my memory of these days, I quote from a letter I wrote in late October, 1944:

> Let me tell you what I did yesterday to give you an idea why I had no time for writing letters. In the morning I wrote a column about entertainment here with a stiff kick in the pants for the USO, demanding more American stars for the front, not for the boys like us in the rear. Then I did a story on the Spanish situation, another on France, another on Churchill's speech to the Commons, another on the Russian front, another on Norway, and odds and ends. In addition, I wrote some heads and went over the copy others had prepared, since the managing editor wants me to check on a lot of things.

Usually we had our own soldier-correspondents at the front in our war zone, but our reports on world news were assembled from a variety of services. The front that required a special effort if our stories were to be up-to-the-minute was the Russian one. When they had particularly good news, the Russians announced it in orders of the day. The only way we could be *au courant* with the latest advances was to listen to the BBC broadcasts at 9 P.M. If the Soviets had liberated another town, we would learn about it when the BBC announcer read the order of the day released by Moscow. The BBC, of course, would pro-

Stanley Meltzoff in his studio in 1975.

nounce the name of a liberated town somewhere in Russia or Eastern Europe in an English version, but our only large, fully detailed map of those territories used Cyrillic letters. Since I was the one who generally wrote about the action in the east and since my acquaintance with the Cyrillic alphabet was superficial at best, I had to scramble to locate the designated town and to write in a hurry so that the news would be in the issue delivered to the front the next morning.

Among my duties it fell to my lot to cover the news of the political situation in Italy. I spent a little time attending the trial of a General Roatta who was accused of Fascist crimes. He managed to escape from custody, and as far as I know his disappearance has remained a mystery.

One day we got a phone call saying there had been a political murder in front of the Quirinale, where the Italian government, such as it was, had its head-quarters. The Piazza Quirinale is one of those vast, magnificent spaces with which Rome abounds, and when I got there, the contending forces were drawn up. For action? A large company of carabinieri carrying their carbines at the ready was in ominous formation in front of the Quirinale. Across the piazza about a hundred yards away was a huge crowd of demonstrators. In the middle of this large, empty cobblestoned space were a puddle of blood and entrails, a man with a cross standing over a corpse, and a placard charging the carabinieri with murder. I walked over to the demonstrators to ask what had happened. A tumult of voices sought to explain, and one of the leaders took my arm and said he would show me. Whereupon we began striding across the piazza toward the body, followed by a huge phalanx of demonstrators. The carabinieri responded by marching toward us, carbines ready.

Suddenly I halted. *What in the world am I doing here*, I thought, *seemingly the point man in a rebellion? I haven't really learned the reason for the demonstration or the shooting, and if there is going to be a bloody showdown, what am I, an American, doing at the head of it?* I am not ashamed to confess that I excused myself and departed posthaste. Despite the threatening gestures by both sides, there was no further bloodshed.

I had better luck with Italian politics when, with the war in Europe over, I headed north to investigate the role, if any, that the *partigiani* had played in the final liberation of Italy. I was in a jeep with cases of C-rations and a companion, Stanley Meltzoff, my roommate and the *S & S* art editor (which meant preparing layouts, not covering art shows). In the north I met a few of the partisan leaders. The one who impressed me most, an intense, incisive, thoughtful man, understated for an Italian, was Umberto Parri. A member of something called the Action Party, he had spent nine years in jail of the twenty he had been involved in fighting Fascism. It was difficult to get him to expand on his activities behind the fighting line. Was he, I speculated, still suppressing some of the details of what the *partigiani* did and how? And if so, why? Had the fear of being found out in the months of secret maneuvers left a psychological mark?

Clearly Parri seemed to be a man with an important contribution to make to a freshly organized Italian democracy, and when such a government was set up, he was chosen as the first premier. But he did not last long. What is the count of postwar Italian premiers? At least fifty in the first fifty years?

A good many of us on *Stars and Stripes* took advantage of the glories Rome had to offer, but some were indifferent to the city and its art, architecture and history. It was the latter group, who remained in the billet to play cards during free time or roamed the streets in pursuit of earthier encounters, whom our first sergeant had in mind when he lectured us at a full unit meeting. As a gesture to the Italians, *Stars and Stripes* had decided to throw a big party for leading Romans. We borrowed the use of an elegant Italian officers' club and prepared to serve drinks and food. To be sure that as hosts we would comport ourselves with proper dignity, our first sergeant told us to dress smartly, to watch our language and, above all, to think twice about whom we might escort to the party. He had spoken sharply on earlier occasions to several men who had brought unmistakable tarts to our mess as dinner guests. Now he wanted to be sure that no disreputable women would cheapen the mood of an elite gathering. "And remember," he thundered as he wound up the meeting, "I don't want you guys to pick up any Tom, Dick or Harry for this party."

Thanks to Stanley, my roommate, I became better acquainted with Rome's incomparable artistic heritage in the course of Saturday afternoon expeditions than would have been possible had I ventured out on my own. Stanley had reached Rome with the *S & S* vanguard shortly after the city's liberation. By the time I arrived, he had, he told me, done the first and second class churches and palaces and was working on third and fourth class. I assured him that I was willing to start at his notion of a lower level. Eventually he relented, and to accommodate me he returned to some of his designated first and second class places.

At one church that was closed, we kept pounding on the door—Stanley insisted there was something choice on the walls, though to my shame I cannot recollect which immortal artist we were after—until a small, gentle Franciscan friar opened it. We told him what we wanted. He replied that no one was to be admitted. We pleaded, argued, offered cigarettes, which he declined, the only Italian I met who did so. When he realized that Stanley had a deep appreciation of the art inside the church as well as knowledge of the church's history, the little friar smiled and led us in. When we left, he escorted us to the door. As we thanked him, he said with a shy smile, "Those cigarettes—I have a friend . . ." I hope the friend enjoyed them.

Stanley was good at persuading guards and caretakers to make exceptions for us. The matchless Villa Julia, with its garden artfully terraced to create the illusion of a large, enchanting cultivated space, was barred to visitors, but Stanley walked us in. When we traveled north, he carried his guidebooks with him and insisted on a number of detours to look at murals by Gian-Baptista Tiepolo, one of his special interests. Either with eloquence or with cigarettes, he always got us admitted.

In Rome there was opportunity to hear music by fine performers. The opera had reopened, and though I was too busy at *Stars and Stripes* to attend more than a couple of times, I was tempted when I saw the announcement that Zandonai's *Francesca da Rimini* was to be done with Maria Caniglia, whose singing I had admired at the Metropolitan Opera. It was an opera I did not know, but when I tried to get tickets, I found they were sold out. I appealed to John Welsch III, whom we called our socialite sergeant, and by golly, he delivered.

He knew the mother of the conductor, Oliviero de Fabritiis, called on her and returned with the glad tidings that she could do nothing for any of the sold-out performances but that I could be her guest at the dress rehearsal. In Europe dress rehearsals more often than not are complete, uninterrupted performances before a full house. I was led into Signora de Fabritiis's box, was introduced to her and sat in the rear studying my fellow guests, elegantly dressed ladies and one fine-looking elderly gentleman with a Van Dyke beard and a pince-nez, to whom our hostess paid special attention. He turned out to be a distinguished professor at Santa Cecilia, Rome's famous conservatory. At intermission time the *professore della musica* made some remarks about Zandonai in the scheme of Italian opera, and I offered a comment. He looked at me with surprise and elaborated on his views, speaking, of course, in Italian. I knew enough Italian by this time to chat easily, particularly when the subject was music. As the conversation grew animated, the *professore* stared at me and my uniform (the only insignia we on *S & S* wore on our Eisenhower jackets was a shoulder pad that said "Correspondent," but I was sitting at an angle where he could not see it). As the lights went down, the professor leaned toward Signora de Fabritiis and in what he thought was a whisper said, "These Americans are amazing," his voice rising in wonderment. "Look at that simple soldier, and listen to the way he talks about music."

The plight of the poor, hungry Italians, always wrenching, seemed especially poignant at Christmastime. On my way to the office on Christmas morning I passed a church where a high dignitary was distributing packages to orphans and refugee families, and I saw family groups coming out of the church. It was a cold, cutting morning, and nearly all the children, as well as the adults, were inadequately dressed for the weather. The moment they were out of the church, the grownups opened the paper bags, extracted loaves of bread and broke off chunks for the children and themselves. They stood there chewing as if they had had no bread for days, possibly weeks.

On Christmas Eve I had set out with some colleagues to watch the Pope celebrate an unusual midnight mass open to the public. The Piazza San Pietro was brilliantly illuminated as it had not been, though Rome was an open city, since the war had come to the country. Michelangelo's glorious dome was sharply etched against the bright moon, and I thought that this was the way the artist and those who completed his design might have envisaged the cathedral. The basilica was packed to capacity, and according to Roman police, at least fifty thousand men, women and children were crowded into the piazza within the embrace of the curves of the Bernini colonnade. Even with our press credentials, we got barely past the open doors. People inside were almost ululating with excitement. Some fainted and were carried out. It was a mob scene, unregulated and almost hysterical. When the Pope was carried out on a litter, there were tremendous roars of *"Viva il Papa"* and continuous bursts of handclapping. It was as if an entire people were exploding in a mixture of hope and anguish during the long wait for peace on earth, good will to men.

On New Year's Eve we had little to celebrate. Some of us remained at the billet, had a drink and listened to the radio, which provided, among other attractions, a transmission of Hitler ranting wildly for the benefit of his countrymen and the great cause that they would bring to triumph before the new year was done.

At no time were the horror and havoc of war brought home more vividly to me than the night we screened *The Battle of San Pietro* in our billet. In the years to come there were more opportunities than one cared to endure to watch the awful televised snatches of action in Vietnam, but I do not know of any filmed record as appallingly eloquent as the one directed by John Huston. This was the truth unadorned. One saw our men charging frontally into a hail of fire and then, many wrapped in sacks, being carried away to be buried. As the film made clear, the frontal assault failed, and San Pietro was taken only after attacks on the flanks. I wondered then and still wonder: was the frontal assault necessary? Yes, I also wonder, as do a multitude of others: was Vietnam necessary?

April 12, 1945—a date older Americans remember. As I wrote in a letter, "What a day and night!" I had been at the office until almost midnight putting the Friday morning paper to bed, and when I got to the billet, I took off my coat and was about to get a bite when the phone rang. The call was from a friend, a civilian who had worked for the Rome section of the Office of War Information. Breathlessly he told me the grim news—Franklin Delano Roosevelt was dead. As we spoke briefly, my voice shook, though I had been forewarned. Some days earlier I had interviewed Edward Flynn, a New York City Democratic Party leader who had been a supporter and associate of FDR, who told me that the President's ability to complete his fourth term was a matter of deep concern to him. I woke everyone in the billet, grabbed a sandwich and trooped with the others back to the office.

We could not allow the edition that had already run off the presses to be distributed among any of our forces, and certainly not among those at the front. Between 12:30 and 3:30 A.M. we turned out a completely new paper. In those three hours I was typewriter happy. As one who had lived through the bitter, troubled and hopeful years of the Roosevelt presidency, I managed to write on and on with hardly any resort to books and files. I could write out of admiration in recounting how the New Deal restored confidence to a despairing nation. I did not leave out critical comment. I remembered how shamelessly Roosevelt and his advisors joined the farce of non-intervention when the duly elected democratic government of Spain was attacked by Francisco Franco's rebels and defeated with the help of Hitler's air force and Mussolini's foot soldiers.

As the staff ground out the edited copy, our soldier-printers set type and made up new pages. The presses rolled, and planes provided by the Army flew the new edition with its somber news to wherever there were Americans. We got numerous congratulatory calls marveling at how we managed to get so much into eight tabloid pages in so short time.

Almost three weeks later there was a reprise of early morning heroics, but this time for a more satisfying reason. I had returned to the billet about 10:30 P.M., relatively early for a change, looking forward to a reasonable bedtime. Again the phone rang, again important news. Hitler was dead. At 11 P.M. I was back at my typewriter, happily pounding away with news that our readers would find heartening, as we did.

Between those two momentous deaths, there was another big story: nothing less than the surrender of the German armies in Italy. I can best convey my sense of the event by quoting from a letter I sent home:

> Now I can tell you a little of the story behind the story. For once I was really a military secret. I first heard about it when we arrived at headquarters in Caserta by plane last Saturday—some brass, four civilian correspondents and I. On Sunday we saw the signing.

I did not describe the signing itself in my letter. Considering the magnitude of the occasion, I would have expected the kind of show once depicted in a colorful film about the Congress of Vienna and the end of another war. This was a drab and colorless affair, formal and stiff. Four high German officers at attention faced an equal number of Allied officers. Key paragraphs of the surrender document were read and the German and Allied officers signed, while the correspondents listened and made notes. The high-ceilinged room in the Caserta palace with its frescoes lent a touch of what seemed like wistful grandeur as well as a measure of irony, for on the ceiling, inscribed in bold letters by the Fascists, was the slogan "Novo ordo incipit"—the new order begins.

To return to my letter:

> I came back to town in an open command car—a windy, bumpy ride that chilled me through and through. I was not supposed to tell anyone, but I had to tell David Golding, the managing editor, and we decided to tell Irving Levinson, our first sergeant, the man in charge of the technical side of getting our paper out.
>
> I locked myself in Bill Mauldin's room upstairs in the office building and wrote the story—and a long, long one it was. Keeping the secret was easy enough; the

Correspondents recording the surrender of the German armies in Italy and western Austria, April 29, 1945. Taubman is fourth from left. Lt. Gen. W. D. Morgan, who signed for the Allies, stands at right in front. The historic signing took exactly twelve minutes.

knowledge that a slip-up on the agreement to surrender might cost even one extra life would be enough to button my lips.

Then on Monday General Mark Clark, who loved publicity, issued his statement about resistance in Italy being virtually eliminated. That statement was issued twenty-four hours after the signing of the surrender documents, and it was feared in the highest circles here that the Germans might think we were pulling a fast one. After that we sat on the story like a bunch of brood hens. We thought it might break earlier than Wednesday. All day Tuesday I hung around the public relations office waiting, and nothing happened. Then at night came the Hitler story, and I was really pooped yesterday. I had to get up at 7 A.M. and go to the PR office, where I sat from 8 A.M. on. Nothing happened even at 2 P.M. when the time came to live up to the surrender deal. By 4 P.M. it looked bad, and the powers that be thought that the Germans were reneging. I went home wearily, thinking to catch a nap. At 5:30 P.M. I was summoned posthaste. I had to be on tap myself because the censor's office had my story under lock and key and wouldn't deliver it to anyone else. They gave us the release an hour ahead of time. We got out our paper, for which we had prepared some preliminary background material, by 8 P.M. It was wonderful to see the excitement on the soldiers' faces. They wouldn't believe it was true until they could read the news, and they kept rushing in for copies of their own paper.

And now a sour note from the same letter:

The big story wasn't all fun. I was boiling mad last Saturday night. Some hulking jerk of a lieutenant colonel insisted that since I was an enlisted man I could not eat and sleep with the civilian correspondents since they were being put up among officers. I don't give a hoot in hell about associating with officers. But the enlisted men's mess was closed by the time I got there and a surly mess sergeant threw me a couple of cold hunks of stew and two pieces of bread. Then I was given a wormy cot to sleep on in a cold room without enough blankets. Fortunately I didn't catch cold. But I seethed with rage, not only at the undemocratic treatment of me personally. But here was I, the only enlisted man on the story, the eyes and ears of all the American troops in the theater, and I was being treated in the usual cavalier manner granted so many troops. The troops, of course, the enlisted men, have done the major part of winning and being killed. The whole attitude toward the enlisted men, as I've experienced from the beginning, has rankled. Fortunately, in our organization there is no such nonsense.

THE STARS AND STRIPES
MEDITERRANEAN

Vol. 2, No. 150, Thursday, May 3, 1945   ITALY EDITION * * TWO LIRE

NAZI ARMIES IN ITALY SURRENDER

By Sgt. HOWARD TAUBMAN

AFHQ, May 2—The German armies in Italy and in part of Austria have surrendered—completely and unconditionally.

The long, bitter, back-breaking campaign of Italy has been crowned with victory. In the theater where the western Allies made their first breach in Adolf Hitler's Fortress Europe, the fighting has ended with the surrender of an entire front.

This front covers not only the rest of Italy but the western area of Austria. The Germans defending the Austrian provinces of Voralberg, Tyrol, Salzburg and part of Carinthia and Styria have surrendered to the Allied might of the Mediterranean Theater

When Stanley and I set out for the north to check on the role of the partisans, the back of our jeep was jammed. We carried four cases of C-rations, extra cans of gasoline and water, canteens, mess kits, personal luggage. If we looked as though we were heading for a vacation rather than an official mission, that was the way it worked out. I suspect our commanding officer guessed it might be so and did not mind. Perhaps we were being rewarded for the long hours we had put in as the war was grinding to an end.

S & S had a small billet in Livorno, used as a delivery center. We stopped there for the night, then moved on to Pisa.

We climbed the leaning tower, as apparently every soldier who had passed through Pisa had done. There are huge bells at the top of the campanile, and we rang them as apparently every soldier had. The people of Pisa, I thought, must be driven batty by the constant clangor. Because the tower does lean markedly, climbing up it made us feel as if we were on a pitching ship and just a little seasick. But the view was worth it—the serene Arno River that had been the center of the long winter siege, and beyond, the hills of the lovely Tuscan landscape so familiar from old paintings.

With Stanley we were never far from art. We looked in on the cathedral, the baptistery and the Campo Santo, that gorgeous close and burial ground, where the walls were partly ruined by bombs. It was good to see that the thirteenth-century frescoes, especially *The Triumph of Death,* were not in ruins. Their simplicity and humanity made one think of Dante.

We went on to Lucca because Stanley insisted there were three or four churches worth seeing. I knew Puccini's birthplace was here, but we did not look for it; his music is a good enough landmark for me. As we drove north we saw that the countryside had been battered. Some villages barely existed. Fields were sealed off because they were still mined. We got the first flat tire of many at a spot in the town of Massa, near La Spezia, luckily beside a small clearing free of mines where we could make a tire change.

We pulled up in Rapallo for the night before a pleasant-looking pensione and were told they could give us a room but had no food to provide a dinner. We produced enough cans of C-rations not only for our meal but also for our hosts'. By means of what alchemy we never found out, our hosts transformed those rations into a tasty, agreeable repast worthy of quality Italian cuisine. We then strolled along the lovely sea wall of the resort town where Ezra Pound had lived. We knew of his anti-American broadcasts and wondered what had led him to such perfidy. We were cheered by the sight of the men who had served as partisans. They looked dashing in their red shirts, neckerchiefs and armbands, their hair worn long. Was all this a reaction to the shaven, blackshirted appearance of the Fascists?

In Genoa the port was all but destroyed, and many buildings were battered. We crossed the Po over a pontoon bridge. North of the river there were fewer signs of the war, save for an abandoned German tank or other vehicle now and then.

While I spent my time talking to partisans and many men and women who had secretly sided with them, Stanley did his thing—hunted down museums and churches. He managed to get to Turin, Bergamo and Pavia and back to Milan each night to regale me with the wonders he had beheld.

Coming to Milan a couple of weeks after armies reached the city and then moved out quickly, Stanley and I were treated as liberators. As we drove through out-of-the-way sections in our jeep, we actually had flowers thrown at us. Unfortunately, no girls climbed into our vehicle to kiss us the way maidens greeted rifle-bearing liberators in Italy and France. I did see a group of self-described Young Communists in front of a neighborhood party headquarters cutting off the hair of two girls. I did not enjoy the sight. Were some of these swaggering hoodlums, I wondered, former members of Fascist mobs joining what they thought was a new leftist tide?

From Milan we drove east, mostly on a fine autostrada that had not been bruised much by fighting. Shortly after leaving Milan, we noticed we were approaching a town called Gorgonzola. "They must make the cheese here," suggested Stanley. "Why don't we get some?"

I scoffed, "Why waste time looking for a cheese factory?"

All the same we stopped to question a passerby. In a moment we were at the cheese factory, and because we were Americans in uniform, liberators here too, we were presented with a splendid wheel of gorgonzola.

We spent the night in Mantua in a queer little room in an old hotel called the Senoner. The British town major gave us carte blanche. We found that much of the town was destroyed, but the palace of the Gonzagas in the heart of what seemed to me one of the simplest and loveliest Italian squares was intact. Thanks to the British town major's hospitality, we were granted admittance, even into rooms that had been designated off-limits. The Mantegna room—walls and ceiling all by this master—still lingers in my memory.

So does, more poignantly, what we encountered in Padua. There, not far from the railroad tracks, we found Mantegna again, this time, in shards. The Eremitani Chapel had been hit by Allied bombers. When we pulled up beside the ruin, we saw that the roof was gone and the jagged remains of a single wall defined part of an enclosure that had been the chapel. Only the lower end of a Mantegna panel could be seen. Monks were on their hands and knees gathering pieces of the wall into great baskets, taking care to brush away the dust that covered the painting. These fragments of wall varied in size from less than a foot to less than an inch.

We asked one of the painstaking gatherers what would be done with these bits and pieces.

"Reassemble as much of the painting as possible and return it to the wall," we were told.

"You mean to what remains of the wall?"

"Yes, to what remains of the wall."

I did not believe such a feat was possible. But the vision of the stricken Eremitani Chapel and the devoted monks haunted me. I promised myself a return visit to see how the Mantegna restorers were getting on with their impossible, self-imposed task. It chanced that in 1962 I was in Italy and driving from Rome to Venice. I made it a point to spend a night in Padua and hastened to the site of the Eremitani. There stood the jagged remains of the wall, and on it was a substantial section of the Mantegna panel. I had brought with me a volume showing the painting when it was unmarred and the chapel walls were intact. The monks had evidently done a remarkable job of gathering and preserving shards, and the restorer, under the guidance of the Italian government's art experts, had managed an unbelievable task of reconstructing art of an invaluable heritage. I wrote a piece about this years-long act of dedication for *The Times*, perhaps exorcising my own 1945 ghosts.

In that 1945 visit we checked out the happily unhit and undamaged Scrovegni Chapel, in which virtually every inch of wall was covered with frescoes by Giotto. To protect these masterpieces from the bombers, the Paduans had piled sandbags on scaffolding up to the ceiling, and when we got there the removal of the sandbags had begun. The scaffolding remained, and we climbed it to examine Giotto's work at close quarters. I had seen Stanley in great excitement even at the third and fourth class churches and palaces. Here he all but exploded as he studied with his nose almost on the paint a glorious Last Judgment. The opportunity of a lifetime! If he didn't literally crow, I have the illusion that he did.

On into Venice, which the British were running. After we parked our jeep in a garage, we piled our baggage, including C-rations and the gorgonzola wheel, into a gondola, then debarked and went looking for a hotel. We discovered that the press was quartered at the Luna. We were supposed to get some sort of permit from the town major, but I talked to the British major in charge of the Luna as if I were a civilian on assignment for *The Times* rather than an enlisted man applying for a room in a hotel reserved for officers. After all we *were* correspondents representing *Stars and Stripes*. The young British major was persuaded; he took us in without a permit.

"It's amazing," Stanley said, "how you condescend to colonels and majors."

"What's amazing," I replied without false modesty, "is how I forget I'm an enlisted man and convince myself I'm talking as a *Times* representative."

As for the room in the Luna, I recall it with affection. It was large, airy, modern, with an amenity we had all but forgotten: a private bath. For 30 lire a day— 30 cents in our money at the time—we got the room and four meals a day, including a brave effort at high tea.

We stayed at the Luna for a week. In the services everyone learns to gold-brick, and this was my zenith of goldbricking. We did some work, but we spent a good deal of our time sightseeing. I can remember a lovely sunny day when we hired a gondola for hours—the price was a couple of cigarette packs—and cruised along the canals while Stanley did watercolors and I stretched out and rejoiced in Venice.

I think we achieved a new high in enlisted man's cheekiness one day when we were approached by two American officers in a corridor at the Luna. We had just emerged from our room with its private bath—the officers had not seen us closing the door behind us. "Hey, soldier," one of them said, "do you know where we can find a bathroom?"

I put on a show of bewilderment. "A bathroom?" I replied. "There's a gents' room downstairs."

They thanked us and took the lift down.

"Oh my aching back," said Stanley, still the prisoner of an inferior enlisted man's psychology.

The meals at this British-run hotel were all right, but compared with the generous *Stars and Stripes* menu, they left us feeling we had not had enough. We had a few extras to fill up on, including our gorgonzola.

In my investigation of the role of the partisans, I found odd reactions from some British officers. When I dropped in at the Allied Military Government offices seeking information about the Italian officials, a British captain said with a laugh, "Why don't you talk to a white man like the colonel?"

An Italian serving as a finance superintendent was booted out of office by the Italian Committee of National Liberation on charges of being a Fascist. While I was in the office of the British lieutenant colonel who was serving as provincial commissioner, his captain in charge of finances came in to report that Venetian civil employees could not be paid their salaries because the departed superintendent was not on hand to sign the papers. "I told the partisans," he said, "that it wasn't a matter of prejudice against them but one of legality." As I listened, I wondered whether the captain hadn't thought to have another finance superintendent appointed. I could not help reflecting that there were some larger illegalities like war, killing, destruction, the ruin of societies, to fret about.

The lieutenant colonel gave me a copy of a report on how the Lido could be used as an army rest center but for the moment was out of bounds because it might have been mined. The report contained an analysis of the Lido hotels and a paragraph on the Palazzo al Mare with this final sentence: "It is very strongly recommended that this hotel is an officers' hotel. It would be badly misused in any other role."

Not all the Italians I met had been partisans. Far from it. One evening we went to deliver a letter to the brother of an Italian who helped us out with maps in Rome. His people were upper middle class. One of his relatives, a fat, comfortable, middle-aged signora, chattered as if she alone had suffered. She said that she had owned two houses in Padua and both were destroyed. "By your bombers," she added accusingly. "Who will pay for them?" Did she think the Allies would reimburse her? I suggested that she try collecting from Mussolini. She was not amused. She went on, "What's going to happen to our Trieste, our Ethiopia, our Albania?" It was as if the Allies owed her an accounting.

After changing tires all the way across northern Italy, we decided to part with our faithful jeep when we returned to Milan. Our *S & S* man stationed in Milan declared he could use it even with undependable wheels, and we persuaded our superiors in Rome that it would make sense to leave it with him while we hitched a ride on one of the Army's planes. Back in Rome we had a delightful surprise. Our living quarters had been shifted to a spacious hotel, the Albergo Capitale, near Santa Maria Maggiore, one of Rome's four cathedrals. Our

Naples office had been closed, and the contingent that had operated there had been brought up to Rome, necessitating more space, but not luxury. Somehow we adapted.

If living quarters on Via 16 Settembre were like being ensconced in a silver foxhole, life at the Albergo Capitale was more comfortable than the grandest of gold foxholes. We had more space, more amenities, the same excellent mess and a roof turned into a garden. It was provided with a bar and with facilities for card games and for the showing of movies. The days were hot in Rome beginning in June—there were trucks to take those who were not working or could manage to goof off to the beach at Ostia—and evenings on the roof were pleasantly cool. The view from the roof at sunset was unforgettable—the campanile and cupola of Santa Maria Maggiore surmounted by the statue of the Virgin and Child sharply etched against the glowing colors of the west and the Appenine foothills beyond.

For a while we had an elevator that worked, unlike the one at Via 16 Settembre, which suffered from the aches of age and neglect and which balked at carrying passengers up and therefore was permitted only for descent. Something went wrong with the Albergo *ascensore* one evening when Jinx Falkenberg, traveling with a USO unit, was a guest, and it got stuck with her in it. We ran a photograph in *S & S* of her clambering out of it, and that day we had an order from a general not to use the elevator again.

"Not even if it is fixed?" we asked.

Jinx Falkenberg in 1942.

"Not even if it is fixed," we were told; "you're in the Army now."

Once it was repaired, however, the general's order was forgotten.

Show biz and sports figures turned up in Rome repeatedly, theoretically to "entertain the troops." When they passed through, they generally visited the *Stars and Stripes* billet. Among the celebrities who were our guests were Frank Sinatra, Joe Louis and Marcel Cerdan, pugilists, and a couple of Hollywood moguls named Balaban and Holman of Paramount. I had the privilege of chatting with them all.

I told Sinatra I had had problems making my way to the entrance of *The Times* on West Forty-third Street past the bobby-soxers who were waiting to enter the Paramount Theater to hear him. He laughed, pleased to be reminded of his admirers.

One afternoon I had bought a ticket and entered the Paramount. It was true: the bobby-soxers really squealed "Frankie! Frankie!" And I could see why. His singing was like a caress.

With Frank Sinatra at the Albergo Capitale in Rome, 1945. David Golding, managing editor at *Stars and Stripes*, is between Taubman and Sinatra. Photograph courtesy of David Golding.

S & S had a number of jeeps at its disposal, and staff members who used them in the evening took to parking them in front of the hotel for the night. One morning we found a wheel gone from a jeep. The next morning another jeep had been deprived of a wheel. Clearly a problem, one that could be solved by simply parking the vehicles in a garage overnight. But we had a young lieutenant who was determined to catch the thief or thieves, and like a well-indoctrinated officer, he organized his forces into a round-the-night watch. According to his battle plan, several of us were to be stationed at windows looking out on the street and were to remain on the alert for two hours until relieved by the next contingent. What were we to do if we saw a wheel thief *in flagrante delicto?* Shoot? We had no weapons. Shout? Yes, but wouldn't that give the perpetrators time for a getaway? Never mind. No thieves appeared during the night. The lieutenant, like a good commander, moved from window to window all through the night, and at daybreak gave the order to conclude the watch. Poor fellow! He underestimated the resourcefulness of the thief or thieves. They got off with two wheels after the watch went to sleep.

Apart from the ending of the war with Japan, which would mean returning home, I had little to look forward to except the usual work at the paper and the agreeable evenings on the roof. Then came another inviting assignment. Vienna, which had been liberated by the Red Army and was under Soviet control, was now to become, with the rest of Austria, the responsibility of the four Allied powers. The diplomatic agreement provided for the formal entry of Allied troops into the Austrian capital. A group of civilian correspondents was flown to Linz to report on the grand cavalcade led by General Mark Clark that would roll into Vienna. The correspondents sat near Linz with the troops that had been assembled for an impressive entrance while the general, for reasons never fully explained, waited in Rome.

The problem may have been unfavorable weather over the Alps. I had stayed on in Rome and had made my own arrangements for a flight to cover the famous entry. The first leg of my trip took me to Verona, where I was to be the only passenger in a small fighter plane. My young pilot returned from a visit to the briefing room with word that the Alps were socked in. "Should we try it anyhow?" he asked.

"Do you think we can get through?" I replied.

"Don't know," he said cheerfully. "Let's try it anyhow."

I pretended to be as happy-go-lucky and adventurous as he. As he strapped me into a parachute and planted me on the only seat behind his, I trembled.

We took off, and as I shivered with trepidation I reflected, *What price Mark Clark's glory to me?* We passed through banks of clouds as we achieved altitude, and the pilot cheerily remarked, "Will we be able to see the peaks when we reach them? If not, it'll be fun."

Some fun! There must have been some connection between his good humor and the way the clouds parted for us as we passed over the highest points of the Alps. We landed safely in Vienna.

For a welcome change I was treated like the other journalists, rather than like an enlisted man unworthy to associate with officers, and installed in a fine hotel with them and with Army brass. The Vienna I saw was a far different and sadder place than the city I had visited in 1935. Not that Vienna was happy in 1935. Dollfuss had been assassinated and a nervous Schussnigg was chancellor. But a great lovable bear of a Hungarian—his name was Emil Vadnay—whose jaw had been partly shot away during World War I, was there on the staff of *The Times*, and he devoted several days to showing me the historic city and its environs with memories of Haydn, Mozart, Beethoven, Schubert, Brahms and the rest that meant so much to a young writer about music.

What I found in late July and early August, 1945, was a hungry, starving city. I had grown accustomed in Naples and Rome to hearing contemptuous Americans revile Italians as natural beggars. Those who had entered Vienna with Clark learned quickly that begging was not an exclusively Italian trait. Americans were approached everywhere with a plea for a piece of bread. The shops were nearly all closed. People waited in line for hours to get their meager rations. With some civilian colleagues I went to interview the burgermeister, Theodore Koerner, a tall, handsome, weary gentleman. He received us in an elegant room in the Rathaus just before lunchtime. As we talked he reached for a briefcase and, asking our pardon, pulled out a single piece of dark bread and observed with a wry smile, "If you will forgive me, I had little breakfast, and this is my lunch."

Then there was the night of the Laval hunt. At 8 P.M. one evening the correspondents were tipped off that Pierre Laval, the Frenchman who had done so much of Hitler's dirty work after the fall of France, had landed in Linz from wherever he had been hiding and had been taken into custody. Obviously, if there was a chance to find and talk to him, it must be seized. A search party was organized. Headquarters provided a command car and a jeep. In the large vehicle were a driver and five correspondents, in the jeep a driver and two of us. I was in the front seat of the command car with the driver and an Englishman named Desmond Tighe of Reuters. If Tighe is still alive, I'd like him to know that I remember him with affection. If Reuters happens to be retroactively annoyed, I submit that after almost half a century, Tighe should be remembered only with fondness.

As we started to roll from our Vienna hotel, Tighe asked the driver to stop at a place where he was able to acquire a bottle of brandy. I realized later that he was already a bit tight. Linz is 120 miles west of Vienna, and in the first hour of our ride Tighe talked and drank. He asked my name, and I told him. "Oh yes," he said, "I've read your stuff." Fifteen minutes later he wanted to know my name again. Apparently it was a matter of courtesy that he inquire my name at regular intervals. He told me about a brother who had pounded rubber in Malaysia and had returned to England to achieve his life's ambition to own a country pub. From time to time he reminded me what a swine Laval had been and what an important story we were after. Then he fell asleep.

He woke when we stopped at a railroad crossing to let a train go by and happened to meet a Red Army detachment. The Russians greeted us with warmth. We tried to explain our mission. I doubt that they understood, though the repetition of the word "Laval" might have meant something to them. They were young and outgoing, and when Tighe offered them a nip from his brandy bottle, several accepted and in turn offered us a shot of vodka. I had heard some Red Army recordings at home, and I asked for "Yesli zaftra," virtually the only Russian words I knew. They instantly began booming out that defiant song which oldtimers who remember the common battle against Nazism may recognize as "If War Comes Tomorrow."

When we reached Linz, we could not find Laval. We woke up officers and men who had seen him. They told us what they could, and though we ended without making contact with the traitor, we gathered some information about where he had been hiding out, where he had been found and what he had said in an effort to explain his treachery. Tighe managed to turn up as we were completing an interview. In a Linz hotel barroom he was offered a drink by a couple of Americans, and we had to go looking for him before we could start back to Vienna. He slept through this drive of more than three hours, and we woke him when we reached Vienna. We were in a hurry to write and file our reports, but I paused to say goodbye to my new friend and to wish him well. "You were good company," he said amiably, "but that wasn't much of a story, was it, old boy?"

After a week in Vienna I had had enough. Whether the Viennese, indeed the Austrians, deserved their fate is still being argued almost half a century later. As one who visited the Mauthausen concentration camp near Linz during that 1945 trip and saw the rows upon rows of small white crosses where the remains of the Nazi victims had been buried, I was haunted by the recent horrors and by the hasty assurances of residents in the neighborhood that they had had no idea of what was going on so near their homes.

Clete Roberts, a correspondent for a radio network, felt as I did, and we decided to return to Rome. In the usual casual way of that period, we negotiated with officers for a ride on a plane and were referred to a young pilot who would be ferrying a DC-3 to Rome via Linz and Salzburg. He was glad to have company, and we took off. When we paused in Linz the weather outlook was most unpromising, but our daring young flyer said, "Why not?" There was little visibility, and Clete and I noticed that we were flying very low. I observed nervously that my recollection of Salzburg, where I had been ten years earlier, was that there were high hills all around it. Clete, an amateur pilot, went up front and noticed that the altimeter was at four hundred feet. And he discovered that our cheerful airman had never flown to Salzburg and was hoping to find it by eye. By now we were flying through dense fog, and Clete persuaded our pilot to return to Linz.

We managed to find cots for the night at the airfield, and the next morning our pilot turned up, jaunty as ever, to invite us to join him in his rounds to Salzburg, Verona and Rome. We thanked him and looked around for a more direct flight and a less sanguine airman. We got lucky. We ran into General Alfred M. Grunther, General Clark's chief of staff, and he offered us a ride direct to Verona. A most amiable, accommodating officer, he then ordered his crew, who were planning to take the plane to Florence for the night, to do so by way of Rome. We gratefully accepted without realizing that the airmen would be late for dates in Florence. They followed orders, of course, but as we were crossing Lake Trasimano they guided the plane into a nose dive that made us think this would be our last flight and then straightened out with equal abruptness for the landing in Rome. As we thanked them and bade them goodbye, I noticed a flicker of amusement in the eyes of the pilot and his navigator.

The war with Japan ended in August, 1945. I had reached my thirty-eighth birthday in July. I knew I would be eligible for discharge any day now. So did my commanding officer at *S & S*. He sought to persuade me to stay on until the end of the year. How would I like a trip to Yugoslavia? What about covering the trials of Goering, Goebbels and the others soon to take place in Nuremberg? There was a smidgeon of temptation in that one. But no. I wanted to be a civilian and back with my family.

At the end of August I was again in Naples at a replacement depot, then soon on the *Santa Barbara* turned into a troopship and sailing west through the Mediterranean and on to Newport News, Virginia, the port from which I had left for Italy. Several other men from *Stars and Stripes* were on board, and we quickly organized a daily news report. Once again I worked in the quarters of the civilian skipper and once again gladly accepted special food perks.

It was a happy voyage across a quiet sea until the afternoon before we were to land. Suddenly we were moving into the violent path of a late summer hurricane. Many of us had gathered on the deck to glimpse a first sight of our own country, and as we stood there, staring into the rays of the setting sun, our ship took a hard, full turn. As the men saw with horror that we were sailing away from the setting sun, there was a spontaneous roar of protest. Hurricane or no hurricane, we would dare all for home. The skipper was unmoved. He continued to head east until the hurricane's worst had blown north. We were considerably delayed in setting foot on home territory. Irritating but endurable. There had been huge, unpredictable delays in ending the war, and some of our former comrades were never going to make it back.

Nora and Bill in 1945, dressed up for   With Bill at home.
Howard's return from the Army.

14

Theater—Bitter and Sweet

I N MY TOUR of duty as drama critic of *The Times*, from mid-1960 until the end of 1965, there were openings on Broadway and off nearly every night, including Saturdays. Some were amusing, provocative, exciting or exhilarating, and therefore a challenge and a pleasure to write about. But a great many were dreary and enervating beyond belief. The curtain would often rise on a handsomely appointed living room, attractive enough to make one ready to move in and set up housekeeping. I formulated a personal rule: if the set is this inviting, beware. And if characters drifted in and began conversation of crushing banality, which clearly was not intended to be banal, I sensed I was doomed. It was regarded then, and I suppose it still is, as impermissible for a critic to bolt before the final curtain, no matter how abysmal the proceedings onstage. I would sit there glancing helplessly at my watch and composing brilliant invective, which I would not use, because game so lackluster should be allowed to crawl away and expire noiselessly. Years later I still bear the scars of those hapless evenings. When a play opens with a delightful, livable set, my spirits fall, though I know that no law requires me to endure a performance for the decor.

It was customary in those days to dash out of the theater the instant the curtain came down and hasten to the office. Opening nights were fixed to begin an hour or so earlier than usual to give the critic time to write. Brooks Atkinson, a man not given to grumbling, would speak nostalgically of his early years on the job when his deadline was 1 A.M., not midnight as it had become. By 1960 the deadline had been driven down to 11:30 P.M. by the exigencies of getting out a larger paper to a constantly widening circulation area. The idea of inviting a critic to previews was proposed but turned down. Tryouts, after all, took place in other cities, and the few productions that preferred previews in town did not want evaluations while they were still working on details.

I had a baptism under fire the night Brendan Behan's *The Hostage* opened. A man of great natural gifts, Behan used song and dance and a thread of a story to offer a wild gloss on the Irish question. Some of it was hilarious and touching; a lot of it was wide of any mark. No matter; it was an unusual, original approach to the theater as staged by Joan Littlewood, herself a woman with a fresh orientation. It deserved a well-considered reaction; an hour of writing time would not have been amiss. But Behan was a man who liked his drink. He arrived for the opening past curtain time and in a convivial mood held court on the sidewalk while the producers held the curtain. It was 11 P.M. when the three acts ended. I do not know how I managed to complete a review in less than thirty minutes. I have recently reread it. It was literate and, I think, just. I am glad the reviewers today have more civilized arrangements.

I believe it is also wise to hold the curtain, as nearly all managements used to do and continue to do, about five minutes past the announced starting time, not merely to accommodate latecomers but to make sure that they do not disturb unduly those who have arrived on time. I feel strongly about this because of the one time I was late for an opening. The play was Arthur Laurents' *Invitation to a March*, with Celeste Holm, Eileen Heckert and a young Jane Fonda, and it was housed in the Music Box on West Forty-fifth Street. It was a night in late October, 1960, when John F. Kennedy was campaigning in New York, and he and his cavalcade had created a massive tie-up north and south of Columbus Circle. Unaware of what presidential politicking was doing to traffic, I started in a taxi from the upper West Side in what seemed like ample time. For long, agitating minutes I sat in an immobilized vehicle while cars and crowds drawn by the candidate's passage blocked every thoroughfare. I got out and walked and ran and walked. I plunged into the theater, stumbled down the darkened aisle and dropped into my seat as my neighbors stared in disapproval. This was the only opening night I attended that started exactly when it announced it would!

In that first season I ran into trouble by making a request that I suppose was naive. Tennessee Williams had a new play coming in, *A Period of Adjustment*. I knew his work and regarded him as one of our finest playwrights. Respecting his achievements, I thought it might be useful to read the play before seeing it.

In the music world, from which I had come, it was not extraordinary to examine a new score before it was performed, and it was routine at the Metropolitan Opera to invite the critics to attend, though not to write about, the dress rehearsal of an important new production. In my view a new play by Williams was *ipso facto* important.

My request generated a kind of panic. The reaction of the producers seemed to be, *What is he up to?* When I was told that the script was not frozen and that changes were still being made, I quickly withdrew my request. But the mere making of such a request evidently upset Williams badly. It turned out that I did not believe *A Period of Adjustment* belonged with his best work. *The Night of the Iguana*, which followed a year or two later, seemed closer to his top quality. Then came *The Milk Train Doesn't Stop Here Anymore*, which I considered a disappointing falling off. Even after it was revised and mounted again, I thought it was Williams in a weak, repetitive mode.

I had visited San Francisco some time after the second failure of this play. As luck would have it, the Actors' Workshop run by Jules Irving and Herbert Blau, who were shortly to be invited to take over the direction of the Lincoln Center Repertory Theater, was presenting this play on my first night in town. I was not avid to see it again, but my purpose in coming to San Francisco was to acquaint myself with the work of the Actors' Workshop. When I arrived at the theater, I was asked, "What have you done to Tennessee Williams?" That afternoon he had been informed that I was in town and was planning to be at the theater that evening, whereupon he not only canceled his plan to attend but packed his bags and fled the city. Too bad, for I would have been proud to meet and know this distinguished American playwright.

My next and last request to read a play before it opened created another furor. This one was for Rolf Hochhuth's *The Deputy*. The play, which had been done abroad in a number of countries, was profoundly controversial. It charged that the Vatican, indeed the Pope, had failed to speak out with proper moral indignation against the slaughter in the Nazi concentration camps. I felt that it would be helpful to know the play if I was to deal intelligently with its essential argument. I explained as much to the representative of the producer, Kermit Bloomgarden, who contended that all that was expected of me was to evaluate what I saw and heard in the theater, and that reading the play was unnecessary. Did ordinary playgoers read the play before they went to a performance? *No*, I thought, *but this may not be an ordinary play*. Did any playgoer, professional critic or not, sacrifice freshness of response by reading a Shakespeare or Chekhov play before seeing it?

I did not waste time in further discussion with the producer or his people. I knew that an English translation of the German original had been published in London, and I cabled the *New York Times* bureau there asking that a copy be purchased and sent air express. I did read *The Deputy* before I saw it. Doing so enhanced my respect for the play's moral fervor, for the intensity of the production and the quality of the performance.

A critic learns to expect criticism. Generally it manifests itself in vituperative mail. Sometimes it is pained, pathetic mail, like the letter from an actor in a play that lasted only a few days who wanted to know how he was to support his family after my review had contributed to throwing him out of a job. Sometimes it takes the form of gossip. On a wet opening night a fellow critic eased himself into a seat behind mine and tapped me on the shoulder. "How's your sinus?" he wanted to know.

"My sinus, why?"

My colleague explained, "As I walked through the lobby I passed a chap worrying about it."

How thoughtful, I thought.

"He says it kills you on wet nights," my neighbor went on, "and you kill the show."

I smiled, though only partly amused. I told my colleague that there was nothing wrong with my sinus any night, dry or wet. In a Sunday article I wrote, "With the season about to begin, I would like to inform my considerate admirer, if that is the word for him, that I rarely get headaches, except from wretched plays and blasting pit bands, that my sinuses are not unduly tender and, having no alternative, I take the weather as I find it."

Direct, face-to-face disagreement was rare. Once at a reception for parents in the home of the headmaster of my son's school, I was introduced to the mother of a student. "Yes, I know who you are," she glared, and turning her back on me, she flounced away. She might at least have told me which review or reviews had angered her.

The most startling confrontation was one with Paddy Chayefsky. I had no doubt about which review had infuriated him. It was some days after the opening and swift demise of his play about Stalin, *The Passion of Josef D.* A group of distinguished Soviet poets and dramatists were on an official visit to the

United States, and Al Hirshfeld, who for decades graced the drama pages of *The Sunday Times* with his witty caricatures, gave a party for them at his town house. Remembering that some of these Russians had received me agreeably in the Soviet Union several years earlier, I decided to make an appearance, though normally I avoided big parties. I chatted with the Russians through an interpreter— I recall that Arbuzov, the playwright, and Voznesensky, the poet, were among the visitors—and then I turned to leave. Al and Dolly Hirshfeld's large living room could accommodate a crowd, and I had made my way past several groups when Chayefsky appeared in my path. He seized my lapels and launched into a tirade. I do not recall his words, only his rage. I did not wish to argue; I said mildly that it was unfortunate, but we simply disagreed about his play. He would not be assuaged. As he stormed at me, other writers, actors, directors, encircled us. Finally he was pulled away, and I was allowed to make my way out.

As I left the Hirshfeld house and strolled down the street, I thought about the encounter. Chayefsky had acted out resentments and frustrations that he could not, at least at that moment, conceal under a veneer of civility. His verbal attack, I confess, had shocked me; it would not have surprised me if he had thrown a punch. It's remarkable, I mused, that such confrontations do not occur more often. It cannot be easy to be subjected to judgments that differ from one's own and that can have so profound an effect on one's career.

S. N. Behrman, a playwright whose sophisticated, wise and witty plays had given me great pleasure during a lifetime of theater-going, wrote me an aggrieved letter, taking issue with my review of *Pengo*. His last play to be produced on Broadway, this was about Lord Duveen, the shrewd art dealer about whom he had written a delightful book. The burden of Behrman's letter seemed to be that it was cheeky of me, relatively a Johnny-come-lately to theater reviewing, to have reservations about his play. I did not mind. Hadn't Behrman earned the right to read a critic a lesson? I replied that I hoped we would both feel better after his next play.

I am sure that my hostess in Houston felt a lot better after having her say about critics. The occasion was my first visit to the Alley Theater in Houston, when it was housed in a modest, converted vestige of a building in an alley and not in the elegant, spacious quarters in which it now functions. The late Nina Vance, the founder and heart of the company, wired when she heard that I was coming. Would I please agree to be the guest of honor at a big party; it would

mean so much to the future of the theater. I could not say no. And it was quite
a party. In a Palladian palazzo in one of Houston's posh suburbs, leaders of the
city's cultural community assembled, and after a splendid buffet supper we were
all invited into a large room hung with old masters, where we seated ourselves
in semicircles facing our hostess. A colloquy began.

I was not aware that my hosts, like other enormously wealthy Texans, had
invested in the Broadway theater and had nothing to show for it but large losses.
I soon found out. My hostess began by asking questions about Brooks Atkinson. Like most of us at the party, she had had, I assume, quite a bit of cham-
pagne, and from questions about my predecessor she modulated into a bitter
attack. I defended Brooks, who really required no defense. Finally, my hostess
summed up her view of Brooks: "He's a son-of-a-bitch!"

I expostulated: "That's going too far."

She had a wicked grin as she added as an afterthought, "You're one too!"

Had I been guilty of disapproving a show she had backed? I did not know.
Anyhow, once a critic, always a son-of-a-bitch.

And always, at least in my case, an admirer of fine theater in its endlessly varied manifestations. Not much in this world is quite as refreshing, exhilarating
and enriching as a work of the imagination for the stage—drama or musical,
comedy or tragedy, farce or fantasy—when all the elements of writing, producing and performing are in happy conjunction. In the kaleidoscope of my
memory of more than six decades of devoted theater attendance, I single out
moments that shine with a nostalgic refulgence. If I linger on performers and
performances more than on the plays themselves, it is because I remember them
as an indivisible unity.

I begin with a performance in a play that I find I did not even mention in
my 1965 book *The Making of the American Theater:* Walter Huston in Sophie
Treadwell's *The Commodore Marries.* Why I start there only the vicissitudes of
memory can explain. I do not recall the story, but Huston's performance as a
retired old salt about to take a wife still resonates in my mind with its sly, hearty
humor.

In the twenties I managed to get a seat in the second balcony for 50 cents for
The Cocoanuts, book by George S. Kaufman and songs by Irving Berlin, in
which the young Marx Brothers had me laughing until it hurt. And mind you,
I was not unfamiliar with the antics of demented vaudevillians; I had haunted
the Palace as a high-schooler when it was the court of last resort for this branch
of the profession.

From another musical comes a recollection of another fond moment: Ed Wynn in *Simple Simon*—book by Wynn himself and Guy Bolton, songs by Richard Rodgers and Lorenz Hart—walking out on the large, empty stage of the Ziegfeld dragging a lariat, wearing a worried, foolish look and giggling in embarrassment. "Either I found a rope," he confided to no one in particular, "or I lost a horse."

An inspired little sequence, without dialogue or song, from *A Funny Thing Happened on the Way to the Forum*—book by Burt Shevelove and Larry Gelbart and songs by Stephen Sondheim—recalls Zero Mostel. It is a moment when Zero Mostel and his male companions are moving from stage right to left, and they pass a line of luscious courtesans moving from stage left to right. As if drawn by a powerful magnet, Mostel deserts his group and falls in behind the girls, and now he is stepping along lightfootedly with just a trace of a wiggle and an undisguised smirk of concupiscence. Charlie Chaplin, who knew how to move with the ineffable delicacy of a dancer, could not have done it better.

The images in memory's kaleidoscope demand individual attention, but there are so many that they receive only fleeting notice: Danny Kaye singing his wife Sylvia's song about all those Russian composers with a virtuoso's speed and accuracy in Kurt Weill's *Lady in the Dark;* Mary Martin in her sinfully demure rendition of Cole Porter's "My Heart Belongs to Daddy"; Howard

Danny Kaye in *Lady in the Dark* in the 1940s.

DaSilva in the elaborately fraudulent lament by Rodgers and Hammerstein, "Pore Jud Is Daid," in *Oklahoma!*

There is Bert Lahr bringing off six different parts in S. J. Perelman's *The Beauty Part*—as the modish husband of a woman of incalculable wealth, as a lady publisher of lurid magazines, a Hollywood producer named Harry Hubris, a wily exotic trying to steal a novel, a cackling, deaf old husband of a millionaire, and a judge dispensing justice in full view of the television public. Unfortunately, not many can share this memory, for *The Beauty Part* opened in late December, 1962, and unable to overcome the handicap of the long newspaper strike in New York, closed quickly.

For comedy that was broad, brilliantly meshed and timed, I recall the perfect interplay of Walter Matthau and Art Carney in Neil Simon's *The Odd Couple*, not forgetting the contribution of Mike Nichols, impossible to isolate and credit for its felicities, nonetheless an indispensable factor.

In another vein, comedy that was delectably broad in its artifice and elegance, I recall Paul Scofield as Don Amedeo de Almeida and Zoe Caldwell as Rosaline

Walter Matthau and Art Carney in *The Odd Couple*, 1965.

in Shakespeare's *Love's Labour's Lost* at Stratford, Ontario, directed by Michael Langham, a master of classical style that remains pertinent for our time.

For sheer brilliance in a role that required unmatched speed, stamina and precision of articulation, I cannot recall anyone more impressive and wildly amusing than Michael Hordern in Tom Stoppard's *Jumpers* at the National Theater in London.

How about the uses of silence? I have never forgotten the final moments of the second act of N. C. Hunter's *Waters of the Moon*, which I saw in a West End theater in London about four decades ago. In the cast were four great ladies of the British theater—Sybil Thorndyke, Edith Evans, Wendy Hiller and Celia Johnson. They were inmates of a home for women of good family who had fallen on hard days, and all four gathered onstage in the scene I remember. Thorndyke is sitting alone on a sofa upstage center, the others at her side. A piece of bad news for Thorndyke arrives. Her friends seek to minimize it by chatter while Thorndyke sits and stares straight ahead of her. The chatter subsides. Thorndyke has not moved, but her seemingly catatonic position is belied by eyes that reflect and communicate unknowable anguish.

Another great performance in which a distinguished actor used his eyes—and eyes alone—to tell us of his humiliation and pain was that of Alec Guinness in Terence Rattigan's *Ross*. Ross, the T. E. Lawrence character, has been assaulted, presumably raped, by Arabs offstage, and he enters onstage haltingly, broken in spirit. And there he stands, wordless for a few moments with his eyes boring their way inwardly, revealing his shame.

I think of Laurette Taylor in Williams' *The Glass Menagerie*, conveying the frayed gentility and the relentless determination of an aging southern belle who would not and dared not give up her illusions. I have seen other actresses play Amanda compellingly and touchingly, but no one reached as deeply into the woman's vulnerable invulnerability.

Jessica Tandy in *A Streetcar Named Desire* caught the painful, desperate vulnerability of another Williams female living under fragile illusions, and with Marlon Brando as the brutal, consuming Kowalski, created moments that haunt my memory. Credit Elia Kazan, the director, for some of the intensity that I cannot forget.

And there was Lee J. Cobb as the hapless Willy Loman in Arthur Miller's *Death of a Salesman*, a rending performance he never equaled.

And Morris Carnovsky, a versatile, resourceful actor, who reached his peak,

Laurette Taylor in *The Glass Menagerie*, 1945.

at least for me, with his King Lear, which he played at the Hollywood Bowl in an outdoor setting that was both a handicap (too big a space to project into) and an asset (invoking all the angry elements to contend against).

And though this *Cherry Orchard* goes back some sixty years—it was at Eva LeGallienne's brave, exciting Civic Repertory in the musky, barnlike Fourteenth Street theater—Alla Nazimova's Madame Ranevsky retains in my memory its marvelous blend of hard-earned gallantry and Russian fecklessness.

I recall the sense of indomitable youth and courage conveyed by the young Joan Plowright when I first saw her in London in Arnold Wesker's *Roots*. She did not need speeches to establish that she would overcome poverty and a lack of education to turn herself into a whole person; the glow of her youth and ardor said it all. She was not introduced to New York in this role, but in She-lagh Delaney's *A Taste of Honey*, where she was impressive but not unforgettable as in *Roots*.

Ralph Richardson did not appear in David Storey's *Early Days* in the United States except on television. I saw him in this role of a crotchety old gentleman forced to live at his daughter's and fiercely resisting his lot, and nearly everyone who approached him, with double talk and conundrums. It was a memorable achievement of cranky humor covering defeat and disenchantment. What made it even more affecting the evening I saw the play in London was Richardson's unmistakable difficulty in remembering his lines. He would stare unseeingly into the distance as the actors around him waited for cues that did not come, and somehow he managed to speak lines that were perfect for the character and a comment on his own predicament.

Bracketed in my memory are two performances of desperation, quiet and unquiet. Both summed up heartbreakingly the situation of men at the end of their tether, both in plays by Harold Pinter. Donald Pleasance as the drifter Davey, picked up by the two odd brothers, in *The Caretaker*, and John Gielgud as the broken loser taken in by the maniacal man of property played by Richardson in *No Man's Land*. Pleasance with his pitiable display of a bold front and Gielgud with momentary explosions of an almost buried pride relapsing into utter defeat—both doing what the theater at its best should do, reminding us of the pity and terror of life.

Nor can I forget John Kani in Athol Fugard's *Master Harold—and the Boys* as the black servant who has tried to seem obedient without servility and who finally erupts at the young white master and reveals so much that people like him have had to deal with in South Africa.

The consuming intensity of Uta Hagen and Arthur Hill in Edward Albee's *Who's Afraid of Virginia Woolf* remains burned into my memory, as do the misery and despair of Frederic March, Florence Eldridge, Jason Robards and Bradford Dillman in Eugene O'Neill's relentlessly truthful tragedy about his family, *Long Day's Journey into Night*.

I have vivid recollections of Laurence Olivier in a rich diversity of roles—Henry V, Hamlet, Lear, Archie Price in John Osborne's *The Entertainer*, Shaw's Caesar—but his achievement in the course of three successive evenings at Expo '67 in Montreal ranks among the most versatile, skillful and courageous in my experience as a theatergoer. By 1967 Olivier, through his leadership and influence, had helped to establish Britain's National Theater, and the company's first visit to North America was anticipated as a major attraction of the Montreal World Fair. Olivier himself was scheduled to appear in all three plays; but some months before the visit, he had to undergo surgery for cancer, and it was announced that he would not be ready to return to the stage even if his recovery proceeded as hoped for.

Like hundreds of others with plans to see Olivier and his new company, I was disappointed but decided to go to Montreal anyhow. When I got there, I heard that Olivier was determined to appear in the opening play, Strindberg's *Dance of Death*, regardless of his medical history. If he had chosen to play the Captain with a measure of restraint, it would have been understandable and forgivable. Nothing of the sort! I have rarely seen a performance of such furious intensity. With Geraldine MacEwen opposite him, this was truly a married couple's dance to the death as only Strindberg's inflamed, vengeful imagination could conceive it.

Brilliantly done, thou good and faithful servant of the drama, one might have thought, but at what exhausting cost? The next two nights the National turned to comedy—Congreve's *Way of the World* and Feydeau's *A Flea in His Ear*. Olivier had discharged his duty; it was not expected that he would appear in small roles in each of these plays as scheduled. Wrong again. Though they were minor parts, he carried them off with his usual flair—the elegance, hauteur and wit of Congreve were reflected not only in the lines but in the very carriage and movement of the player, and in the Feydeau there was a disarming, comic simplicity in the role of a bewildered, bumbling servant. I found it hard to believe that this was Olivier on the stage, not only because of his shaky physical condition and the energy he had used up in the long Strindberg role but also because his realizations did not seem to be acting but were utterly convincing embodiments of character and personality.

Olivier wrote in his autobiographical books and spoke at length in television interviews about the challenge, the work and the unexpected forces that influence a life in the theater. He once remarked to me that the best thing that happened to him was the five flops he appeared in during his beginning years as a professional. He learned more from those failures, he thought, than he could have learned from an immediate big success.

But how to explain the sudden illumination of a special gift for the theater from a totally unpredictable source? I don't know the answer, but I remember such a moment. It occurred in a production of a play by Emanuel Robles in an adaptation by Lillian Hellman. It was called *Montserrat*, and it dealt with the taking and killing of hostages in reprisal for a political murder. In one scene the hostages were lined up against the rear wall, each waiting his or her turn to be questioned and shot. The actors playing the hostages had either no lines or at most one or two. At the performance I saw some time after the opening, discipline and concentration presumably had slackened. All but one of the hostages slouched indifferently as if what was to happen to them in the drama no longer involved them. The exception was a young girl who stood in an attitude of fear and terror as if her life depended, as indeed it did, on what was being argued in front of her. That young actress was Julie Harris.

Some years later, in the summer of 1960, I saw Harris at another stage of her development. She was playing Juliet at the Shakespeare Festival in Stratford, Ontario. It was a lovely performance, but how radiant and ardent it was I realized through a twelve-year-old boy's reaction. My son Philip was with me. I had taken him with some reluctance. Wasn't *Romeo and Juliet*, despite its youthful lovers, a bit too much for him at twelve? I underestimated the play and the boy, and especially Julie Harris. As we were leaving the theater, the lad almost walked through a glass door. He seemed to be in a trance as we went to our parked car. Had the play affected him so? It came out slowly: he confessed he had fallen in love. With Juliet or Julie? I shall never know, nor will he.

I remember the night when *High Spirits*, a musical based on Noel Coward's *Blithe Spirit*, opened. In the evening's high spot, Bea Lillie, playing Madame Arcati, a raffish medium, sat in her boudoir in nightgown, nightcap and slippers adorned with bunnies and sang a song of cheerful self-adulation. It was so delightful a turn that the applause literally stopped the show. What the audience seemed to demand was an encore. Miss Lillie was wise enough to know that a reprise might hurt the flow of the musical. With the greatest naturalness she did a brief business of travestying a ballerina, which was the kind of thing Madame Arcati in *High Spirits* might have done. Again there was prolonged, thunderous applause. What to do now to keep the show afloat? Miss Lillie responded with a deliciously comic series of mock curtsies of a prima ballerina gushing with gratitude. And now *High Spirits* could carry on.

Several weeks after the opening, I met Miss Lillie and I mentioned the ballerina sequence, inquiring whether it had been rehearsed when the musical was being prepared. Not at all. She had improvised it because it seemed the only thing to do. Now it had become a fixed part in the play, the contribution of a greatly gifted performer.

The mystery of talent was exemplified for me in another way at the opening of *The Hollow Crown*, which was not a full play but a kind of reading—a colorful, glamorous reading—of passages from memoirs and letters telling of the kingly or queenly state, including Richard II's "For within the hollow crown that rounds the mortal temples of a king keeps Death his court and there the antic sits." The set resembled a rather ordinary living room, and the four actors—three men and a woman from Britain's Royal Shakespeare Company—sat in stuffed chairs waiting their turn. The woman was Dorothy Tutin, whom I had admired years before as Viola in *Twelfth Night* at Stratford-upon-Avon, and she was the last to speak. From my seat in the third row on the aisle, I was astonished to observe how unglamorous she seemed. Her round face looked puffy, her figure was plump and even her clothes were not striking. *It's no good being this close to the stage,* I thought. *Can this be the actress who was so enchanting as Viola?* Now it was her turn. She stood up, adjusted her stole with an imperious gesture, moved forward and began to speak her lines. A transformation! A woman wearing a modest twentieth-century gown had become in a miraculous flash the young, radiant, commanding Elizabeth I.

The memory of Richard Burton conjures up a performance of a different order, extraordinary in its own way. It has been said repeatedly that Burton had it in him to be one of the greatest actors of all time but frittered away his gifts. When I first saw him a long time ago in Stratford-upon-Avon, he was a young, mercurial, dazzling Prince Hal. His Hamlet in modern rehearsal clothes, directed by Gielgud, had excitement if not the depth one would have liked. His King Arthur in *Camelot* was full of vitality and charm. The performance I remember particularly, however, did not take place on a stage.

Six of us were gathered for a Sunday morning television causerie on the theater. The panel consisted of Harold Clurman, designated as the moderator, Elia Kazan, Robert Preston, Edward Albee, Burton and me. We sat at a longish table with glasses of water before us. We were introduced, then there was a commercial. While it was being aired and we were off camera, Burton bent down, brought up a brown paper bag he had stashed under his chair, extracted a liter of vodka, got rid of the water in his glass and filled it from the bottle, then returned the bottle to its bag and its hiding place. He proceeded to converse about the theater; at least some of the time it was wise and witty talk. As I need hardly explain, the panel was lively and argumentative, and the liveliest and most argumentative panelist was Burton. There were periodic breaks for commercials, and during each Burton refilled his glass from his bottle under his chair. By the time the session approached its conclusion, Burton had killed the bottle, had succeeded in taking over the role of moderator and had become so dominant that he posed questions and answered them himself. What did he do that day for an encore?

Richard Burton with Christine Ebersole in *Camelot*, 1980.

I know what Alfred Lunt did to occupy himself when he was away from the theater early in the 1950s: he staged opera. I was fortunate enough to watch him at work during a number of rehearsals and observe how he managed to eliminate the gaucheries that passed for "acting" in the opera house. His part in the Metropolitan's 1951 revival of Mozart's *Così fan tutte* helped to turn it into a triumph in which music and action were seamlessly united.

The plot of *Così* is, of course, silly. One must suspend tons of disbelief if one is to credit the notion that two young women in love, however flighty and insipid they might be, would not recognize their supposedly departed lovers in exaggerated Turkish disguises. To Lunt, who had played in Molnar's *The Guardsman* many years earlier with a panache that swept away disbelief, the *Così* was a challenge: how to make it match the music's unending genius for laughter and, when least expected, for honest emotion—in short, how to transcend credibility and capture the opera's enchantment?

Lunt was a worrier at work. "For an actor of advancing years," he told me mournfully, "this is a fine thing to get into. Rudolf Bing's instructions were to make it light, gay and elegant. Does he think I'm Madame Lazanga who guarantees to teach ballet in six easy lessons?" He groaned, "I'm slow and need more time, lots of it."

During the summer at Ten Chimneys, his home in Genessee Depot, Wisconsin, he studied the Lorenzo Da Ponte libretto and its English translation by Thomas and Ruth Martin and listened to recordings until he knew the opera by heart. He corresponded with Rolf Gerard, the designer, and conferred with him repeatedly when he returned to New York. He asked Fritz Stiedry, the conductor, for permission to sit in on all musical rehearsals, even the earliest with piano. He fretted that he would not have enough time with the cast. Musically it was a polished one since it comprised Eleanor Steber, Blanche Thebom, Patrice Munsel, Richard Tucker, Frank Guarrera and John Brownlee, but how would it respond to his requirement for elegance and wit in acting style?

"Each move," he told them, "is like a step in a minuet." To the women he said, "If you beat your breast as they like to do in opera, I'll kill you." To the men, "You have to feel at home in those eighteenth-century lace-filled costumes." And he got the flavor and mood he wanted. In the huge old opera house on Broadway between Thirty-ninth and Fortieth Streets, *Così* emerged as a wonderful *jeu d'esprit* with an illusion of intimacy one would expect in a small, exquisite eighteenth-century court theater. To make the necessary spirit of artifice seem believable, Lunt hammered away on the absolute need for everyone onstage to be unaware of artifice. And when Mozart, with Fiordiligi's second-act aria, moves into the real world of a troubled, vulnerable heart, Lunt knew it was his job to get out of the way: "When Fiordiligi goes soaring off into the heavens, I told Steber to forget me and to just stand there and sing."

Lunt went shopping for props and paid for them out of his own pocket. He found the right wine glasses at 18 cents apiece and painted them himself. His wife, Lynn Fontanne, was caught up in the adventure. She bought linen and lace to make handkerchiefs for the cast, hand-rolling them and stitching the hems with infinite care. Though he had admonished Bing that he was paying his director too much to stage a production that would have six performances in a season, Lunt managed to end up with hardly any money to show for the months he poured into his assignment. By the time he finished buying tickets for his friends, he felt lucky to break even.

As opening night approached, he had become so attached to what he was doing that, like any eager actor longing to be onstage, he could not resist an urge to be part of it. He donned the livery of an eighteenth-century flunky, and as Stiedry and the orchestra played the sparkling overture, Lunt emerged from the wings carrying a taper and with precision and grace went through the motions of lighting the footlights arranged to simulate candles.

My article in *The Sunday Times* about Lunt's experience in opera had a bit of fun with his fears and seeming insecurity. It was headed "Threnody by Lunt." Some days after it appeared, he introduced me to his wife. "Oh, I enjoyed what you wrote," she said, and she laughed with that touch of mischief just this side of malice that I remembered so well from *The Guardsman*, Noel Coward's *Design for Living*, Robert E. Sherwood's *Reunion in Vienna* and many other plays. "It's the kind of thing Alexander Woollcott would have written, and how Alfred deserves it."

In December, 1968, I received a letter from Ten Chimneys. With it was a penciled enclosure, an unfinished note dated December 6, 1965, on the stationery of the Passavant Pavilion of Northwestern Memorial Hospital in Chicago.

"Your book"—the reference was to *The Making of the American Theater*—"is giving me such pleasure," the note began. It continued:

> Perfect reading for the place I'm in—takes my mind away and into such happy days—days I might have forgotten. We did *The Young Mrs. Winthrop* at Carroll College followed by *You Never Can Tell*—then *Pillars of Society* (1910–11). We did all the Charles Hoyt farces at the Castle Square in Boston. Charles K. Harris lived around the corner from us in Milwaukee, Eighteenth Street it was. You see, I was first taken to the theater in 1896 . . .

The accompanying letter explained:

> I just came across a little note written some three years ago while in hospital indulging in pneumonia, but found your book much more enjoyable—and still do.
>
> While we are in New York during the next few months I wonder if you would care to have lunch with me, say at the Players.

I would have relished lunching with Alfred Lunt at the Players or anywhere else, but alas, we did not get together. I thought I was too busy, traveling in the United States and Europe. I am ashamed to say that excuses do not excuse; it was unforgivably remiss of me. When I was ready to call, Alfred Lunt was dead.

He lives vividly in my memory in a long line of shining roles, especially his last in Friedrich Dürrenmatt's mordant *The Visit*. I cannot forget the moment

when he is sitting on the ground, beaten by the wife (Fontanne, of course) he
had scorned, a vision of misery and defeat. But I like to remember him best as
the flunky lighting the footlights for his *Così* and setting the tone for an elegance of acting style that was very much his own and which he had succeeded
in grafting, if only for a while, on a cast of opera singers.

The most remarkable ensemble work I ever saw was at the Berliner Ensemble, the East Berlin theater that Bertolt Brecht established with unlimited financial support from the East German government. I saw magical performances of
Brecht's *Arturo Ui* and *The Three Penny Opera*. After Brecht's death the theater
was run by his widow, Helene Weigel, who played Mother Courage with a
memorable blend of compassion and rage.

Not far behind the Berliner Ensemble were some of the Theater Guild's productions of Shaw with a fine group of actors headed by the Lunts.

My most difficult time as a theater reviewer occurred during the long newspaper strike that began in 1962 and lasted for four painful months. After the
curtain I hurried back to the office on West Forty-third Street and wrote a short
review, then went to the quarters of WQXR and read and taped it for broadcast later that evening. Next I walked or taxied to the NBC building, where I
wrote another version of the review, donned makeup and read it on camera after
Frank Field finished his weather forecast. Then the day's work really began. I
would hurry back to the office to write a full-length review to be published the
next morning in the International and West Coast editions of *The Times*. This
version would be distributed to the thousands of newspapers in the United
States and abroad that subscribed to *The Times* Syndicate. Is this a picture of a
man talking to himself? On CBS Walter Kerr of the *Herald Tribune* was reading his reviews. Those with an interest in the productions stared at two television sets, as Lyndon Johnson was said to do in his eagerness to keep up with his
treatment by the media. I do believe that our TV reviews sparked a prolifera-
tion of opening-night reviews on radio and television. I suspect that there is too
much of this now!

15

Grace Notes

I T WAS TO BE a temporary assignment. I was walking down the corridor in the rear of the vast third-floor newsroom of *The New York Times* when I was clapped briskly on the shoulder. The hand was Frederick T. Birchall's.

I had no idea that the big boss was aware that I existed, let alone able to call me by name. Freddy Birchall, as we reporters, veteran or barely fledged like me, called him behind his back, had the title of acting managing editor because, according to tradition, Adolph S. Ochs, the owner, would not give an Englishman the full title of managing editor, which in fact Freddy Birchall was. And a more feisty one I never encountered.

"Laddie," he said, "I'd like you to move into the Music Department."

I demurred. I knew and loved music. Olin Downes, chief music critic, whose acquaintance I had made, had asked for me. But I did not see myself being shunted off into a fringe department when I had visions of dealing with presidents and prime ministers.

"It'll be for a short while, laddie," Birchall assured me, "at most two years, I promise."

I joined the Music Department in September, 1930, and left it in September, 1960. I wonder how long I would have stayed if the promise had been of a permanent connection. Had it been up to me, I would have remained longer, but the executive editor, Turner Catledge, backed by Orvil E. Dryfoos, publisher of *The Times*, insisted that I shift from chief music critic to chief drama critic. In my remaining years on *The Times*—and in fifteen years as a consultant to Exxon Corporation in its distinguished heyday of commitment to the arts on television—my affection for music and musicians was undiminished.

And so it has remained. In six decades I have had countless close contacts as well as some glancing ones with practitioners of the art, and it cheers me to linger on some of the most memorable.

Early on there was an inadvertent brush—the precise word—with Mary Garden. I had just heard her in a recital and had been entranced by the skill with which she used a voice that James Huneker, who once served as *The Times* music critic, described as "a sonorous mirage" when she was at the height of her powers. When I heard her she was in her sixties, and it was remarkable what subtleties she could achieve with the shadow of a voice and the gifts of a true actor's rich personality.

I went around to interview her with the awe one would have for a goddess, the kind a later generation of admirers had for Maria Callas. I had read about Garden's storied Mélisande in the premiere of Debussy's opera. I had read Huneker's *The Painted Veil,* supposedly based on her life, and remembered passages once considered highly erotic. Blame it on my callowness, but I did not think her particularly seductive, even though in her chic, tight-fitting silk dress she did not look her age.

Orvil Dryfoos in 1961.

Turner Catledge in 1964.

She took immediate charge of the interview. Criticism? She brought her palms together. "That's how close criticism is to rudeness." Her voice? "I've had little voice as such all my career. How can they say I've lost it?"

I was seated in an armchair. She invited me to join her on the sofa. I took the corner farthest from her. She reached for my hand and drew me near her. Holding it, she spoke of her first encounter with Debussy's music in a musty hotel at Aix-les-Bains where she was leafing through an old copy of *L'Illustration* and paused at a page of music, a Debussy ariette. "It was so sensual," she said, "so sensual, I ripped out the page. So sensual, so sensual," she murmured as she guided my hand to stroke her breast. Oh, I was a proper young man, ashamed for the goddess, and fled as soon as I could.

How a certain colleague, a gossipy sort, would have relished this story! He was the chap who regaled me from time to time with tidbits about who in the music world did what, to and with whom. One evening as we strolled away from Carnegie Hall, he seemed to be savoring an especially juicy morsel. "I was at a party the other night," he said with a nice air of hesitancy and concern, "and someone was saying you were so good to Suzanne Sten because," a delicate pause, "because she sleeps with you."

Mary Garden in 1937.

"How interesting," I said with a calmness that must have been a letdown to my colleague. But granting that he had actually heard such gossip and not invented it, I wondered about its origin. I had never written any criticism, favorable or unfavorable, of Suzanne Sten, nor had I ever seen her on or off the stage. I knew she was a well-regarded soprano, and I remembered photographs that showed her to be a fine-looking woman. To make sure that my memory was not playing me false, I went through the Sten folder in the *Times* morgue, as the archive of all that appeared in the paper about thousands of people was called, and found that in fact I had never reviewed Suzanne Sten.

How, I wondered, *do such rumors get floated? Does someone with a grievance against a critic invent them as a form of vengeance?* One day I glanced at a flyer announcing a Sten recital and noticed that her accompanist would be Leo Taubman. Aha, that must be the man. Leo and I were not related. We chanced to be fellow guests at a lunch, and I said, "I see that you are Suzanne Sten's accompanist."

He nodded.

I decided to be presumptuous. "Forgive me for being personal," I said, "but are you and she especially friendly?"

He laughed and laughed. "Very friendly. She is my wife and has been for some time."

Considering that my contact with Charles Ives lasted no more than a couple of hours, I have no right to regard it as a close one, yet I came away with a sense of warmth and intimacy that normally would take months and years to achieve. It was extraordinary that the meeting took place at all. Ives was almost seventy-five, a man whose health was so fragile that he saw hardly anyone. I had heard and admired the "Concord" Sonata for piano, in which he sought to epitomize the world of Emerson, Hawthorne, the Alcotts and Thoreau. I had heard a rare program of his music when his Third Symphony had its first performance thirty-five years after it was completed. A remote, lonely figure in the music world, he had pursued his vocation for composing while becoming one of the country's ablest and most successful insurance men.

His was a story worth telling as fully as possible, but we had not done so in *The Times*. As one who had written many profiles of musicians for *The Times Magazine*, I dared to propose a piece on Ives to Lester Markel, the redoubtable Sunday editor who liked to generate his own ideas. He was not excited.

"It's time we did an American composer," I argued.

"But why Ives?"

I tried to explain. No sale—yet.

"What's the news peg?"

"On October 20, 1949, he will be seventy-five, and it's time we did something," I persisted.

"Let's try it," he said without enthusiasm, "and we'll see how it comes out."

Now came the hardest part—to get an appointment. Through friends of Ives it was finally arranged that he would see me when up to it, and that could be known only at the last minute. One morning I had a call from Mrs. Ives to say that he was having a good day, I could come if I wished. I drove up from New York to their gracious, simple house high on a Connecticut hill, oddly enough not far from where I now live.

Harmony Twitchell Ives was on the porch waiting for me. Inside the house there was the pounding of a cane. We entered. There stood a gaunt, wiry man, bearded, erect with the cane's support, the image of a Yankee patriarch. His eyes were bright and alert. "It's good of you," he said, "to come and see this old broom." He moved toward a couple of straight-backed armchairs near a large window facing west. Though he used the cane, his walk was springy and his gestures volatile. He pointed his stick toward the window: "That's Danbury on the other side of the mountain. That's where I was born and grew up and learned a little about music. Pa taught me what I know."

At thirteen Charles became the organist of Danbury's West Street Congregational Church. At Yale he studied with Horatio Parker, a leading American composer. Even before coming to Yale, Charles had begun what all but his father considered his outlandish experiments. At twenty he wrote "Song for Harvest Season," using a stanza from an old hymn and setting it for voice, cornet, trombone and organ pedal, each in a different way. Parker's reaction was, "Ives, must you hog all the keys?"

Ives' eyes danced as he recalled Parker's question. Beating time with his cane, he sang a four-square tune by Haydn, improvising these words: "First you write in C. Then you write in G. Then go back to C again, and no one calls you wrong."

Throughout the visit he would burst into song, making up words about the staid music world with its "old ladies, male and female." Occasionally he stopped short, panting for breath, and I looked in alarm at Mrs. Ives, who nodded reassuringly. "Don't know why I get excited," he said as he recovered his breath, and he began chanting again, "No one gives a damn, what a fool I am."

With his business flourishing and demanding full working days, including weekends, when did he compose? Mrs. Ives answered: "Evenings, free weekends, vacations. He could hardly wait for dinner to be over, and he was at the piano. He went to bed at 2 or 3 A.M." Ives broke in. "We never went anywhere, and she didn't mind, and she never told me to be good and write something nice that people would like."

He had to write as he saw fit. That meant drawing on the experiences and memories of his boyhood and youth, conjuring up the tone of barn dances, revival meetings, Indians, Halloween, the Housatonic at Stockbridge, a football game, a lefthanded pitcher, a Decoration Day parade, the village volunteer firemen, town meetings, harvest time, the country store, minstrel airs played by country fiddlers. But his music went beyond literalism and jesting: it transmuted memories and natural sounds into personal tonal visions.

Several times during our talk he got so excited he had to lie down. I looked at Mrs. Ives for a signal to leave, and her answering glance seemed to say, *Be patient, it will pass.* When I was ready to go—I declined an invitation from him to "stay and have a potato"—he led me into his study, where the floor was covered with piles of photostated scores. Did I have any use for any of the music?

"I'd like whatever can be spared," I said. I walked out carrying a heap of scores. I no longer remember what scores or how many. They are now in the archives of Cornell.

My only meeting with Sergei Rachmaninoff was even shorter than the one with Ives, yet it left an equally indelible impression. I was commissioned to write an article about him for *Collier's*, and when I called his manager for an appointment, I was told that he had no time for me in New York but if I wished to come to Chicago, he could give me thirty minutes. *Crazy*, I thought—*all the way to Chicago for thirty minutes.* It was 1939 and one did not casually catch a flight; one traveled by train.

Collier's had arranged for a photographer to meet me at the Blackstone Hotel, and when we entered the pianist's suite, he received us coolly. He hadn't expected picture-taking but agreed with good enough grace to a few. The photographer asked him to sit at the keyboard, and he sat there, looking just as forbidding, his face somber and expressionless, as he normally did at Carnegie Hall.

"Please play a few chords," the photographer said.

Rachmaninoff stared at him coldly. "Do you know what my fee is?"

The photographer thought he was joking, and so did I. We were wrong.

The photographer was dismissed in a hurry, and Rachmaninoff turned to me. "Shall we begin?" He drew one of those old-fashioned, bulky Ingersoll watches from his vest pocket and placed it on a table near him. "Thirty minutes, yes." Precisely thirty minutes later he stood up, returned the watch to his pocket and bade me goodbye. The most usable thing he told me was that he could not stand the C-sharp minor Prelude, his best-known and most frequently played piece, and that he would never play it again. For this a couple of days spent traveling to and from Chicago? Using other sources, all in New York, I put together an acceptable piece. I have never forgotten Rachmaninoff's Ingersoll.

I recall a flap in which we in the *Times* Music Department were embroiled with Rachmaninoff's family. Gina Bachauer had made a flaming debut as a pianist. The truth was Bachauer was a dynamo of a pianist. (Later I wrote of her "furious intensity," which was nothing like Horowitz's.) I asked Harold

Sergei Rachmaninoff, 1939.

Schonberg to interview her for the Sunday paper. We were interested in discovering her musical background. Harold reported that she said she had studied with Rachmaninoff. I got an indignant call from the Russian pianist's family and agreed to receive a visit from Rachmaninoff's widow and his daughter.

They came to complain, in Harold's presence, that Rachmaninoff had never taught Bachauer. We listened to their protest and promised to publish a few lines carrying their denial. I could not understand what upset them. Was it that they felt there was an implication of some sort of intimacy between Rachmaninoff and Bachauer, a well-set-up figure of a woman? I assured them there was no such implication. They left content with the promise of a correction. I never heard from the Rachmaninoff family again.

Years after my meeting with Ives, I chatted with Paul Hindemith, who was teaching at Yale, and wondered what influence he would have had on a young talent like Ives. *Probably none*, I thought, and though Ives was not mentioned, Hindemith confirmed my speculation by insisting that composing could not be taught, that a composer could only learn and that the most useful way to learn was to work directly with musicians, to get a thorough grounding in the voice, the instruments, the broad theory and the past of music.

Paul Hindemith, 1939.

A man of lively intelligence, Hindemith was in a provocative mood. He had no patience with the concept "American composer," dismissing it as a stale nationalistic appeal. He decried the pampering of young Americans who wished to compose—all those prizes, awards, scholarships, fellowships and other devices to give potential composers the opportunity and freedom to learn their craft. "You are pampering these young people," he said. "You are delaying the day when they must get to work. Because of your wealth and dislike for paying taxes, you have worked out ways to give money away." He cited examples of Yale graduate students who found so many sources of support that it was a decade before they began to make their way as musicians. And with a wry smile, he added, "I signed their applications. I didn't have the courage to say no."

A man of principle, Hindemith exiled himself from Nazi Germany and spent many years in the United States. I don't think he was being falsely modest when he dismissed the possibility that his music would survive. There were only two composers in the last fifty years—and this was 1960—whose music, in his view, would survive: Stravinsky and Bartók. "They," he said, "are the only composers." But what was Hindemith? "I am," he replied, "simply a musician." A proud affirmation from a man whose music—at least some, such as *Mathis der Maler* and *Nobilissima Visione*—has survived.

Igor Stravinsky, I am sure, had no doubt about his music—neither its durability nor who should judge it. As for the opinions of music critics, he dismissed them out of hand. Perhaps he had a point. I have no doubt that he was being provocative when we met, but I am sure he meant it when he declared that the only persons with the right to judge his music were those who had accomplished as much as—or more than—he had. I did not ask him who would pass that test.

I wondered why he had agreed to talk to me. He insisted that there must be no direct quotes because no interviewer can reproduce a photographic copy of words, gestures and inflections. He had seen too much mischief from inaccurate quotes, he said. But why had he let me come to talk with him? Could it be that despite his severe views of interviewers, he didn't mind attention in *The Times?*

I was amused when he declared—and this is a quote I set down the minute I left his presence—"I have a strong conducting technique." Other conductors, he said, inject themselves, whereas he conducted his own music objectively. In later years I heard him conduct his own music "objectively," or to use a more fitting word, "dully."

Igor Stravinsky, 1948.

I met Stravinsky on other occasions and never found him agreeable—probably my fault or that of my occupation, for I have heard and read descriptions of his warmth and geniality. I remember a concert at the Red Rocks amphitheater near Denver when he conducted and his son, Soulima, was the soloist in his father's Capriccio for Piano and Orchestra. It was not an eloquent performance. At a party afterwards, I noticed that Stravinsky virtually snarled at Soulima as if he were responsible for the shortcomings of the performance.

Arnold Schoenberg I found no more agreeable. There was an occasion when the Juilliard School planned a Schoenberg program and suggested that he write a few hundred words for a program note. What he wrote was sent to me. It was lively and informative, and I offered to publish it under his signature in *The Sunday Times*. The Juilliard man said he would ask for Schoenberg's approval and then called to give the go ahead.

We ran the piece under Schoenberg's signature, and *The Times* sent him a check for $100. I knew that Schoenberg was having a hard time financially, and though the payment was small, it amounted to something at a time when the dollar bought a lot more than it does now. I received a vituperative letter from Schoenberg, calling me all sorts of names for betraying him by publishing his remarks in *The Times*. I still do not understand what made him so furious.

I would add Schoenberg's name to Hindemith's as a giant of the twentieth century. Some would agree, many might disagree. One who evidently disagreed was Alexander Zemlinsky, Schoenberg's teacher and father-in-law. I met him at a lunch given by Artur Bodanzky, the Metropolitan Opera's Wagner conductor when that wing of the repertory was dominated by Kirsten Flagstad and Lauritz Melchior. Zemlinsky, like Schoenberg, was small, sharp-tongued, acidulous. We discussed his son-in-law's latest music. Zemlinsky dismissed it with a sentence: "I don't understand it."

The composer who, like Anton Webern and Alban Berg disciples, did understand Schoenberg and his theories thoroughly and knew how to turn them to his purpose was Luigi Dallapiccola. A tiny man with a reserved manner that masked the stoutness of his convictions, he argued, I remember, that serialism, the twelve-tone row, could be molded to yield lyricism with a richness and profile of its own. An Italian, Dallapiccola could not and would not deny the lyricism in his blood. He had not performed much in the United States, but two of his larger works, *Job* and *Il Prigioniero*, impressed me as persuasive evidence for his thesis.

Another composer who ranks among the great of our century was Ernest Bloch. My respect for him preceded our first meeting, which enhanced it. We had been invited to be the luncheon guests of my *Times* colleague Hubbard Hutchinson, who had studied with Bloch. Hubbard, a bachelor, had a charming walkup apartment with a terrace in one of those old buildings in Manhattan's West Forties, now replaced mostly by unvarying tall boxes. He also had money and a cook, something not easy to attain on our *Times* salaries in the early thirties. Hubbard unfortunately died of leukemia when he was in his thirties.

When I arrived for lunch, Bloch was there. No Hubbard; indeed Hubbard did not appear at all. At the office the next day he apologized but did not explain. Without our host, we asked for a drink, then another. We decided to proceed with lunch. It went famously. Bloch was not a man to stand on ceremony. We were friends in a few minutes; in a few more I was his confidant. His talk and his appearance, the eyes sparkling and a fringe of gray hair standing out like Albert Einstein's, were full of temperament. I could understand why Romain Rolland chose Bloch as a model for a section of his powerful novel about a composer's life, *Jean Christophe*.

I met Bloch for the last time almost twenty years later. He was living on the edge of the Pacific in Newport, Oregon. He was seventy, and he put on a semblance of weariness and indifference. The world had passed him by, he sighed, and he was resigned. I said something favorable and, to him, irritating about certain far-out experimentalists, and the blood of the old fighter boiled up. His eyes blazed, his short, stocky body leaned forward and his high-pitched voice poured forth in analysis and excoriation.

Like Hindemith and Stravinsky and Schoenberg and Rachmaninoff, he had a profound belief in the high mission of being a composer. I remember a story he had told me long ago about his decision at the age of eleven to dedicate himself to that purpose. "I made a vow," he said, "and I wrote it on paper, buried it under stones and built a fire on the stones to consecrate the vow."

His music reflected his character; it followed no fashions. A performer once complained about a C-sharp chord injected into a passage like a stinging jab to the jaw. Its effect, Bloch was advised, was too violent; he should have a smoother transition to the unexpected chord. Bloch replied after some thought that he would make no change.

"It doesn't make sense," he was warned.

He replied, "It does to me. I will figure out its logic later."

Ernest Bloch, 1934.

Bloch did not enjoy being called a Jewish composer simply because he was of Jewish origin and wrote *Schelomo, Three Jewish Poems,* the *Israel Symphony,* a setting of the Sacred Service and other pieces of Jewish inspiration. "I wrote a great deal that had no Jewish source," he declared. "Must we look for roots in everything?"

And yet we look. The roots are inescapable. The big question remains: are they transcended as they were in Mussorgsky, Tchaikovsky, Dvořák, Sibelius, Villa-Lobos and Vaughan Williams?

Ralph Vaughan Williams was the most reticent composer I ever encountered. In 1939, when I was in London, he agreed to see me provided I wrote nothing about the meeting. I accepted the unusual condition. We met for tea at the Royal College of Music. A burly, tweedy, shaggy man, he talked about the state of English music (only fair), the qualities of the new generation of composers (promising) and Nazism (monstrous). About himself, hardly a word. As a later biographer wrote, "He has a great deal of music and very little biography." A quarter of a century later when we met again in New York, he lacked something more precious, his hearing. Still tweedy and shaggy but oh, how sad! He employed an ear trumpet to achieve the merest wisp of communication. Was Beethoven's reliance on written notes the better way?

What of American music? Ives made no secret of roots he sought out. Nor did Aaron Copland in his deliberate popular vein, as in his ballet scores for *Appalachian Spring, Rodeo* and *Billy the Kid.* Like Ives, he had another vein, more austere and more demanding. He devoted years and endless energy promoting the cause of American composers.

One day in the early 1950s I was walking down Broadway with Copland. "Would you do me a favor?" he asked.

"Yes, what?"

"Please ask Olin Downes to stop referring to me as 'the young American composer.'"

I nodded.

"After all," he went on, "I'm over fifty. When do I stop being a young American composer?"

I had no answer. In my opinion, he remained a young American composer until after his death in 1990. Much of his music remains youthful.

Associated with Copland in his concern for the American composer was Roger Sessions, a rumpled, unpretentious man who wrote music of great, still unappreciated depth. I am sure they would have agreed with Walter Piston, a reserved, thoughtful man who wrote some lively pieces, when he exclaimed impatiently, "It is all American music if it is written by Americans." It is American whether it has what appears to be the rigorous intellectuality of Elliott Carter, the wit and vivacity of Virgil Thomson, the simplest minimalism of Philip Glass or the gravity of Samuel Barber as revealed in the Adagio for Strings or the lovely quintet in *Vanessa*.

Several years before Barber's death, I approached him with the promise of a large commission, which might be offered by the Philip Morris Corporation, for a work to be performed in connection with the opening of a new plant in Virginia. He was dubious. What could he write for such a commission? Perhaps a big cantata, I suggested, using the writings of Thomas Jefferson. The idea appealed to him. He devoted weeks to reading Jefferson; in a way he became a Jeffersonian expert. Then he told me he could not find anything that struck him as right and inevitable, therefore he could not consider the commission.

And who could be regarded as more American than Leonard Bernstein, who wrote the scores for such Broadway shows as *Wonderful Town*, *West Side Story* and *Candide*, as well as sober, probing music like the symphonic *Age of Anxiety* and *The Chichester Psalms?* If there were a designation of all-purpose American musician, who would be more richly entitled to it than Bernstein? But why merely American musician? Why not, as in fact he was, world musician? Or to return to Hindemith's proud, honest self-characterization, simply musician.

Bernstein's versatility was extraordinary. He conducted, played the piano, wrote music, made records, appeared on television. Among his many gifts, his talent for discourse about music was not the least. I remember long ago tuning in on the CBS Sunday afternoon program "Omnibus," when he gave a vividly informative talk on how Beethoven struggled to shape a symphony to suit his inner ear. Bernstein had measures of music painted on the studio floor to illustrate how the composer worked away at changes and improvements. I wrote an appreciative piece for *The Times*, praising Bernstein for writing and delivering a brilliant talk. Soon I received an indignant protest from a man who claimed to have written the text. I sent the letter to Bernstein, who replied with one giving the man full credit.

I doubt that he used the scripts of other writers when he began his "previews" at the New York Philharmonic on Thursday nights. It was, to quote him, "no crime to be gay in Carnegie Hall," and he would tell jokes, play the piano, indulge in bursts of song. He was educator and entertainer as well as interpreter. In his eagerness to share his enthusiasms, he would occasionally oversell a piece, or in his desire to explore the anatomy of a composition he would dissect too much, drawing excessive attention to details.

Then Bernstein decreed that Thursday nights were to be regarded as a kind of dress rehearsal, and critics were disinvited and told to attend Friday afternoon concerts. Call me a male chauvinist pig, but the audiences, made up mostly of women, were casual about their concert-going. Quite a few came late and left early. And the charm bracelets! They tinkled and chimed, often in counterpoint with shimmering *pianissimo*s. I blessed Bernstein when he relented and let the critics resume Thursday attendance. I was prepared to indulge his most euphoric "previews."

Bernstein became one of the dominant conductors of our time. His seventieth birthday in 1988 became a year-long observance that spilled over into

Leonard Bernstein and his wife, Felicia Montealegre, in 1964.

Bernstein conducting the Metropolitan Opera Orchestra, 1969.

adjoining years. He achieved the status of the leading conductors of earlier generations, legendary figures like Arturo Toscanini, Serge Koussevitzky, Leopold Stokowski, Bruno Walter, George Szell, Fritz Reiner, Thomas Beecham, Wilhelm Furtwängler, Willem Mengelberg and Pierre Monteux. Having reached the heights, would he become the subject of an effort at "debunking" as Toscanini has? Yes, he has.

I have little to add to what I wrote about Toscanini in my book *The Maestro* (New York, 1951). In his commitment to music, he was, one could justly say, demonic. Occasionally in his last years he resorted to fast tempos, and there were moments that seemed driven. But not many. For within those tempos he achieved balance, lucidity and a conviction that what one was hearing had to be at that moment exactly as it sounded. Slow movements, even when pushed a bit, did not lose their depth. And never did the music he conducted lose its ardent humanity. I go back to his records to check my memory, and I find two Verdi performances that remind me of the essential Toscanini: the prelude to the last act of *Traviata*, heart-rending in its simplicity and economy, and all of

With Arturo Toscanini, 1950. Photograph by Seymour Friedman.

In Texas with Toscanini, gathering material for *The Maestro*.

Falstaff, which, under his guidance, is a sweet, laughing summing up of an old genius's farewell to youth and age and human folly.

When *The Maestro,* an unauthorized biography, was published, I sent Toscanini a copy but received no acknowledgment. His son, Walter, who had made himself his father's archivist and undoubtedly resented my intrusion into his domain, let it be known that his father never looked at the book, but I heard otherwise. I had a report that someone walking into Toscanini's bedroom in his palatial villa in New York's Riverdale section discovered him with his myopic eyes close to the open pages.

In preparing the book, I did not turn to Walter for assistance, for I knew how jealously he guarded the data about his father. Did he plan a book himself? If he did, too bad he did not get around to it. Decades later it is not amiss to reveal that two of my best sources were Toscanini's daughters—Wally, the Countess Castelbarco, and Wanda, Mrs. Vladimir Horowitz. Shortly after publication, at a gathering at the Toscanini villa, a woman who was a kind of chief of protocol, self-appointed, in the maestro's service, delivered a tirade against me and my book. Since I was not there, the target had to be Wanda, known to be my friend. Wanda, like all the Toscaninis, could be excitable, and she gave as well as she got, insisting that a man like her father who had been before the

Toscanini and (left to right) Wally, Wanda and Walter in 1950.

public so long and so compellingly had to expect to have books written about him. Books about Toscanini continued to appear after mine.

Discs and tapes offer a broad representation of Toscanini as a conductor. Unfortunately, there is no comprehensive record of his early years at La Scala and the Metropolitan Opera. There was a set of kinescopes of his appearances on television. He did ten telecasts for NBC. In 1960, three years after his death, I went up to Riverdale and as Walter's guest sat through showings of these kines. I had been asked to speak at a Toscanini memorial meeting being organized by an Italian-American society. My first reaction was to decline; it would make little sense to talk about a man whose music spoke for him far more eloquently than anyone's words. Someone mentioned the kinescopes, and I said that if they were usable, they could make a memorial occasion truly memorable.

The kinescopes reflected rudimentary television. The visual images were catch-as-catch-can, and the sound was not what it should have been. Yet here was Toscanini *redivivus*. However, the celluloid in Walter's copies was beginning to crumble. An irreplaceable visual record would be gone if RCA, NBC's parent company and owner of the kinescopes, did not transfer them to an enduring medium.

Toscanini conducting the NBC Symphony, 1950.

I chose selections from the music of Rossini, Brahms, Verdi and Wagner, and I spoke briefly to the gathering in the Sert Room at the Waldorf-Astoria before showing each kine. I know I was deeply moved; I noted how shaken others were. We ended with no less a warhorse than "The Ride of the Valkyries," and the sight of the old warrior's flaming spirit calling up this surging music seemed to me a renewed affirmation of man's unconquerable spirit.

At the meeting's end General David Sarnoff, RCA chairman and the man who created the NBC Symphony for Toscanini and assured its existence for sixteen years, thanked me and mentioned the deep feelings it had stirred. I replied that the emotions it generated could not have been possible without the kines. Wouldn't it be another admirable RCA contribution to preserve these kines in permanent form? Sarnoff agreed, but whether he did anything I do not know. Not too long ago several bits from those kines were included in a television recollection of Toscanini, his family and his music.

Toscanini functioned as a conductor until he was eighty-six. His final concert with the NBC Symphony was for him a tragic one. He knew that it would be followed by the dissolution of the orchestra, and he was distressed. I attended the last rehearsal for this concert in Studio H in Radio City. After the last downbeat he stood on the podium like a person in mourning. The baton dropped from his hand. No one in the orchestra moved to pick it up. Jimmy Dolan, the orchestra's librarian, recovered and kept it when Toscanini used another one for the final concert. Dolan presented the fallen baton to me. In a simple frame, it hangs in my home.

Leopold Stokowski was an ingenious, adventurous musician who liked playing the role of a great conductor, and at times he was just that. In his subtly European accent—was it inevitable or calculated?—he could be loftily distant and philosophical. I once accepted an assignment to do a profile of him for a magazine, and I asked for an appointment. He refused, saying he wanted no article. Relying on material garnered from friends and associates, I wrote the piece anyhow and heard indirectly that he liked it.

In his lofty philosophical vein he spoke to me many years ago: "I believe that painting, sculpture, architecture and all the other arts are more solid, whereas music is as ethereal as pure spirit. Because music lies so high, life's changes touch it later. We have had American painting stemming from American life; our architecture is obviously that. It will come in music—perhaps not so soon."

"Hasn't it come," I asked, "in jazz and the popular field?"

Leopold Stokowski rehearsing an Army band in 1941.

"Music," he went on as if I had not put a question, "is not what is written; it is not instruments, not air vibrations—it is all those things and more. It is extraordinarily non-material, so remote, so deep inside us, a voice of divinity."

In another vein he could reach out and excite young people. After a concert in a college town he was met by a group of fifty or sixty students, and they invited him and some of his orchestra to join them for a snack. He accepted, and they marched him to a favorite spot, a large room where several hundred were assembled at long tables. As the beer flowed, the students began to sing American folk songs. Stokowski sang with them. Then he enjoined his musicians of Italian extraction to sing Italian folk songs and those of German background to offer German folk songs. As the party gained in fervor, he leaped onto a bench and conducted.

He never lost his magnetism. In the 1960s he agreed to conduct a collection of undertrained and undertalented instrumentalists, students at Riverdale Country School, where his son was enrolled. My son Philip, whom I can only describe as a pre-amateur fiddler, was a member of that ensemble, and I

Stokowski (at right) with stage director Nathaniel Merrill in 1961. Photograph by Sam Falk.

attended the performance, which took place after one rehearsal with Stokowski. What he accomplished with this band was sheer sorcery. The youngsters did not merely play together and in time; they sounded almost professional and made music worthy of professionals.

Stokowski was restless and imaginative. He devised lighting effects that put an aureole around his golden, wavy locks when he was on the podium and dimmed the rest of the stage. He made films with Deanna Durbin and Walt Disney. He took a romantic holiday with Greta Garbo, later married young Gloria Vanderbilt. He reseated the orchestra, moving the cellos to the conductor's right where the second violins had been traditionally. His example is still followed by some, and I still think that this arrangement results in an imbalance of sound, especially in the classical repertory.

He was the true begetter of the rich, lush Philadelphia Orchestra sound, which Eugene Ormandy, his successor, nurtured for decades. In 1958 when the orchestra under Ormandy visited the Soviet Union, Stokowski appeared unexpectedly as guest conductor of the Moscow orchestra. I was concluding a working trip to the Soviet Union at the time, and my last evening in Moscow I was dining with William J. Jorden and Max Frankel, *The Times* correspondents, and their wives when Stokowski entered the dining room at the National Hotel. I introduced him to my companions. At a distant table he dined alone, and when he finished, he came by to say goodbye. He was conducting the next night, and I wished him good luck. He stared at me. "I do not need good luck," he said severely. "If you know your métier, you do not need luck, and I know mine." I thought there might be a flicker of amusement in his eye, but no. He strode out of the dining room with the air of a man who had disposed of another example of empty small talk.

During the same visit, Ormandy invited me to lunch with him and Mrs. Ormandy at the Rossiya Hotel, promising as much caviar as I could consume. He happened to be very fond of caviar and had ordered a lot. At one point I asked for a napkin. Proud of his Russian, he conferred with the waiter, who trotted off and returned, smiling and carrying aloft a true prize, a roll of toilet paper.

Eugene Ormandy, 1971.

On the subject of food in the Soviet Union, I recall the Czarist dinner Sol Hurok arranged for Nora and me on our first Soviet visit. It took place at the Metropole Hotel in Moscow. He always did things with a grand gesture. The high point of the occasion occurred when the waiters, in elegant uniforms, marched in carrying flaming squabs on the tips of swords, and we felt like royalty. It was a magnificent show and a tasty meal. Typical Hurok. Who knows what it cost him in tips and bribes?

It was said of Serge Koussevitzky that his first wife's wealth turned a talented double-bass player into a world-famous conductor. It was said of him that fundamentally he was not a born conductor. I heard members of his Boston Symphony poke fun at his stick technique, but members of orchestras are not noted for adulation of their drillmasters. Year after year he managed to get performances of distinction from this orchestra. His strength was in music that demanded the passionate, dramatic and emotional gesture, and he thrived on Tchaikovsky.

Serge Koussevitzky conducting the Boston Symphony at Tanglewood, 1937.

Like Stokowski, he made a point of presenting music by living composers. From the moment the means were available to him, he befriended composers. With his first wife, Nathalie, he established in 1909 the Éditions Russes de Musique, a publishing firm, with the profits to go to Russian composers. As head of the Boston Symphony from 1925 to 1949, he introduced the works of contemporaries, especially Americans; he gave them commissions to write pieces they could not afford to undertake; he set up a foundation to underwrite commissions and support in other forms. More than anyone else he built Tanglewood into an international institution and he created the Berkshire Music Center, the training ground for generations of outstanding musicians.

When the Boston Symphony management was engaged in a knockdown battle with James C. Petrillo and the American Federation of Musicians over whether the orchestra could continue as the only major non-union ensemble in the country, it was Koussevitzky who had led the way toward acceptance of the union. He had been chafing because the Boston Symphony was losing radio and recording engagements, and seeking an end to confrontation and turmoil, he urged a change of policy on the orchestra's trustees. When the board refused, Koussevitzky reminded it that it was not the Boston Symphony. "We the musicians are the orchestra," he admonished the trustees. "Without you we are still an orchestra, but without us what are you?"

Like so many performers, Koussevitzky could be a bit of a ham. At Tanglewood one year he was doing a new work that I wanted to write about. Knowing that I would have to be elsewhere on the night of the performance, I asked Koussevitzky for permission to attend the final rehearsal. "Of course, of course."

I arrived early; I was the entire audience. It was a mild day, but Koussevitzky appeared wearing his favorite cape. He seemed not to see me. He mounted the stage and ceremonially shook the hands of the first-desk men. Was this routine procedure at rehearsals? A wink from a friend in the orchestra told me otherwise. Then Koussevitzky doffed the cape and got down to business. This was no stop-and-go rehearsal. He worked up a head of steam, his face grew red and his veins bulged as they were wont to do so alarmingly. It was a performance fit for a full house. When it was finished, Koussevitzky wrapped the cape around his shoulders, and in the slow, magisterial gait he liked to employ, walked off the stage and approached me. "Forgive us," he said with a straight face, "we were only practicing."

It was the summer of 1948. Koussevitzky was in his lovely home overlook-

ing Tanglewood. He had announced his retirement from the Boston Symphony
at the end of the 1948–49 season, and the orchestra management had named
Charles Munch as his successor. I had had lunch with Koussevitzky and was
preparing to go. As we stood saying our farewells, he asked whether I knew
Munch and his conducting.

"Very little," I replied.

"You know what I do here and in Boston," he continued, "how much work
and how much devotion."

I nodded.

"Do you really think"—it was a question I chose not to answer—"that
Munch can handle it?"

As his years in authority proved, Munch could. He made a point of devot-
ing at least a quarter of each program to contemporary music. After a concert
that included two difficult pieces—Stravinsky's *Canticum Sacrum* and Sessions'
Third Symphony—he was battered by letters of protest from subscribers. In
reply he wrote, "I understand your point of view since you come to concerts
for amusement and distraction or perhaps for consolation, surely for pleasure,"
and ended by pleading for active participation in an exchange among performer, creator and public.

Taubman and Charles Munch help themselves to a Chinese dinner, *c.* 1954. At right is
George Judd, manager of the Boston Symphony.

Munch could be tempestuous. At a dinner party at the home of Alfred Wallenstein, the conductor of the Los Angeles Philharmonic, he began to discuss traditions and standards of his parents' and grandparents' generations and compared them with the indifference and looseness he encountered in mid-twentieth-century studies and performance. As his discourse increased in passion, he rose from his chair and thundered at the gathering of ten. Suddenly he realized that his vehemence was out of proportion to the occasion. He picked up his chair, slammed it down and dashed out of the room.

But he could also purr like a pussycat. After a concert in El Paso, he was the guest of honor at a reception. The guests seemed to be in awe of the famous conductor and had little conversation to interest him. He sat off by himself, and as I happened to be in El Paso and at the reception, I went over to salute him. "Tell me, *mon ami*," he whispered, "will there be food?" He had had drink after drink, and since he had not eaten since lunch, he found canapés to be a poor substitute for a meal. The answer to his question came immediately—more canapés. He continued to drink and to become more gallant in his responses to those who approached him. After midnight George Judd, the courtly manager of the Boston Symphony, got Munch out of the party. I left with him. "And now we shall eat," Munch exclaimed. But where? Room service at the hotel was closed down, and restaurants were dark. We cruised in a taxi until we found a roadside diner where Munch, chuckling wryly at Texas hospitality, gobbled a couple of hamburgers.

George Szell had the reputation of being the most arrogant of conductors. Certainly he was one of the most arrogant, but he had a lot to be arrogant about. He turned the Cleveland Orchestra into one of the best in the world. It has been argued that conductors who have been pianists, as Szell had, do not equal those who have been string players in the subtleties they achieve with an orchestra. Having heard the Cleveland under Szell, I have my doubts. But I have none about his conviction that he was always right.

At the request of Louis Seltzer, editor of the *Cleveland Plain Dealer*, I was sent by *The Times* to address a meeting of the orchestra's supporters. I don't recall exactly what I said, but I know I set out to be critical of the way orchestras were run and maintained and about the behavior of audiences. At a dinner party following the talk, Szell took issue with my remarks. Surprised, I said I didn't know he had been in the audience. He hadn't but had received reliable reports. How would he react, I asked, if I based a review of one of his concerts

George Szell, 1950.

on hearsay? His information was reliable, he remarked coolly, and he wanted me to know I had been guilty of demagoguery.

In 1956 I devoted the entire music page in *The Sunday Times* to an examination of what was wrong with the New York Philharmonic and why. I had an immediate phone call from Cleveland; Szell would be in New York in a couple of days and must talk with me. Why? He would not discuss the matter on the phone. When we met in his New York pied-à-terre, he spread out a copy of my article and launched into a detailed analysis of my analysis, ticking off places where I was wrong and where I was right. I was at first irritated, then amused at his unmitigated self-assurance. I gave a passing thought to analyzing his analysis of my analysis but decided that he would not be amused.

Sir Thomas Beecham could be as arrogant as Szell—and a lot more amusing. With my late colleague Irving Kolodin, I sat with him one lovely evening in an English garden and listened as he decried the musical scene despite growing audiences and increasing private and public support. "Half the dilettanti seem to be scribbling notes," he said, "and what is more remarkable, getting them played." No one in mid-European music, he averred, had written a hun-

Sir Thomas Beecham, 1942.

dred good bars in the past twenty-five years. The reason? His answer—was he serious?—was: Marxism.

When I met Bruno Walter, he was distant and withdrawn. We were staying at the same hotel in Edinburgh in 1951 when he shared the conducting duties for the New York Philharmonic's visit to the festival. When I sought to draw him out, he was correct and uncommunicative. I wondered why. A friend explained that he had been hurt by my review of his autobiography, *Theme and Variations.* Back home I reread my review; as I had remembered, it was largely complimentary. I did refer to his surprise that the Nazis turned out to be aggressive toward culture by saying that "one is surprised that he needed so much time to find out."

The conductor on my conscience is Dimitri Mitropoulos. In my extended analysis of the New York Philharmonic (April 29, 1956), I criticized him for the way in which he as musical director had allowed the orchestra's standards of performance to decline. I was well aware that my observations would do him no good, even cause him pain, but I believed that it was my duty to speak out. Mitropoulos was a good, kind, generous man. When I was preparing a profile for *The Times Magazine* in 1950, I spent some time with him. The man who was taking over as permanent conductor of the Philharmonic lived in a small, ascetic apartment in a second-class hotel. In Minneapolis, where he had headed the orchestra, he had made his home in a dormitory at the university. His private philanthropies were so numerous that his friends were forced to set up a modest annuity fund.

My article, he wrote to a friend, "cost" him "a big grief." He gave up the job and was succeeded by Leonard Bernstein. I did not intend to harm a good man or to help open the way for another good man. My aim was to make sure that the Philharmonic would regain its health and prestige.

Of the solo musicians I have known, was pianist Artur Rubinstein the most extroverted? To get to know him, to relish him as a raconteur with an endless flow of delightful stories told with an actor's flair, was to feel that here was a virtuoso performer without a touch of neurosis. In his autobiography, he wrote of contemplating suicide long ago. I find that hard to believe about the man I knew, a man of vitality, a musician who could balance romanticism and rationalism with appealing sensitivity and expansiveness. He was at home with all sorts of conditions of men and women—artists, politicians, taxi drivers, waiters, royalty, heads of state. And for each he could trot out an apt story. The only musician I knew who could rival him in abundance and pertinence of stories, complete with dialects, was the cellist Gregor Piatigorsky.

Rubinstein enjoyed recalling a time when he was assailed by a stubborn case of hoarseness. The press was full of the perils of smoking. Must he give up Havana cigars? The prudent thing to do was to consult a throat specialist, who examined him for thirty minutes. "I searched his face for a clue," Rubinstein recalled. "It was expressionless. He told me to come back the next day. I didn't sleep that night."

The next day another long examination and again an ominous silence. "Tell me!" Rubinstein exclaimed. "I can stand the truth. I've lived a full, rich life. What's wrong with me?"

The physician looked at him coldly and said, "You talk too much."

Rubinstein insisted that he had no use for anniversaries. In 1956, when he arranged to offer five concerts in two weeks, playing seventeen different concertos, he denied that the enterprise was a commemoration of his American debut in 1906. "No, no," he cried. "What happens on the fifty-first or fifty-second anniversary? Is a fellow dead?" Yet he underwrote the costs of the orchestra and conductor. Of course, there was no fear of a deficit; the box-office take covered expenses and left something more than a widow's mite for the pianist. And of course, it was pride in the anniversary of a long career that prompted him to undertake so back-breaking a chore.

He brought it off in grand style. And more than twenty years later, in his late eighties, he was still playing with enormous vitality. A short man, Rubinstein exuded the impression of rock-like strength. His sturdy, broad-shouldered body, his rough-hewn face and his massive head covered with gray curls gave him the appearance of a much bigger man when he sat at the piano. I once suggested that he looked leonine. He pointed to a photograph of himself with Albert Einstein which sat on the piano in the place of honor and confided, "What I like about it is that it makes Einstein look like a broken-down musician and me like an ancient philosopher."

Artur Rubinstein in 1947.

One of the best Rubinstein stories I know did not come from him but from another pianist, Maryla Jonas, who, unheralded, played a stunning debut recital in New York in 1947.

Maryla Jonas had been a child prodigy in Poland and had grown up to have a career of consequence. With the German invasion of Poland in 1939, her world collapsed. Her home was bombed out, and after Warsaw succumbed, her husband and her three brothers disappeared. After long, painful months she managed to reach Rio de Janeiro, where her sister lived. When word reached them that their parents and brothers and her husband had perished, Maryla had a breakdown.

Rubinstein appeared in Rio in the early forties. He had known Maryla in Warsaw and called on her. Appalled that she had quit playing, he appealed to her that it was her obligation as a Pole to remind the world that her country stood for something and to work and help rescue other Poles from their Nazi-dominated homeland. She agreed with everything he said, but her mind was numb and her fingers stiff.

One morning Rubinstein phoned and invited her to the Municipal Theater to hear him rehearse his program for that evening. He played with unusual fervor for a practice session. She listened. Memories brushed her mind but did not rouse her from apathy. Rubinstein stood up and called to her. Would she be good enough to try the piano while he went to the back of the hall to test the acoustics. She realized much later that he had often played in that hall. She refused at first, and he made a great show of being offended. At last, indifferently, she sat down at the keyboard. Her fingers drew out of the hazy past recollections of Mozart, Beethoven and Chopin. She did not notice the minutes and hours slipping by, nor was she conscious that the hall was filling with the audience for Rubinstein's recital, due to start at 8 P.M. It was 7:30 when she arose. There were tears in her sister's eyes—and her own. Rubinstein was still there. He had barely time to change into concert gear, and he had not eaten. A few days later he arranged for her to play at a private gathering of musicians, an introduction that led to a recital and, after several more years of work, to a renewed career.

In contrast to Rubinstein was pianist Rudolf Serkin, who gave the appearance of being an introvert. To watch him walk out on the stage, his head bent slightly away from the audience, was to observe a man in a hurry to be at his task, not merely because he loved it but also because he seemed ill at ease when the audience expressed its affection for him. I have known few musicians who were more open, responsive and warmhearted. At the piano he was all passion and intensity. His performances were controlled and proportioned, but occasionally they would break the bounds he had imposed and become supercharged. One wondered in such moments whether this was the way Beethoven improvised.

Serkin was a musician's musician, and Marlboro stands as his gift to musicians. For a time he headed the Curtis Institute of Music, a training ground for the elite among the promising, where his generosity and vision had their influence. But at Marlboro one found the quintessential Serkin. There he preached and practiced the cultivation of chamber music, which he called a democracy of art. There he encouraged all participating musicians—virtuosos in the bud, leading orchestral players freed from the tyranny of conductors, and established soloists—to reach more deeply into their own feelings and resources than they were accustomed to do.

Rudolf Serkin, 1957.

I visited the Marlboro Festival in Vermont in 1956 when it was new, and there was Serkin fussing over every detail, even the menu for a buffet supper. I wrote enthusiastically about Marlboro, and he never forgot. Years later he would express his gratitude with a warm embrace as if I, not he, had created Marlboro.

There is a bit of narcissism in most of us and a good deal in some performers. I would nominate Wanda Landowska, harpsichordist and pianist, as one with more than most. I met her at a friend's house, where she assumed that she was the center of attraction. It was rewarding to hear her talk about her research into seventeenth- and eighteenth-century music and a bit strange to listen to her musings on how her students and admirers loved her, like the person who presented her with a beautiful harpsichord and like the unfortunate who actually committed suicide because Landowska would not teach her.

Tiny, seemingly fragile, she did what she wanted exactly as she wished to do it. She gave a series of three recitals at Town Hall in New York devoted to Bach's

Wanda Landowska, 1951.

Well-Tempered Clavier, providing eight preludes and fugues at each recital—in other words, less than an hour of music. I asked her mildly whether that was sufficient for an evening, and she replied, "One prelude and fugue should be enough."

She could not abide shoes when she played, and she would walk out on the stage in her stockings. I treasure a memory of a taxi drawing up in front of Town Hall before one of her Bach evenings and from it emerging two women followed by Landowska. She stood, closed her eyes, waited for her companions to put their arms around her and tote her into the hall. I should add that her Bach was fine enough to justify her self-regard.

Vladimir Horowitz kept an autographed photograph of Rachmaninoff, whom he admired as a pianist and composer, in a place of honor on top of his piano. Horowitz took an innocent delight when celebrated people sought to meet him and establish a friendship. When he bought a house in New Milford, Connecticut, he became friends with people who lived nearby, including Arthur Miller, Richard Widmark, Cleve Grey and his wife, Francine Duplessix, Alexan-

Vladimir Horowitz, 1940.

der Lieberman and his wife (who would come and speak Russian with him), and Frederic March and his wife, Florence Eldridge.

One day Horowitz told me excitedly of a new friend, William Buckley. I had to tell him that I did not like Buckley's politics or writing.

Disappointed, he said, "But he's learning to play Bach on the harpsichord!"

One must not mistake the persona a performer chooses to offer the public for the caliber of the performance. Jascha Heifetz was accused at times of being a splendid, heartless violin-playing machine. Anyone with ears to hear, anyone who did not listen with the eyes, knew this charge was rubbish. For me and many others he was a nonpareil of violinists. He had everything—technique in superabundance, purity of tone, taste, loftiness of feeling.

I can assure you that he was not always stone-faced. I saw him smile; I heard him laugh. But he liked to do things his way. I had occasion some years ago to telephone him a number of times at his home in Beverly Hills. He never came to the phone directly; someone would take my number and say Heifetz would call back. Invariably he did. But why this roundabout procedure? His friends would explain: that's Heifetz.

At his home in Beverly Hills or Malibu, he could be a genial host. If you accepted an invitation to play table tennis, knowing he was an expert, and did not get beaten badly, you moved up a notch in his esteem. If you were invited to his July 4 party at Malibu, you might begin to think he regarded you as a friend. I was in California on that day one year and found that he orchestrated the event as if it were a White House fete. Some guests, presumably his closest friends, were asked to come at 4 P.M., some at 6 (I made that batch) and some at 8. Anyhow, it was a delightful party.

Heifetz was the guest at a publisher's lunch at *The Times* one day, and in an expansive mood he talked about his early career. I remarked that he ought to write his memoirs. His instant response: would I help? If I could, I said, I would try.

Several years later he phoned from Beverly Hills. "I am ready to do the book," he said. "When can you come?"

Startled, I had forgotten the casual exchange at the publisher's lunch. "I can't just pick up and go," I said.

He was insistent. "Why not?"

I said I had obligations to *The Times*. He would call the publisher and arrange everything. I remonstrated that I did not wish him to call the publisher. He was miffed. Did he ever write the book? I believe not.

Fritz Kreisler's public persona was the opposite of Heifetz's. With his portly figure, gray hair and mustache and kindly glance, he exuded an air of benevolence. His violin playing reinforced that impression. It was warm and mellow, like an excellent wine that had matured wisely and well. He could play with brilliance when he chose, but his emphasis was on inwardness. When he was eighty and retired from concertizing, he told me that what he deplored most was the fear of sentiment. "Listen to how fast some very well-known violinists take the last movement of the Mendelssohn concerto, as if they're afraid of feeling."

He was unhappy at the direction composition had taken. He had been a friend of Arnold Schoenberg in Berlin when they were young and remembered that when shown the manuscript of *Verklärte Nacht*, he had suggested that it needed more than the three instruments the composer had required. Schoenberg had added three more. Years later he attended a concert devoted to Schoenberg's latest music. After the concert he told Schoenberg that only one song meant anything to him. Kreisler chuckled as he quoted the composer's response: "Have I fallen so low in my art that Fritz Kreisler likes any parts of it?"

Kreisler could probably have made a career as a pianist. I once heard him play at a private gathering without any advance notice or preparation, and though he did not have the technical address of a fiery virtuoso—nor would he have sought it—his performance had the characteristics of his violin playing— mellow tone, vivacious yet relaxed rhythm and, yes, sentiment.

There was a time when Mischa Elman, another remarkable violinist, enjoyed such wide public esteem that he was thought by many to belong beside Heifetz and Kreisler on the highest pinnacle. The lush opulence of his tone was celebrated. Poor Mischa. Despite his celebrity and success, he labored under the shadows of Heifetz and Kreisler. Nearly everyone had heard the story of the night when a young Heifetz made his American debut in 1917. Elman, sitting in a Carnegie Hall box beside Leopold Godowsky, a great pianist and sardonic wit, complained that it was a hot night, and Godowsky replied, "Not for pianists." I asked Elman about that story, and he said, "Not true, and what's more, it *was* a warm night."

To prove that he could laugh at himself, Elman told me two stories:

A stranger came backstage after a recital, carrying a violin case, and his opening remark was, "I didn't come to hear you play but to show you this fiddle."

In a taxi one evening Elman was pleased to hear good music coming from the radio. He complimented the cabbie, who replied, "I like music, especially Elman and Heifetz, but I can't afford concerts."

Elman handed the driver a large tip and said, "Here, go to a concert." The cabbie was grateful. "Now I can go and hear Heifetz."

Speaking of violinists, I have met few musicians to match the energy of Isaac Stern. His involvement in numerous causes—such as saving Carnegie Hall or dashing off to Israel at a moment's notice to offer support in a crisis—seems only to have enriched his music-making. Years ago I was on a private tennis court in Pittsfield, Massachusetts, at Tanglewood Festival time when Stern showed up, not to play, just to visit. His friends ribbed him about his growing portliness and advised him to play tennis, if he could.

"Damn it," he shouted, "I can play as well as anyone on the court!"

"Prove it!" he was challenged.

He borrowed sneakers and a racquet, took off his shirt and marched out in his undershirt and trousers. And damn it, he could play!

With Isaac Stern, *c.* 1951. Photograph by Dan Weiner of Brackman Associates.

Ready for tennis. Photograph by Dan Weiner of Brackman Associates.

Sometime later, at a dinner party in Connecticut, Stern announced that he would have to leave after dessert, for he had promised to appear at a New York television studio in a tribute to Jack Benny, who had just died. It was snowing, and the roads were slippery. Could he make it to New York in time? A small plane was waiting for him at an airport twenty miles away, but would it be able to fly? Isaac took off, the plane made it, and so did he. "After all," he said as he left the party, "Jack was a dear friend."

Oscar Levant, the American pianist and composer, was an imp and a good musician. As he said of himself, he made quite a career playing George Gershwin. He poked fun at himself and could not resist the impulse to do something capricious that amused him. You may remember him as a bright, humorous star of the television show "Information Please" and the author of three autobiographical books, *A Smattering of Ignorance* (1940), *Memoirs of an Amnesiac* (1965) and *The Unimportance of Being Oscar* (1968).

Once I was in California, staying at the Beverly Wilshire, on a musical mission in Los Angeles. The phone in my room rang. It was Oscar's chipper voice: "I've come to take you out to dinner."

"How did you know I was here?"

He chuckled, pleased at being mysterious. In a moment the doorbell rang. There stood Oscar, a happy grin on his face. "Ready for dinner?"

Where could I find better, more amusing company?

He drove me out to his home and introduced me to his wife, whose eye was cold. I could see she did not enjoy a surprise guest.

"Let's go somewhere else," I suggested to Oscar, who disregarded his wife's coolness. He went into the kitchen and busied himself, emerging with two plates of cold cuts, and seated us at a table on a balcony, while his wife glared. He set to and urged me to eat. It turned out to be a good meal, eaten companionably. When we finished our coffee he jumped up. "Let's go," he said.

"Where?"

"To the Gershwins'."

He drove us to Ira Gershwin's, where he announced that we had come to pay a surprise visit. Ira was warm. His wife, Lenore, was as cold as Oscar's. "What is the object of your visit?" Ira asked.

"Oscar's whim," I said, thoroughly embarrassed. I needn't have been. The Gershwins were delightful, if unwilling and unprepared, hosts. Finally Oscar relented and took me back to my hotel. Years later I got to meet his charming daughter, Marcia, who spoke of her father as though he were a favorite entertainer. Marcia was married to Jerry Tallmer, a good drama critic on the New York *Post*, whose work I respected.

If you write as many reviews as I have over the years, you are bound to hear of some unexpected reactions. Mstislav Rostropovich, the self-exiled Soviet cellist, told a group of *Times* editors how grateful he was to me. It seems that in 1956, after his first American concert following his flight from the Soviets, he lay awake pondering what to do. Stay in the United States and seek a career? In the middle of the night he decided to go for a walk to clear his mind. He passed a newsstand where he could obtain an early edition of *The Times*. In it was a favorable, welcoming review I had written of his concert, and he decided that the review would justify his staying in the U.S. His career as a solo artist never wavered, and he became conductor of the National Symphony Orchestra of Washington, D.C., a post he held until 1994. He thanked *The Times* profusely. I had only done what he richly deserved.

Mstislav Rostropovich at Juilliard in 1975. Photograph by Paul
Hosefros.

16

On Wings of Song

I VALUE REFINEMENT in song with all that it connotes—delicacy of phrasing, nuances of color, subtle flexibility of rhythm within a framework of steadiness, a deep understanding of the composer's wishes. But I am bound to confess that I get a bang out of a glorious voice at the full, not bellowing, of course, but rising to the composer's challenge.

Fortunate the singer who combines refinement and power. Such a voice belonged to Enrico Caruso, whose career remains one of the most storied of the twentieth century. I was not lucky enough to hear him in the flesh, yet I feel he was one of my familiars. Like many of my generation, I grew up on his recordings. In my home we could afford only a modest collection; it was all Caruso. I remember the newsboys dashing through the streets of Manhattan in the summer of 1921 crying, "Extra, extra! Caruso is dead!" It was shocking news, like a death in the family. Even today, when I listen to the reprocessed Caruso records and tapes and marvel at how much of the golden power of that voice has been retained, my pleasure is tinged by the memory of that sad day in 1921.

From the beginning of my duties in the Music Department of *The Times*, I encountered a number of persons who had worked closely with Caruso, Gatti-Casazza, Toscanini, other conductors, and singers like Antonio Scotti.

I even ran into an actor—Edward McNamara, who had been a Patterson, New Jersey, policeman and who overnight made a huge success on Broadway in Preston Sturges' play *Strictly Dishonorable*—who had been a Caruso protégé. Blessed with a big, raw natural tenor, McNamara had so impressed Caruso that he offered to become his teacher. McNamara would come to Caruso's suite in the Vanderbilt Hotel and vocalize under the master's tutelage. One day Caruso urged McNamara to sing louder and louder, and the young Irishman roared until he thought he would burst. "Louder!" Caruso commanded, until McNamara cried, "But why?"

"Because," Caruso yelled, laughing delightedly, "you're singing over Scotti's bedroom and he's sick!"

I heard and saw Scotti in his last years. His Scarpia, the first in the United States, remained a study in silken malevolence, though the voice was severely diminished. I remember sitting with him in January, 1933, in his suite at the Hotel Ansonia, on the morning of his farewell appearance at the Met. He was sixty-seven then, an advanced age for a singer, and his voice was almost gone, but he was still a convincing actor. Like the old lady counting her medals, he was recalling and showing mementos of the women he had loved; Ina Claire and Geraldine Farrar were the names and photographs he lingered over.

Farrar, a beautiful woman who starred in silent films, was a magnet for others at the Met. One of her admirers was Toscanini, who had come to the Met

Enrico Caruso as John of Leyden in Meyerbeer's *Le Prophète,* 1921.

Antonio Scotti as Scarpia in Puccini's *Tosca, c.* 1932.

Geraldine Farrar as Cio-Cio-San in   Geraldine Farrar at home in 1949.
Puccini's *Madame Butterfly, c.* 1909.

with Gatti-Casazza in 1908 but left in 1915 because of his rivalry with Antonio
Scotti for the affections of Farrar. Years later, when he was the conductor of the
NBC Symphony, Samuel Chotzinoff, who had persuaded the maestro to return
to New York to head the orchestra General David Sarnoff had created for him,
induced Toscanini to bring the ensemble to Ridgefield, Connecticut, for a concert as a benefit for the library. Farrar lived in Ridgefield and served on the committee to arrange the benefit. She invited Toscanini to dinner after the concert.
I attended the concert, a glowing occasion. Chotzie later told me that Toscanini,
who had a large capacity for irritability, grumbled after the dinner chez Farrar,
"That woman, after all our years together, she did not remember that I hate
fish!"

Giuseppe De Luca, a little man with a broad chest and a light, supple baritone used with bel canto grace, became my friend because, in one of my early
reviews, I inadvertently omitted his name as the Lescaut in a performance of
Massenet's *Manon.* I received an unexpected phone call from him, and in a con-
spirator's voice he requested that I meet him at the Met. I reasoned that some-

thing important was afoot and hastened to the opera house. De Luca met me in the press room, led me down darkened corridors, stopped and faced me and demanded, with the dramatic tension he might have used in one of his fine, credible Rigolettos, "Caro, what have you against me?"

"Nothing."

"Then why did you leave out my name in this morning's review?"

De Luca was in a *Don Carlo* with Feodor Chaliapin and could not prevail upon him to behave like a considerate colleague. Aware that Chaliapin towered over him, De Luca, the Rodrigo, begged the basso, who was singing Philip II, to keep a reasonable distance when they were onstage together. Mischievously Chaliapin kept approaching De Luca, who kept retreating. De Luca could not escape him. Finally, De Luca had to bow before departing. He got down on one knee, shook his fist at Chaliapin and cried, "Son of a bitch!" loudly enough to startle the prompter.

Gatti-Casazza told me that Chaliapin, in his appearances at the Met in the 1920s, tried to run the shows he was in. De Luca provided details. In preparations for the *Don Carlo* revival, Chaliapin apparently saw fit to instruct everyone—the conductor, the régisseur, the designer and the singers. As resentments intensified, the rehearsals became anarchic, and Gatti-Casazza was summoned. The impressive figure of the general manager, moving with its accustomed weightiness, stood before Chaliapin. As De Luca reconstructed the scene more than two decades later, Gatti began with an exclamation, "Eh, Bolsheviko!"

Startled, Chaliapin was silent.

Gatti: "Your job is to sing, eh? If you don't want to, there's the door. If you do, keep quiet!"

The majestic figure of Gatti turned and strode off the stage, and De Luca swore that Chaliapin actually wept. And sang.

At the age of fifty-nine, De Luca retired from the Met. At seventy he returned to the United States for a song recital. Though the voice, never large, was diminished, De Luca could still cause it to do his bidding.

"Why not?" he remarked later; he had spent two years as a beginner on nothing but scales. As for nerves, he had them, of course, badly, but had learned long ago that the way to cope was to breathe slowly and deeply three times and to start: "Then the heart becomes quiet, the stomach goes back from the throat to where it belongs, and you can sing."

It is the mark of a fine artist that he or she can communicate the essence of music as effectively as ever when the voice has narrowed and paled. Chaliapin, in his last years, could manage the feat *in excelsis*.

In one of his last American appearances, he was mesmerizing. The rich, smooth sonority of his voice, which was so impressive in his early recordings, could be heard only in scattered phrases. But how he caught the flavor of the song! And how he acted! A facial expression, a gesture, a movement—they all counted. In Mussorgsky's "Song of the Flea," a tall man in white tie and tails on a cold, bare Town Hall stage conjured up the very image of old Russia.

So enchanting was the persona Chaliapin created that when he sang "Song of the Flea," you felt like scratching. I remember a story he liked to tell. He was in Paris, woke up one night, and could not go back to sleep. He dressed, went for a walk, and went over a role he was studying. As he walked, he was accosted by a streetwalker and declined her invitation.

"What are you doing?" she asked.

"I walk," he said, "and I work."

She extended a hand and exclaimed, "Comrade!"

Paul Robeson, at the height of his powers, had a bass voice that in texture and resonance compared with the best, but it had never been trained adequately. I remember hearing him in a recital where in the first half he sang with ease and richness and in the second turned breathy and hoarse. A pity he had not learned how to properly use a remarkable natural gift.

Elisabeth Schumann, who had learned how to use her voice skillfully, sang magically in the twilight of her career, though her soprano became thin and her range constricted. Choosing songs that did not require a demanding range, she managed to convey a wealth of emotion by ingenious use of the narrow compass that remained.

I have heard other singers who achieved artistic wonders though their vocal means were limited. I think of Maggie Teyte, Povla Frijsh, Bidù Sayão; Victoria de los Angeles, whose voice in its prime was as beautiful as any I've heard, but who knew the value of skill in her later years; Richard Tauber, who made the most of his voice and who, like Chaliapin and Mary Garden, could turn a colorless concert stage into an ambience of delight; Maria Callas, whose lovely soprano became shrill and strident at the top in her last years when she pushed it beyond its means but who, nevertheless, could still be penetrating in her emotional grasp of a character.

Friedrich Schorr, an ornament of the Wagner wing of the Met in the 1920s and 1930s, had a similar gift. In his palmiest vocal days, his Wotan, Amfortas, Kurwenal and Hans Sachs were nobly sung, but never was the humanity of the role, even of the god Wotan, more touchingly conveyed than when Schorr's voice could no longer sustain the fullness of the grand line.

Gatti once remarked to me that Schorr was one of his two favorite singers. Considering the grand roster of notable singers who had appeared under his management in ten years at La Scala and twenty-seven at the Met, I wondered who could be the other—Caruso, Farrar, Scotti, Bori, Jeritza, Flagstad (whom he introduced to America in his last season at the Met)—who? He never told me.

Schorr, an intelligent man, could take a sardonic view of his world of opera. He regaled me once with some of the idiocies he had contended with. When new sets were created for *The Ring* at the Met, he found that the way down from a height in *Die Walküre* was narrow, precipitous and twisting. As Wotan, he wore a patch on one eye, and since he was shortsighted and could not wear his customary eyeglasses, he could barely see with the other. Irked because he also had to watch the conductor and sing as he made the perilous descent, he

Feodor Chaliapin as Mefistofele in Boito's opera of the same name, Moscow, 1902.

Friedrich Schorr as the Wanderer in Wagner's *Siegfried*, 1939.

grabbed the designer by the arm, led him up to the height and demanded that he descend blindfolded.

Once, he said, an opera house saw fit to chop a large part of the second act, including much of Wotan's music, out of *Die Walküre*, and another time a conductor chose to eliminate half of the beautifully bittersweet "Wahn, Wahn" monologue in *Die Meistersinger*. As for the vagaries of conductors' tempos—and which experienced singer had not muttered about that problem?—Schorr remembered that Richard Strauss, an able conductor, raced through *Die Walküre* faster than anyone he had worked with, and that Siegfried Wagner, a less than inspired one, dragged through this music-drama, requiring fifteen minutes more than anyone he had appeared with.

To ardent Wagnerites, the late 1930s were the years when Wagner was in the ascendant at the Met. What could be more thrilling than the Love Duet in *Tristan und Isolde* when Kirsten Flagstad and Lauritz Melchior were at the top of their form? Or more moving than the long third-act vigil for Tristan and Kurwenal when Melchior and Schorr were there to fill it with longing and compassion?

Flagstad arrived at the Met without advance fanfare—truly a sleeper, if one dares to so designate a singer with so large, perfectly placed and dominating a voice. Though the other elements for a strong Wagner wing, including the conductor Artur Bodanzky, were in place, she was the catalyst who led it into pre-eminence. Her debut as Sieglinde was impressive enough, but her first Isolde was what set the town on its ear. That first Isolde, as she confided later, gave her momentary trouble as she was about to launch into the Liebestod.

The trouble arose from her gift of absolute pitch. After Tristan dies, Isolde's phrase is "Bleibst du mir stumm," which starts on a G-sharp. Flagstad, concentrating on her task, was not listening to the orchestra; she was sure she could depend on her own ear and equally certain that the phrase began on a C-natural. She began with C-natural and sang three measures, all transposed upward, before she realized what she was doing. "I understood later," she told me, "why the dead Tristan's eyes opened in amazement, why the prompter motioned wildly, why there was something strange in Bodanzky's gesture."

When Flagstad left the Met early in World War II, Helen Traubel filled the dramatic-soprano breach in the Wagner repertory with conviction, but no one was Flagstad's equal until Birgit Nilsson, relatively unheralded, made her debut at the Met in the 1959–60 season as Isolde. In my review for *The Times* I wrote

Kirsten Flagstad as Isolde in a 1937 production at Covent Garden, London.

Birgit Nilsson as Isolde in 1959. Photograph by Sam Falk.

that her Isolde was the best since Flagstad's, and the report appeared on page one. Nilsson's success was, in any case, assured, but a review on page one gave it additional impetus. Some days later I happened to be at a dress rehearsal of a new production at the Met, and during a break Rudolf Bing introduced me to Nilsson. A big, hearty woman, Nilsson smiled and addressed me: "Has he," she said, nodding to Bing, "told you that my review is going to cost him a lot of money?"

I don't see why outstanding singers, like glamorous athletes, should not be shrewdly aware of their worth. Ljuba Welitsch, who as a mature woman made a sensual spitfire out of Strauss's Salome in her Met debut, later told me that she was so confident of her ability that when Edward Johnson assured her there would be no more than fifty in the house during the press rehearsal, she warned that if there were more, she would expect a full-performance fee. When the debut performance was over and she was taking curtain calls, she had so thoroughly gauged the excitement of the audience that she urged Margaret Carson, the Met's press representative, to begin arranging press interviews.

Welitsch was one of the last of a breed of self-assured, domineering, demanding prima donnas, at least one of the last I have known well. She was flamboyant in appearance. She dyed her hair a vivid copper color and, of course, wore no wig as Salome. A good thing, too: as Salome's desire became heated, Welitsch ran her hand through her hair with such intensity that a wig might have been dislodged. Asked to do Tosca, she declined until she felt the Cavaradossi and Scarpia would be singers of, to quote her cheerful lack of false modesty, "equal stature." A magazine ran a caricature of her as Salome, and some of her friends thought it so rough that they wanted to keep it from her. When she saw it, she ordered extra copies. When she told me that one day she would like to sing Musetta, I wondered why she would wish for the secondary soprano role.

"Because I am special in it," she replied. "I used to sing the little-girl roles. I was small, slim, beautiful girl."

I continued to look dubious.

"It is true," she said as if responding to the doubt in my mind, "now I am ripe woman," and she glanced at her low-cut dress. "I still make Musetta interesting."

She did do a Musetta. I went to see it. Sorry, Ljuba, it was a caricature.

I last saw Welitsch in Vienna in 1973. Margaret Carson was there and called her, and she invited us to lunch in an elegant restaurant. With her was a Baron something or other, a practiced *cavaliere servente.* Welitsch, still brilliantly copper-haired, still flamboyantly dressed, was in great form. Now a successful film actress, she was still full of vivacity and lively stories, still without a trace of false modesty. "I hear you were a success, a so-called friend said to me when I got back to Vienna after my first Met season," she recalled, "and I answered, 'I was a sensation!'" And she went on, "I was at a dinner party recently and a woman said to me, 'My husband so admires you,' and I said, 'Don't you?'"

Rosa Ponselle was a prima donna of the old school. Her voice was one of the most beautiful I have heard, warm, mellow, finely controlled, wide in range. She could sing Violetta in *Traviata* effectively though not play it with flexibility and lightness, just as Renata Tebaldi could sing radiantly a Cio-Cio-San in *Butterfly* but could not, because of her size, escape an impression of heaviness. Possibly because I heard Ponselle first in *La Forza del destino*, I am convinced that no one has ever sung "Pace, pace, mio Dio!" more ravishingly, and there were performances when Zinka Milanov handled the aria beautifully.

Ponselle, a temperamental woman, fretted about repeating the same roles, mostly by Verdi, but they were suited to the dark velvet of her voice. She played the title role in Charles Wakefield Cadman's *Shanewis*, an opera about an Indian maiden. She made her entrance, perfectly costumed to look like an American Indian woman, with feathered headdress. When she came onstage, the moon was shining, and whether it was her idea or the stage director's, she took the classic, clichéd Indian stance—her right hand over her eyes, as if to keep out the sun's glare. It was a ludicrous entrance and hurt whatever chances the little opera had.

Ponselle was a prima donna in the capricious mold, the result, I believe, of a basic nervous tension when she approached a role or a performance. In the later years of her career, her tension increased. An hour before a performance she once arrived at the Met and told Edward Johnson, the handsome tenor turned general manager and successor to Gatti-Casazza, that she could not sing. "If you can't, you can't," he told her, and suggested a little walk. He led her outside the theater—the old Met, that is—and walked her around the block. He forgot, he told me, how many circuits they made around the building before she calmed down and agreed to sing. "It was a lovely performance," Johnson remarked.

Rosa Ponselle as Violetta in Verdi's *La Traviata,*
c. 1932.

A prima donna–tenor altercation pitted Moravian-born soprano Maria Jeritza against Beniamino Gigli. After a performance of *Tosca*, the two upstaged each other during the curtain calls. When the applause faded, Jeritza appeared and told the audience, "Gigli has been mean to me." It seems that when they got backstage, he planted a kick where he thought it would teach her a lesson. Remember, this was the Met, not the Bowery.

Lotte Lehmann was a first lady of song, though not a prima donna in the sense of a leading soprano who threw her weight around, like, to mention a prima donna of the old school, Frances Alda (who was married to Gatti-Casazza from 1910 to 1928). I knew Alda only after she had retired, when she was married to my friend Ray Vir Den, who headed an advertising agency and was president of the Dutch Treat Club.

Lehmann was the luncheon guest of the Dutch Treat Club one Tuesday. The program usually consisted of fifteen minutes of performance by a singer, instrumentalist or actor and then a talk by a major figure in the news. As we sat at the head table, Lehmann whispered instructions to me, and I relayed them to Vir Den. As the time approached for her to sing, she requested that the members and guests stop smoking. Vir Den asked the crowd in the ballroom of the Ambassador Hotel to douse their cigarettes, cigars and pipes. Then Lehmann, in a whisper that was barely audible, said that she did not wish to speak until after she had sung. I transmitted this intelligence to Vir Den. The moment came for Vir Den to introduce our guest, and he began: "I have been sitting here for the last half-hour listening to Taubman trying to tell *me* how to behave toward a prima donna."

Lucrezia Bori, though she had plenty of temperament in performance, never flaunted it offstage. I knew her well as a singer and, after her retirement from opera, as an ardent worker to preserve and sustain the Met in its years of financial troubles, and I neither saw nor heard of any evidence of prima-donna-ism. Even as a young woman, this descendant of the Borgias had the character to make cool judgments about herself and her career. In 1910, when the Met, in its first trip abroad, played a season in Paris, Toscanini would not do Puccini's *Manon Lescaut* unless he had a young soprano with the freshness and ardor of the heedless girl of the Abbé Prévost's tale, and no one in the company met his uncompromising standards. With Gatti and Puccini, he auditioned the young Bori, then twenty-two, in Milan. She was engaged and sang charmingly opposite Caruso and Amato. Invited to join the Met that fall, Bori declined. She thought that she ought to spend the next two years at La Scala, broadening and honing her repertory. When she opened the season in the fall of 1912 in *Manon Lescaut* with Caruso and Scotti, she was an immediate success.

In 1916 she underwent several operations to remove nodules on her vocal cords. Five years of patient retraining ensued before she could return to the stage. When you asked Bori about that period, she shrugged. There was no self-pity in her. In 1936, while still singing with style, she retired. Like Farrar in the 1920s, she had no intention of being heard at less than her best.

When Bori was in her prime, she was one of the Met's great attractions, not only in New York but wherever the company appeared on tour. For many years a visit by the Met became a peak of the social season, in no city more than Atlanta. Parties were arranged and guest lists established weeks and months in advance, and the hosts who could promise the presence of Met stars were obviously those with the most.

A story I heard about such a party involved Bori. Was it apocryphal? When I asked her about it years later, she simply smiled enigmatically. As the tale has it, Asa Candler, the founder of the Coca-Cola Company, was particularly taken with Bori, excited by her singing and acting and charmed by her lively personality. He took her aside and made an unusual offer: he would let her buy some stock, an offer made to only a choice few, in his company. A conservative investor, Bori wanted to know what Coca-Cola was like. Candler described it, and Bori asked for permission to taste the fairly new concoction. A European, accustomed to dry wines of excellent vintage, Bori rolled it around in her mouth and winced at the sweetness of the brew. She thanked Candler kindly for his offer, but no, she did not think she wanted to invest in this drink.

I remember walking up Fifth Avenue with Bori and Edward Johnson on a wintry day in 1957 after Toscanini's funeral at St. Patrick's, and the conversation was full of nostalgic recollections. These two had sung together frequently, always as the romantic leads. Some who did not understand that Bori was not the marrying kind and that Johnson, after the death of his young wife in Italy a long time ago, chose not to remarry, sought to push such a marriage by providing gossip items to columnists. I mentioned these efforts as we strolled up Fifth Avenue, and they both laughed, as they had laughed when the gossip appeared in print. As long-time comrades in song, they seemed to understand and value each other more than some married couples.

Johnson, a skilled performer himself, remembered when he had encountered

Edward Johnson, holding a gift upon his retirement as general manager of the Met in 1950. With him in foreground are (left to right) Lawrence Tibbett; Jenny Cervini, the Met wardrobe mistress; and Lucrezia Bori.

an unforeseen block. He was singing at Ravinia Park, the outdoor arena in Highland Park, near Chicago. He was trying to project a high *fortissimo* when an insect flew into his mouth. He understood the hazards of singing.

Johnson also recalled the time in Italy when, to get a chance in opera, he used the *nom de guerre* of Edoardo di Giovanni. He was married, and his wife was known as Signora Johnson. Johnson's Italian colleagues in the opera house would wink knowingly when they encountered her with him.

No one was close enough to wink at Teresa Stich-Randall, a gifted and attractive young American soprano, when she undertook an astonishing feat in Florence one summer. I had seen Marjorie Lawrence as Brünnhilde mount a horse and seem to ride into the flames in the final scene of *Götterdämmerung* at the Met. I had witnessed bassos singing Boris Godunov plunge off a high throne at the risk of broken bones. I had never seen a singer in a bathing suit doing an aria in a lake.

Herbert Graf, staging Weber's *Oberon* in the Boboli Gardens behind the Pitti Palace for a Maggio Musicale, proposed that the young American, as the

Daughter of the Sea, swim several hundred feet across the lake, pull herself up beside a statue and do her aria. She brought off the feat—singing and swimming—with flair. "But," I asked her, "wasn't it cold?"

"No," she said, "not after swimming to the statue"—and certainly not after the aria, when the audience roared its approval and delight.

Stich-Randall, who had sung enchantingly as Nanetta in the concert version of *Falstaff* conducted by Toscanini, was wise to be in Europe, where she had opportunities to appear in a variety of roles and opera houses. After World War II many Americans seized the opportunity for such experience abroad, experience that very few could get at home. Sena Jurinac, a soprano of distinction when I first heard her in the early 1950s, touched on this subject in a conversation we had in Munich in 1951. "Do you realize," she said, "how many times I have already sung Cherubino? More than two hundred." And that was when Jurinac was still in the early stages of her career. The year before, she had sung Dorabella in *Così fan tutte* at Glyndebourne and some days later switched to Fiordiligi, the former role demanding lightness and flightiness and the latter a sudden honesty and intensity, and had brought off the change with compelling conviction. In the sixties I heard her again, this time as an elegant and touching Marschallin in *Der Rosenkavalier*.

How many Americans get to sing two hundred Cherubinos? Certainly none in the United States. And yet—I can think of a number of Americans who built major careers without much European preparation. Lawrence Tibbett was an early example. Later ones were Jan Peerce, Richard Tucker and Leonard Warren. Having achieved star status at the Met, singers had the opportunities to undertake a wide range of roles. Indeed, singers from abroad, once established at the Met, were encouraged to appear in a great diversity of roles. Ezio Pinza, the owner of a velvety basso cantante, became an international, versatile star at the Met as he ranged over the entire repertory—Verdi, Donizetti, Gounod, Mozart, Mussorgsky and Wagner.

Peerce, Tucker and Warren—somehow they are linked in my memories. Warren, the baritone, sang often with one or the other tenor. They appeared mostly in Italian opera, and these three, all born in New York City, not one of Italian extraction, enunciated Italian with more accuracy and savor than many Italian-born singers. I listened recently to the recording of the concert version of *Traviata* conducted by Toscanini and was astonished once again at Peerce's impeccable Italianate style as Alfredo.

In 1958 I was in Moscow when Warren made guest appearances at the Bolshoi. His Rigoletto won the Russians completely. I had heard him many times in the role at the Met; he outdid himself at the Bolshoi. At the final rehearsal, attended by a throng of Soviet singers, he started by singing half-voice. A message came backstage pleading with him to sing full-voice, as the Russian singers would not be able to hear him in the night performance. Warren gladly went through the third act full-voice, and the Russian singers stood up and shouted in appreciation.

While I enjoyed Peerce and Tucker in performance, I have fond memories of each in other settings. In 1948, the Met paid its first visit to the West Coast since the 1906 San Francisco earthquake, when a bewildered company was caught there during the disaster, and I accompanied the troupe on the train to Los Angeles. While we were en route somewhere in western Texas, Peerce came by my compartment in the afternoon and suggested that I join him and several friends in the dining car for dinner. "Be sure to come early," he said. "I have a surprise."

When I got there, he was presiding at a table not far from the galley. Clearly he had made arrangements with the kitchen crew. It was the first night of Passover, and as a Jew who observed the traditions of this faith, he had assembled the makings of a Passover feast. He apologized that he could not also provide the full setting of a proper seder, but by eating the right food and drinking the right order of wines, we would not be too remote from the spirit of the occasion.

Some years later I was in San Francisco to write about the opera season by the excellent company there. Tucker was making guest appearances, and we ran into each other at the hotel one morning. "What are you doing this afternoon?" he asked challengingly.

"Why?"

"I'm going out to the racetrack," he said. "Care to join us?"

His tone suggested that a music critic should not be interested, let alone know anything about horse racing. I pretended to be dubious and let him work at persuading me.

Since I knew little about the horses at this track, I did not bother to look at the *Racing Form;* I made my bets by watching the odds board. Tucker kept studying the *Racing Form* and, I gathered from his comments, losing big bets, while guying me about the amateur way I chose to bet. Before the last race, fed up with his bad luck, he thrust his program into my hands. "Here," he said disgustedly, "you pick them."

I said, "Let me have the *Racing Form.*"

"What for?" he hooted.

I examined it, with Tucker urging me to quit the comedy: "You know you can't read that thing."

I proposed two horses for a quinella.

"How come this one?" he argued.

I didn't explain that I had noticed "this one" had been running in sprints, tended to make up ground at the end and was a good, long price. I gestured vaguely.

"Okay, okay, let's bet," Tucker said.

We bet: I chanced $2, Tucker a lot more. The quinella came in at better than $50. Tucker insisted on being the host that evening at an expensive feast. After that he would always greet me with the words "beginner's luck."

Jussi Bjoerling was a tenor who, when at the top of his form, could pour out tones that compared favorably with any of the strong-voiced tenors I ever heard, whether Giacomo Lauri-Volpi, Giovanni Martinelli, Mario del Monaco or

Jussi Bjoerling as Riccardo in Verdi's *Un Ballo in maschera,* 1940.

even, I sometimes thought, Caruso. Bjoerling was a guest once at the Dutch Treat Club and noticed that in the gathering were Richard Crooks, Charles Kullman and Frederick Jagel, all tenor colleagues at the Met. As he rose to sing, he whispered mischievously, "Shall we show them?" Whereupon he sang "Che gelida manina" from *Bohème* and ended with a high C of such beauty and power that it still rings in my inner ear. When he sat down, he murmured, "How do you think my friends liked that?"

17

Anecdotage: Odds and Ends
of a Career in the Arts

I N MY YEARS in New York there were frequent debut recitals in the afternoon at Town Hall, given in hope that the aspiring debutants would attract critical attention. Some of us felt it our duty to attend. Often we would slip into a back seat after the recital had begun. I remember one recital in particular when a group of critics sat in a row. Some were asleep. Francis D. Perkins of the *Herald Tribune* came bustling in, quite a bit late, dripping with rain from a heavy shower. It was a deplorable debut. One of my colleagues muttered, "Poor Frank doesn't know enough to stay out in the rain."

At *The Times,* critics sometimes fought for their rights. John Martin, our dance critic, was a non-person for a while. His reviews did not bear any identification of their authorship. When Mary Wigman, the innovative German dancer, made her American debut, John wrote an all-out rave review, which appeared in the early edition. Edwin James, the fine Virginia gentleman who was seemingly training to take over as managing editor, was working in the bull pen, where the night editors functioned. He read John's galley, was irritated by the bounteous praise and ordered that the review be cut down to two paragraphs for the next edition.

The next morning the phone rang endlessly in the large area where John and the Music Department worked. We did not know how to deal with readers' complaints about the abbreviated review. I had a brainstorm. I said, "Let's transfer all calls to Osmund Phillips," a middle-level executive who worked in the managing editor's office. Mr. Phillips, a severe, dour man who wore wing-tips and boiled collars, had some supervising duties. A man who rarely smiled, he often passed by our area and looked us over, never without his habitual frown. After dealing with the calls for a couple of hours, he ordered Martin to sign his reviews. Later, Sol Hurok, who had brought Wigman to New York and had seen the full review in the early edition, ran all of John's review in an ad headed "All the News That's Fit to Print."

On some evenings, there would be four or five men in the bull pen. *The Times,* after all, is comprehensive and requires extensive editorial care. Occasionally time would hang heavy on the hands of these editors, and they would make it pass by playing such games as Categories.

You know, you have a list of categories, and the challenge is to complete the board by filling in appropriate names. One evening, as I walked by the bull pen, I was asked to adjudicate a dispute over the rubric "composers." One chap—who shall remain nameless—had been challenged to name a composer whose name began with an "L." He had written "Lohengrin," composer of *The Wedding March.* The perpetrator glowered at me when I said, "Wrong man."

As a young, daring music editor, I used language with verve. At least once, I was challenged over a word choice. Theodore Bernstein, an editor at *The Times,* was in charge after the dayside editors had gone home. The guardian of correct English usage, he was also the author of *The Times'* style book. One day he phoned me to ask whether I knew what a "panache" was. I had used the word to comment on an actor's style of acting. I answered quickly, "a feather plume." He slammed the phone down, irked, I suppose, that he had not caught me *in flagrante delicto.* Bernstein edited a bulletin called "Winners and Sinners," praising a fresh turn of phrase or condemning gaffes of expression. I remember when I wrote of the people who stood in line all night to buy standing room for the Metropolitan Opera opening, "They also serve who only wait to stand." He appreciated this as a variation of the John Milton line, "They also serve who only stand and wait."

The Vivian Beaumont Theater—like the Met, a New York cultural landmark—was the last of the Lincoln Center buildings to open. It was turned over to the Lincoln Center Theater, which Elia Kazan and Robert Whitehead ran. The theater opened with an ambitious production, which I found as unimpressive as it was meant to be impressive. I sat in my aisle seat, thinking what a fine home the theater could make for the new company, when a small, sturdy woman rose from her aisle seat at the other side of the auditorium and strode with determination toward me.

"I am Vivian Beaumont," she said.

I said I was pleased to meet someone who could make such a rich gift.

"What did you think of the production?" she asked.

I replied that I never discussed my critical reactions.

"Oh, come off it!" she exclaimed. "I am Vivian Beaumont."

Matching her tone tit for tat, I said, "You can find what I think in tomorrow's *Times*."

Such contrariness is common to critics. Is any species of humankind more perverse?

In the final count, life can be as perverse as man. I think of Giulio Gatti-Casazza, manager of the Metropolitan Opera for twenty-seven years, and his much younger wife, Rosina Galli, chief ballerina of the Met. In 1935 Nora and I visited him at his retirement villa on Lago Maggiore. He loved to sit and watch the sun set on the lake against a backdrop of mountains. He purred with satisfaction. But Rosina grumbled. It was too quiet. She was stuck out in the country. "Please," she begged, "help me to persuade him to live elsewhere." I doubt that he would have listened to such impudence. In any case, I assumed that

Giulio Gatti-Casazza with Rosina Galli, his wife, in 1934.

Gatti at his villa on Lago Maggiore, Italy, 1935.

since he was much older, change would be inevitable. As it turned out, Rosina died years ahead of him.

Gatti's last years in New York were trying. Early in 1930 the Metropolitan Opera announced it was in financial straits and was canceling the next season. A "Save the Met" campaign began. The leading singers, except for Beniamino Gigli, agreed to accept cuts in fees. The Met Opera Guild was launched with the leadership of Mrs. August Belmont and Lucrezia Bori. Gatti-Casazza smarted and felt humiliated. He pointed out that the company, during good years, had built up a nest egg, which was now gone.

One day he invited me up to his office. With a glint in his eye, he said he was going to commit an indiscretion. Because the *Herald Tribune* had run an editorial questioning the need for the Met to continue, he leaked the information to me that significant support for the Met had come forward. I had an exclusive that made page one, and he had his revenge. Clearly the foreign-born manager had learned how to play the media game.

Gatti-Casazza was a man of great reserve and dignity, a big man, bearded and every inch the head of a major opera company. With the Met's future in doubt, he was persuaded he could help it survive if he related the details of his fabulous career as chief of La Scala in Milan, with Toscanini as his principal collaborator, then as chief at the Met with the same uncompromising partner conducting. The story was to be published as a serial in the *Saturday Evening Post.* I was honored to be asked to assist him in the writing. But how? He did not speak English, nor I Italian. I suggested French. Neither of us was comfortable in this language. I managed to locate a stenographer who knew French. We met in Mr. Gatti's rooms at the Savoy Plaza in New York during a sizzling, humid July. He kept the windows closed for fear of drafts.

We worked effectively together. When the notes of our conversations were transcribed, I mailed them to Gatti, who had sailed to Italy for his vacation. He obviously was not satisfied and replied with a batch of notes in Italian. With the help of an Italian secretary at the Met, I found I had a pile of colorful, entertaining material for the serial.

Gatti would not sanction publication of the *Post* stories in book form. After he died, however, his surviving brother and heir, Giuseppe, granted Scribner's permission to publish. Years later the book, *Memories of the Opera,* was reissued by Vienna House; a 1980 Riverrun Press edition is still in print. I believe the series in the *Saturday Evening Post* and in book form made friends for opera and the Met. It is still good reading, and I recommend it to everyone who is fond of opera and its traditions.

Opera companies' perennial problems with money inspire creative responses. Rudolf Bing, who became general manager of the Met in 1950, once invited me to lunch to request that I write an editorial suggesting that the Met give him a raise. I told him I had no influence getting a raise for myself, much less for the manager of the Met. Anyhow, I would never intrude on the Met's affairs.

Ardent supporter though I was, I sometimes added to the Met's problems. At one time Cyril Ritchard, a Broadway and West End figure of importance, restaged *The Marriage of Figaro* at the Met. I found fault with his vulgarizing the staging by having a clothesline in the Countess's boudoir with her underthings hanging from it. When I was appointed drama critic to succeed Brooks Atkinson in 1960, Ritchard sent a telegram to Rudolf Bing that said, "Oh, to be back at the Met!"

Will directors in the theater and opera house ever stop tinkering and "improving" works they stage? I doubt it. I remember a 1986 production of

Carmen that Karajan conducted at Salzburg. *Carmen* does not need help or alteration. For this production Karajan imported a group of flamenco dancers and singers and seated them at right center. After Carmen finished the Seguidilla, they began to sing and dance in flamenco style, which was an intrusion. Perfect use of flamenco singing and dancing was made in the film *The Flamenco Carmen* by Spanish filmmaker Carlos Saura, using Antonio Gades's singers and dancers. Could it be that Karajan was seduced by this magical achievement into trying his experiment?

Every now and then an event restores even a critic's faith. In 1957 there was a festival of Pan-American music. Horacio Palacios, who had made a lot of money in Caracas real estate, underwrote it. He brought composers from all the Americas to Venezuela, and provided an orchestra. Among the composers were Aaron Copland, Virgil Thomson, Carlos Chávez, Alberto Ginastera and Juan Castro of Argentina, and Roque Cordero of Panama. The Venezuelan dictator, Jimenez, a pompous, fat little man, had a wicker armchair placed on one of the concrete steps of the amphitheater and sat through the performances like a king.

There was to be a premiere of an opera by Chávez. Having completed it especially for this occasion, he did not have time to prepare the parts. In a perfect example of harmony, his fellow composers rallied round and proceeded to copy out the parts.

In my early theater-going days, I had a romantic view of the producer-directors like Arthur Hopkins, Winthrop Ames and Jed Harris who flourished on Broadway. I recently expressed this attitude to my friend Haila Stoddard, an actress-producer and experienced Broadway hand. She explained their secret as remarkably accurate casting. What kind of guidance did Hopkins give his actors? "He used a simple phrase," she said. "Be better." Remembering some of his productions, I should say it was an effective appeal.

Of thousands of musical and dramatic performances I attended through my years on *The Times,* one of the most memorable was a poetry reading by Andrei Voznesensky, Soviet poet, in Moscow in 1987. The huge house, the Vakhtangov Theater, was packed. The poet held the stage for four hours without a break. The audience did not budge. I did not understand a word but watched with fascination and admiration as he fielded written requests sent through the audience by its members, reciting poems asked for and responding to political questions as well. I was able to follow the action because my son Philip and his wife

Composers copying out parts at the festival of Pan-American music in Caracas, Venezuela, in 1957. Carlos Chávez is standing at far left; Aaron Copland, in light-colored glasses, is at the table in front of Chávez. The group effort enabled Chávez to meet his deadline. Photograph by Joseph Fabry.

Andrei Voznesensky at his dacha in Peredelkino, near Moscow, in 1986. Photograph by Philip Taubman.

Felicity Barringer, both correspondents for *The Times,* translated for us. Bravo Andrei!

The year before, when Philip and Felicity were stationed in Moscow, my second wife, Lori, and I decided to visit them and their two boys. We stopped in Munich, where I had many friends thanks to my work as a consultant for Exxon on the PBS television series "Great Performances." Exxon had bought many operas and concert performances from the Unitel/Beta Group for the series, and my friends at this company insisted on presenting me with two tote bags filled with musical videos to take to my family.

At the Moscow airport, Soviet customs regarded those tote bags with suspicion. Why did I carry so many videos? I was approached by countless customs officers. We tried as many languages. Russian? *Nyet!* English? No one understood a word. French? *Mais non!* Italian? *No!* Finally, German? *Nein!* Was I going to open a video shop? "No," I cried piteously. "This is only entertainment for our children, so far from home."

No, I could not take the cassettes into Moscow. They would be kept at the airport. Full of suspicion, I believed the Soviets would help themselves to my gifts. I remembered there was a cassette of *Madame Butterfly* that had been

Philip and Felicity with their son Michael, 1981.

processed for the Japanese market, with subtitles in Japanese. What would the Soviets make of that?

When we reached my son's flat, he assured me he would get the videos by asking the foreign office to help. No such luck.

On our way out of the Soviet Union, we again received the full Soviet customs treatment. I was led into an office, where a clerk produced my two tote bags, the cassettes still in them, and handed them to me with a gracious little speech. A clerk produced a bill for several rubles.

"What is this?" I asked.

"A storage charge" was the answer.

I protested, "I have no rubles." The clerk pointed to my wallet. I opened it and drew out a $1 bill. That settled the claim. We took the tote bags onto our British Air plane and carried our treasures to our London hotel. Eventually the videos reached my son's apartment in Moscow. The London bureau of *The Times,* headed by Howell Raines, had found a way to deliver the musical prizes. The moral of the story: don't try to reason with customs officers in any language.

Unlike Boris Godunov, the troubled protagonist of Mussorgsky's magnificent opera based on Pushkin's poem, who was haunted by the true and false Dimitris, I had an amusing encounter with the true and false George Cavanides. Preparing for a visit to Greece to look in on the Athens Festival of 1962, I got in touch with the Greek Tourist Bureau in New York. They advised me to get in touch with George Cavanides in the prime minister's office. In Athens I tried to reach him by phone and failed. When I told a new Greek friend of my difficulty, he knew what to do. "Just tell the hotel telephone operator to get you George Cavanides." I did, and presently there was George Cavanides on the phone.

I made my pitch to him about the importance of my mission as a critic of *The New York Times.* The poor man, who spoke English, said he had never heard of me. I pleaded that I needed to meet him. He said I must come to his office in Piraeus. I argued it would be best if he came to my hotel. He demurred, he was too busy.

Finally, he gave in and promised to come for a drink. Several days later he appeared with a companion, whom I took to be a bodyguard. He was a charming, agreeable gentleman who was bewildered by my conversation until it dawned on me that this must be the wrong George Cavanides. He insisted he had no government position but was merely a ship owner. We had a friendly drink, he invited me to take a ride on one of his ships and we parted amicably. Back in my room, I told the hotel operator I was looking for the George Cavanides in the prime minister's office, and in a minute she had him on the phone. We met for a drink, and presently he was promising to arrange for me to meet Prime Minister Caramanlis, which was not part of my mission in Athens. I enjoyed meeting the prime minister, a genial, courtly gentleman. The true George Cavanides proved to be as helpful as promised in New York. Alas, I never took advantage of the false George Cavanides' invitation to sail on one of his ships.

On one of my trips to London, I was invited to see a documentary on Jessye Norman made by the British Arts Council. The famous singer was shown about to enter a building through a revolving door. Miss Norman, as we all know, is a large woman, and she was having trouble dealing with the door. Her guide suggested, "Try entering sideways." Miss Norman's self-deprecating reply (echoing a remark made by another large singer, Ernestine Schumann-Heink, decades before): "But I have no sideways." Thank goodness for prima donnas who can laugh at themselves.

And thank goodness for illusion, essential to art. I recall seeing Galina Ulanova and Margot Fonteyn dance the role of Juliet—Ulanova with the Bolshoi Ballet, Fonteyn with the Royal Ballet. Both were at an age when dancing this part would seem too demanding, yet they moved like teenage girls. It was easy to believe they were madly in love and young enough to dare all.

I believe in seizing the opportunity. Sometimes good things result. There were people in the music world who wanted to prove that Americans could compete with the brilliant young Soviet virtuosos who kept winning the international contests. People at the Juilliard School in New York were determined to find a pianist who could win the Tchaikovsky piano competition in Moscow. Mark Schubart, assistant dean of the Juilliard School, and his associates decided that a young Texan named Van Cliburn had the talent and urged him to go to Moscow.

He played so well that he won the heart of the Soviet public. Max Frankel, who became the executive editor of *The New York Times* in 1986 and retired in July, 1994, was then a Moscow correspondent. He perceived that the Soviet public favored Cliburn and would not tolerate having the first prize go to someone else, even a Soviet musician. *The Times* played his report on page one. As it

Galina Ulanova as Juliet, 1959.

turned out, Cliburn won the contest; his victory was forced on the judges by the public. The result: a ticker-tape parade celebrated his return to New York, and Cliburn became a world figure.

The U.S. pavilion and theater at Expo '58 in Belgium were designed by Edward Stone, the architect of the U.S. embassy in New Delhi, a lovely building that reminded me of the architecture in Venice. The U.S. pavilion had a similar airiness and was greatly admired. With the fair winding up, Howard Cullman, the presidential appointee charged with Expo '58, one day wondered what would happen to the pavilion and theater. I suggested, "Give them to the city of Brussels." Cullman liked the idea and authorized me to write an article for *The Times* announcing that this would be done. He seized an opportunity to create good will for the U.S. in Belgium. I hope the city made creative use of the building, but I have not been back to check.

Otto Klemperer had been a distinguished conductor in pre-Hitler Germany, migrated to the United States when the Nazis came to power, then suffered a

serious ailment in 1939 and could not get work. He would come to the *Times*
offices, ask to see me and wait patiently in the reception room for a chance to
talk music, looking miserable. His aim, I'm sure, was to remain involved in the
music world. He persisted, returned to Germany after the war and resumed his
career with great success, making guest appearances around the world and especially making impressive recordings.

His son Werner Klemperer, Len Cariou and Austin Pendelton enabled the
Roundabout Theater to seize the opportunity to produce a play, David Pow-
nall's *Master Class,* which seemed impossible to cast. It was a bitter, boisterous
play about a master class conducted by a manic Josef Stalin, who was instruct-
ing Shostakovich and Prokofiev on how to write music. I had seen it delightfully done in London. Where could one find actors to play the Soviet composers, indeed to play Shostakovich and Prokofiev playing Shostakovich and
Prokofiev at the piano?

Pendelton (as Shostakovich) and Klemperer (as Prokofiev) were convincing.
With Len Cariou as a roaring, ranting Stalin smashing shellac records in dis-
gust, *Master Class* was a production that delighted and had a lot to say. It was
full of pity and terror.

I recall a time when I failed to advise seizing the opportunity. One day I
received a note from Arthur Hays Sulzberger saying *The Times* had an opportunity to acquire a television broadcasting license, and asking what action I
would recommend. I replied that it would be wise to be cautious. To become a
broadcaster might involve *The Times* in difficult and entangling relationships.
If *The Times* set out to hire creative people and performers, might not such activities lead to embarrassing encounters? Programs would not be easy to come up
with. Later, conversing with Jack Gould, *The Times'* excellent radio and television critic, I found he had received a similar note from Mr. Sulzberger and had
replied in the same vein.

I now see that our advice was bad. Years later *The Times* bought a couple of
television stations. Such licenses to broadcast are worth a lot of money. The
New York *Daily News* applied for a license and got one, Channel 11 in New
York. I am sure it is profitable. What I didn't know—perhaps Jack did—was
that the owner of a license could affiliate with a network and have access to
ample programming. If Mr. Sulzberger based his decision not to apply for a
license on our advice, he made a mistake, because we were wrong.

Mea culpa! Alas for this missed opportunity.

18

Suspected—of What?

I T WAS THE autumn of 1955. Olin Downes, my friend and colleague, had died in August, and I had returned from my vacation to be designated as his successor. We had worked together in harmony and close friendship for twenty-five years; during the first five of those years I was a neophyte learning from him, and in the following twenty I was, as music editor, his close associate, relishing his zest for discovery and controversy, whether in the arts or in politics.

One of my first tasks as chief music critic was to recommend the engagement of someone to fill a vacant position in the department. When I proposed Olin's son, Edward, to Turner Catledge, executive editor, he seemed dubious. "Do we want to encourage the establishment of dynasties in any department?" he asked. I replied that Edward was not only a sound musical scholar and a graceful writer but also a gentleman. Knowing Olin's penchant for stirring up excitement, even in areas having little to do with the music world, Catledge said, "Are you sure?" I was sure. Edward was an asset for *The Times* until he left for other commitments, such as becoming quizmaster in the intermissions of the Saturday afternoon radio broadcasts from the Metropolitan Opera.

At the same time I recommended that Ross Parmenter become my successor as music editor, a job he performed efficiently and loyally.

Only a few weeks had passed since I assumed my new duties when I received a subpoena from an Eastland subcommittee of the United States Senate. Whatever its formal title, it was on the hunt for subversives. Like the House Com-

Music critics at *The Times, c.* 1956, were (left to right) Ross Parmenter, Taubman, Harold Schonberg, John Briggs and Edward Downes. Photograph by Arnold Newman.

mittee on Un-American Activities, like the Senate's Government Operation Committee headed by Joseph McCarthy, the subcommittee chaired by Senator James O. Eastland of Mississippi was looking to unearth Communists and other dangerous radicals. But like McCarthy, the Red hunters were out for all sorts of other game—individuals and organizations with truly democratic views and programs. Often they were engaged in personal vendettas, determined to destroy the reputations of people they envied or did not like. McCarthy's motive, beyond his professed aim to cleanse the State Department, the Army, the country, of those who were undermining the republic, was clearly to promote the career of Joseph McCarthy.

But McCarthy had had his day of reckoning. In the fall of 1954, the Senate at long last had voted to censure him. But in June, 1955, after licking his wounds for some months, he tried to stir up opposition to a plan for a summit meeting between Eisenhower and Khrushchev in Geneva. To the distress of Senator

William F. Knowland and other Republican leaders, McCarthy offered a resolution demanding that the President get prior agreement from the Soviet Union
to discuss the satellite nations as a precondition to any conference. The Demo-
crats, braver than most of them had been in the days when McCarthy terrorized any opposition as well as "dangerous radicals," would not let the Republicans kill the resolution or permit McCarthy to withdraw it. They insisted on a
roll call vote, and the resolution was beaten seventy-seven to four.

But why was I being honored with a subpoena in late 1955? Nor was I the
only *Times*man to be so dignified. Fourteen others had been summoned to testify in New York.

As for myself, I could think of no reason. I examined my past conscientiously.
I had voted for Roosevelt, Truman and Stevenson, though I had no party affili-
ation. I had joined the Newspaper Guild when it was formed in 1933 and had
served on some of its committees, even testifying against *The Times* when it was
defending itself at a Labor Relations Board hearing. I had spent some weeks in
the Soviet Union in 1935, writing about its musical life for *The Times*. In 1946
I had agreed to help Frances Perkins, FDR's secretary of labor, by editing her
fine memoir, *The Roosevelt I Knew*. In the summer of 1955 I had edited Marian
Anderson's autobiography, *My Lord, What a Morning*, but that book was not to
be issued until 1956. Come to think of it, I was a veteran: I had served my country in uniform during World War II. What in the world warranted my sum-
mons to the Eastland subcommittee?

What about *The Times?* The fact that fifteen of us had been subpoenaed
would indicate that someone was eager to embarrass the newspaper. But why?

Over the years I had read *The Times* carefully. Even if I was not fascinated
by the news of the world, as a conscientious newsman I would have watched
how my paper was writing and playing the news. I have to confess that I had
had reservations. During the Spanish Civil War, *The Times*, it seemed to me,
had been at such pains to be even-handed in its treatment of the government
and Franco's forces that the latter got the better breaks in coverage. During the
years of McCarthy's depredations, *The Times*, it seemed to me, had been far too
lax in playing up his accusations without sufficient effort to check and analyze
them immediately and had not given equal prominence to the defenses of the
accused.

On the other hand, the venality of the McCarthy circus had finally roused
The Times to protest on its editorial pages. Not as soon as did Edward R. Mur-

Joseph McCarthy presiding over a hearing in New York in 1953.

row on CBS and some others, but finally it did speak out forcefully and eloquently. After the hearings in the dispute between McCarthy and the United
States Army ended, a 1955 *Times* editorial said in part:

> Whether Mr. McCarthy was attempting to impose his own idea of "security" on
> the Army, whether he was attempting to interfere with the promotion system of
> the Army, whether he was attempting to impugn the integrity of the highest offi-
> cers of the Army, whether he was encouraging anarchy within the Army, it all leads
> to the same conclusion, founded not on what some hostile witness may have said.
> The conclusion is that Senator McCarthy as a legislative official of the United
> States was using—and gives every evidence of intending to continue to use—his
> high position to undermine the structure of this Government for his own purpose
> under the guise of fighting Communists and communism.
>
> There is a second great issue to emerge from the tangled mass of thirty-six days
> of hearings. In fighting his desperate battle against the Army, against the President,
> against the millions of Americans who detest communism but who believe in
> America and what America stands for, Senator McCarthy had time and time again
> displayed methods, tactics, techniques that are not new to him but might well
> have been a revelation to many who for the first time have seen him perform

before their very eyes. Whether he (or someone acting for him) submits a faked picture, whether he flourishes a false letter, whether he crashes by brute force of vocal power into the testimony of his aides when they are hardpressed, whether he denounces as a Communist or Communist sympathizer any and every person who disputes or disagrees with him, whether he impugns without shame and without equivocation the motives of honorable men, whether he vilifies persons who have nothing to do with the case, whether he shows his contempt for the orderly processes of even this hearing, whether he drags the vast reach of his fertile imagination, all these actions can lead but to one conclusion. That conclusion is that here is a man who has disgraced the Senate, who is unfit to head a Senatorial investigation and whose record at the very least imposes on the Senate the obligation to assume some control over its own committees.

Mr. McCarthy has condemned himself by his own words and his own actions before the vast public that he tirelessly and rightly proclaims is the jury that in the last analysis will decide this case. In the larger sense, it is the case of Senator McCarthy not vs Stevens, not vs. the Army, not vs. the President, not vs. the Senate, but Senator McCarthy vs. the constitutional government of the United States.

An editorial written with rare and justified passion. It surely contributed to the beginning of the end of McCarthy. But McCarthyism was not finished. It assumed a less frantic and irrational form in the Eastland subcommittee, and when *The Times* in mid-1955 published another long, powerful editorial condemning the latest investigations and their anti-democratic procedures, it seemed to be time to teach *The Times* a lesson. Otherwise, why summon fifteen staff members before a committee? Was there the slightest scintilla of evidence that the columns of *The Times* had been tainted by subversive doctrine?

Of course not. If the subpoenas were vindictive in intent or at the least a warning to the owners and management of *The Times* that their product was under constant scrutiny, say for the Eastland subcommittee that it behaved with more moderation than McCarthy. Whereas McCarthy proclaimed his charges far and wide, getting the maximum publicity for them and himself, the Eastland subcommittee served its subpoenas quietly.

When I received mine, I did not know that fourteen others had been summoned. I went around to the office of the managing editor. Catledge had already heard from some of the others. He had only one question: "Have you anything you want to tell me?" What he obviously wanted to know was whether I was about to make some embarrassing revelation to the investigators. He did not say so, but in effect he was worrying about how I might reply to the question "Are you now or have you ever been a Communist?" and about whether, if I chose not to answer, I would take the Fifth Amendment.

I told Catledge that I had nothing to tell him. He smiled, relieved. He had already explored with *Times* reporters covering the federal courthouse in lower Manhattan how I could enter and leave by a side door without encountering representatives of the media who had gotten wind of the subpoenas and were waiting to talk to the recipients.

The questioning took place in a small room. If any of my *Times* colleagues had preceded me, I had no indication. I was seated alone on one side of a large table. Opposite me were three men and a woman stenographer. I am sure of the identity of two of the men, though no one bothered to introduce himself. They were Senator Thomas Henning of Missouri and Jay G. Sourwine, the committee's chief counsel. The third, an elderly gentleman, whom I assumed to be Senator Eastland, never said a word.

Sourwine, a big, blustering sort of man, began by asking whether I was willing to take an oath to tell the truth and nothing but the truth and warning me, if I did take the oath, what the consequences might be if I were found not to have told it. Rather odd, I thought, to warn an experienced newspaperman of what taking the oath might mean. Was this routine procedure or a way of making a witness nervous?

I took the oath, then Sourwine popped the expected question: was I or had I ever been a Communist? He prefaced this with a suave reminder that I was free to plead under the Fifth Amendment that I refused to incriminate myself. I said I had no hesitation in replying, "No, I am not a Communist, nor have I ever been one."

Had I supported Communist causes? I said I did not know what Communist causes were unless they were expressly identified as Communist. Had I signed Communist petitions? I said I never signed petitions of any kind. Had I associated with Communists? I said I was not in the habit of checking out the party affiliations of either my friends or other people I chanced to meet.

The sparring between Sourwine and me went on for some minutes. With the air of a man who had been dallying long enough, Sourwine pulled a sheet of paper from his file, and holding it close to his chest, declared portentously,

"Now I ask you, didn't you serve on an important committee in the presidential campaign of 1948?"

I stared at him and at the sheet of paper in disbelief. "No, I served on no such committee."

"What if I show you"—Sourwine sounded as if he was ready for the kill—"a list, a list of the names of the national committee supporting Henry A. Wallace for President?"

"I cannot help it," I replied, "if my name is on such a list. I did not serve on such a committee. I did not authorize the use of my name. If it's there, it's unauthorized and a mistake."

As I talked, I suddenly realized what had happened. My predecessor, Olin Downes, had indeed been a member of the national committee to elect Wallace. An old Wilsonian, he had believed in the need for the League of Nations, and late at night, after we had finished writing our reviews, we would sit around and chat, and he would work up a head of steam over the refusal of the United States to join the League. In 1948, hopeful that the new United Nations would become a force for world peace and distressed at developments in the Cold War, he had decided to give up his normal allegiance to the Democratic Party and to support Wallace.

Clearly Sourwine and his staff had discovered that the chief music critic of *The Times* had not only endorsed but even campaigned, in a minimal way, for Wallace. And they had done the natural thing in subpoenaing the chief music critic of *The Times*. What had evidently escaped their notice was that Downes had died some weeks earlier.

Sourwine seemed not to be put off by my assurance under oath that I had not been on the national committee for Wallace. He pursued his line of inquiry, asking the same question in various ways. I might have, were I debating with him as an equal rather than as a witness under oath, challenged his assumption that supporting Wallace was somehow suspect and perhaps subversive. My only thought was that I wanted to get out of there, that the scene was both distasteful and offensive.

After hammering away, Sourwine said, still clinging to the sheet of paper close to his chest, "What if I showed you that your name is listed on the roster of the Wallace national committee?"

Once more I contended that if it was there, it was without my knowledge or permission. But by this time Senator Henning, who must have been bored by a series of questions and answers that arrived at the same dead end, turned to Sourwine and asked whether he could examine the sheet of paper. Sourwine refused to hand it to him. Henning, red in the face, demanded to see it at once. Sourwine held back. Henning looked at the silent man at the table, presumably Eastland, who waved a commanding hand at Sourwine. Slowly, reluctantly, Sourwine handed the sheet of paper to Henning.

The senator from Missouri examined the paper. He stood up angrily, pushing his chair back so violently that it almost turned over. Glaring at Sourwine, he shouted, "This is a disgrace!" He waved the sheet of paper so that I could see both sides. It was blank.

"I move," Henning thundered, "that this man be immediately excused and that everything in the record about him be expunged. And as for you!" he glared at Sourwine. He then escorted me to the door, apologizing that I had been put to all this trouble.

An honorable man, Senator Henning. *The Times,* of course, survived the investigation. I quote in part from an eloquent editorial that appeared early in January, 1956:

A few employees of this newspaper who have appeared before the Eastland subcommittee have pleaded the Fifth Amendment. A few others have testified to membership in the Communist party over periods terminating at various dates in the past. So far as we are aware, no present member of the Communist party had been found among the more than four thousand employees on our rolls.

The policy of this newspaper with regard to the employment of Communist party members had been stated many times, and may be stated here again. We would not knowingly employ a Communist party member in the news or editorial departments of this paper, because we would not trust his ability to report the news objectively or to comment on it honestly, and the discovery of Communist party membership on the part of such an employee would lead to his immediate dismissal.

In the case of those employees who have testified to some Communist association in the past, or who have pleaded the Fifth Amendment for reasons of their own, it will be our policy to judge each case on its own merits, in the light of each individual's responsibilities in our organization and of the degree to which his relations with this newspaper entitle him to possess our confidence.

We may say this, however. We do not believe in the doctrine of irredeemable sin. We think it possible to atone through good performance for past error, and we have tried to supply the security and the favorable working conditions which should exist in a democracy and which would encourage men who were once misled to reconsider and to reshape their political thinking.

We have judged these men, and we shall continue to judge them, by the quality of their work and by our confidence in their ability to perform that work satisfactorily. It is our own business to decide whom we shall employ and not employ. We do not propose to hand over that function to the Eastland subcommittee.

Nor do we propose to permit the Eastland subcommittee or any other agency outside this office, to determine in any way the policies of this newspaper. It seems to us quite obvious that the Eastland investigation has been aimed with particular emphasis at *The New York Times*. This is evident from several facts: from the heavy concentration of subpoenas served on employees of this newspaper, from the nature of the examination conducted at earlier hearings by the subcommittee's counsel, Mr. Sourwine, and from the counsel's effort, at these hearings, to demonstrate some connection between a witness's one-time association with the Communist party and the character of the news published in this paper.

It seems to us to be a further obvious conclusion that *The Times* has been singled out for this attack precisely because of the vigor of its opposition to many of the things for which Mr. Eastland, his colleague Mr. Jenner and the subcommittee's counsel stand—that is, because we have condemned segregation in the Southern schools; because we have challenged the high-handed and abusive methods employed by various Congressional committees; because we have denounced McCarthyism and all its works; because we have attacked the narrow and bigoted restrictions of the McCarran Immigration Act; because we have criticized a "security system" which conceals the accuser from his victim; because we have insisted that the true spirit of American democracy demands a scrupulous respect for the rights of even the lowliest individual and a high standard of fair play.

The editorial ended with a ringing affirmation that "long after Senator Eastland and his present subcommittee are forgotten, and long after McCarthyism is a dim, unwelcome memory, that long after the Congressional committee has learned that it cannot tamper successfully with a free press, *The New York Times* will still be speaking for the men who make it, and only for the men who make it, and speaking, without fear of favor, the truth as it sees it."

I was proud then to be associated with that newspaper. I am certain, however, that if that editorial were to be written today, it would be speaking of "the men and women" who make *The Times.*

I have often wondered why a decent man like Senator Henning, seeing that the subcommittee counsel was inventing charges based on a blank sheet of paper, did not rise up in public wrath against a committee counsel like Sourwine. Indeed, I have speculated about how countless men and women, in and out of office, could sit silently for so long while a shameless, self-promoting fanatic like McCarthy could intimidate and almost paralyze a nation. How many of the sheets of paper purporting to list the names of dangerous subversives, which he flaunted so tirelessly and so ominously, were blank?

Olin Downes had a favorite story. When he was a brash young music critic on *The Boston Post,* a somewhat raffish newspaper reaching a similar audience, he wrote a piece in which he used the word "increment." His editor reprimanded him for employing such language. Downes defended himself, saying, "You mean *excrement.*" The editor thundered, *"Increment, excrement,* Downes, it's all shit to the readers of *The Boston Post!"* Which seems to me an apt comment on witch hunts, and committees that conduct them.

19

TV—No Vast Wasteland Here

IT BEGAN WITH a chance meeting at a lunch, and it turned into an immensely gratifying involvement that lasted for fifteen years. I am proud of what "Great Performances," largely supported by grants from the Exxon Corporation, achieved during those years when it helped to prove that television in America need not be a vast wasteland. I regret deeply that Exxon saw fit to withdraw its support of "Great Performances" as of June, 1988—indeed to eliminate nearly all its contributions to the arts, an area where Exxon for decades had been a vastly influential corporate leader.

I happened to be a guest at the annual awards lunch held late in 1971 by the New York Business Committee for the Arts and found myself at a table with Exxon executives. Trygve T. Tonnessen, a manager in the Public Affairs Department, inquired whether I had seen an Exxon-supported series called "Vibrations." I had; it was a potpourri of music, drama and dance assembled from televised performances abroad. Though some of the bits were attractive, they lacked coherence and a binding purpose. My reply intimated as much.

"If you had the choice," he asked, "what would you advise Exxon to do on television in the arts?"

"The entire work," I said.

"What entire work?"

I was not prepared to be specific, but if Exxon wished to support the arts on television in an exciting way, I suggested undertaking three programs as an experiment—a major drama, a major musical work and a major dance work. A good listener and a thoughtful man, Tonnessen said we must meet again, and we had lunch a couple of times in 1972 during my last months at *The Times.*

Late in 1972 when I had retired, Tryg, as I came to call him, phoned to inquire whether I would read a pair of proposals submitted by WNET or Channel 13 in New York and give him and his colleagues my opinion. They were prospectuses for "Theater in America" and for a mini-series on the Adams family. I met with Tryg and his colleagues in Public Affairs, Harold Roser and John Irwin. I observed that the theater project had exciting potential and warned against certain pitfalls. I had reservations about the Adams proposal. Without my knowing it at the time, Exxon made a grant toward a pilot episode, and when it was screened in 1973, it was apparent that many elements had gone wrong. Exxon did not pursue the project. It was taken over by Arco, was completed after large, painful cost overruns and aired with moderate success.

As for "Theater in America," Exxon committed itself to be the major funder for a first season that would comprise eleven new productions from theaters in the United States plus repetitions of eight plays produced by WNET in previous seasons. All that remained to be done—and what a job that proved to be!—was to identify and shoot the eleven new productions. Early in 1973 I had a call from Tryg. Would I be willing to sign on as an advisor for the year? I learned later that the other person considered for the consultancy was John Houseman. As a friend and admirer of John and his remarkable career, I still feel flattered.

There was never any doubt in my mind or anyone else's at Exxon or WNET about my role: I was to be a consultant, that is to say, an advisor, not a decision maker. No one at Exxon made final decisions. Artistic control was the province of WNET and the Public Broadcasting System, of which it was not only a member but one of its principal production centers. I will not pretend that there were no disagreements. There were times when Jac Venza, executive producer, chose programs that some of us at Exxon were unhappy with, and I assume that Jac accepted programs we pressed on him when his heart was not in it. For the better part of fifteen years it was a good marriage with inevitable tiffs but with a sustaining mutual respect and, yes, affection.

I have read repeatedly in articles by careless writers that Exxon censored programs on "Great Performances." Merrill Brockway, the imaginative director of our first programs in the "Dance in America" component, charged that Exxon had ordered the making of a dance program he did not favor. As far as I know,

Exxon never interfered in any way with any dance program. Perhaps someone at WNET who wished to do the program Brockway disapproved, attributed refusal to Exxon. A couple of programs on "Dance in America"—none Brockway's responsibility, by the way—were so disappointing that I wished Exxon had been able to proscribe them.

While Stephen Stamas was vice-president for public affairs and Clifton C. Garvin, Jr., was chairman, Exxon, an acknowledged pillar of measured conservatism, was more daring and innovative in its programming goals for television than many of the people who ran PBS and some of its member stations. Station managers complained that some programs were not popular enough, that they were too highbrow, too elitist. They appealed to the Washington headquarters of PBS. They expressed their disaffection to Exxon personnel. And they did just what the crass commercial networks did with programs they considered highbrow art—exiled them to the airwaves' Sunday afternoon ghetto.

I am sure that Stamas, a former Rhodes scholar (who became president of the New York Philharmonic in 1984), who was supervising officer during the greater part of Exxon's commitment to "Great Performances," had to deal with angry criticism of some programs by his superiors. But he held fast to his conviction that the best was good enough for the general public, and he clearly had Garvin's support.

The aim in that first season of "Theater in America" was to reflect the diversity and energy of theater across the country. We knew that there were regional companies and small, adventurous ensembles in New York capable of doing impressive work. In my years as drama critic and critic-at-large at *The Times*, I had seen the work of these companies and sensed that they were a growing force. I remember that some oldtimers among Broadway producers found fault with the time and space I devoted to such reports; my main business as drama critic, they insisted, was the Broadway theater. Nowadays producers are alert to the work being done Off Broadway and in the regional theaters. Without the productions transferred from these venues to Broadway, the Broadway theater would be even more barren than it has become.

In 1973 Jac traveled up and down the land, as did his associates, and so did I. Jac and I took scouting trips together frequently; I have recollections of being in airplanes with Jac through a good deal of 1973, sitting through dreary performances that had been recommended for our consideration and seeking consolation in the region's highly regarded restaurants.

Jac and I saw eye to eye more often than not. The best example of how we functioned under the pressure of putting together so wide-ranging a season in a relatively short time—think of how many months, even years, a commercial network requires to produce one first-rate production—involves *Feasting with Panthers*.

It was a Friday. I was at home in Danbury, Connecticut, relaxed, getting ready for lunch and then a long walk along rural roads. The phone rang; Jac had just heard interesting comment about a production by the Trinity Square Repertory in Providence. It was closing the next night, and he could not make it. Could I? Not the next night; only tonight.

Feasting with Panthers more than justified the trip to Providence, including the late-night return to Danbury (much as I cared about drama, I did not intend to miss my year-round Saturday morning tennis game in Danbury). It proved to be a fresh, original approach to a sensitive, touching subject—Oscar Wilde in Reading Gaol. Adrian Hall, director of the Providence company, and his musician associate Richard Cumming had created a remarkably affecting play-with-music that abjured realism, yet was profoundly true.

The action began with Wilde's arrival in Reading Gaol and his being placed in an isolation cell for speaking to another prisoner while they were exercising in lockstep. Scenes from his life and work thronged Wilde's memory, mingling surrealistically with harsh prison routine. In a vision of a scene from *The Importance of Being Earnest*, the Reading Gaol warden, a severe man, became a bewigged Lady Bracknell. A recollection of *Salome* had Wilde talking to a bare-bosomed young man with a girl's breasts outlined on his chest. Intervals of music intensified the impact of memory's phantasmagoria alternating with real encounters with prison officers, guards and other prisoners and visits by wife and friends. Most of the lines spoken were Wilde's, drawn especially from "The Ballad of Reading Gaol" and "De Profundis." Hall's staging and Richard Kneeland's Wilde conveyed the wry humor as well as the bitterness and pathos of Wilde's predicament.

The next morning, even before I left for my tennis appointment, I called Jac and told him that he must get to Providence. He did, and immediately after the performance, he initiated negotiations to bring the play to television.

A quick dissolve; it is months later. I was in a New York screening room looking at something that we might consider for future use, when I was summoned to a telephone. A Stamas subordinate was at the other end, urging me to come to his office immediately. When I arrived, I was confronted by a grim, unhappy man. He had been looking at the tapes of *Feasting with Panthers* and was mightily displeased. How could I have approved a work of this sort? The gist of his displeasure—I did not keep a diary and I refrain from using quotes—was that it was in awfully bad taste, all that attention to homosexuality. I argued that it was an impressive, moving work, and Exxon should be proud to be connected with it. His retort: Exxon cannot be associated with stuff of this kind; it must be eliminated from the schedule or Exxon must be dropped from the credits. I stared at him incredulously. After all, I pointed out, the cast is large, the crew at the taping was sizable, too many people would know that Exxon had pulled out.

There were meetings with other executives, and it was agreed that Exxon could not disassociate itself from the production. It was suggested that the political way to minimize Exxon embarrassment would be to schedule *Feasting with Panthers* well along in the series. WNET assented, and poor, haunted Wilde was assigned the tenth slot, exactly midway in the nineteen-week season.

The series got off to a respectable start with Gorky's *Enemies* and the Kaufman-Lardner *June Moon*, stumbled with an unsatisfying *King Lear*, a New York Shakespeare Festival's Central Park production, and an inadequate *Touch of the Poet* by Eugene O'Neill. At last the airing of *Feasting with Panthers*, and with it a strong imprimatur of success for "Theater in America." John J. O'Connor in his *New York Times* review hailed it as one of the finest plays ever produced on television anywhere, and in a follow-up Sunday article held forth at length on its quality and significance. There was great satisfaction at Exxon, though the executive who had given me a hard time never said a word to me about the play's enormous success.

Another ticklish problem concerned Leonard Bernstein's *Mass*. It was on the schedule largely because of my urging. I had seen it at its 1971 premiere during the grand opening of the Kennedy Center in Washington, and though it was condescended to, even savaged, by some of the nation's music critics, I found a lot of merit in it. Early in 1973 I saw a production at Yale, mostly by students, conducted by John Mauceri, himself a graduate student, and was stirred by the youthful fire and commitment, which the piece clearly needed. I persuaded Venza to include it in our season.

The taping was to take place in Vienna, where the Yale company had been invited to give six performances. My colleagues at Exxon thought that it might be useful if I were in Vienna for the taping. Late one evening I had an agitated telephone call from an Exxon colleague in New York. Two members of the Exxon board—both Catholics, I was told—had expressed concern that *Mass* was blasphemous. What could they be told? I explained that I did not think it was irreverent; on the contrary, it was passionately committed to the things of the spirit. My caller was firm: *my* assurances would not suffice.

I promised to investigate the next morning. Bernstein, it turned out, had just arrived from Rome, where he had been conducting a concert at the Vatican at the Pope's invitation with the Holy Father in attendance. Surely that could not be an indication that the Church frowned on the *Mass*, let alone its composer. I wandered into St. Stephen's Cathedral, and there posted on the walls inside the entry were three-sheet advertisements for *Mass*, placed there, as I found after careful checking, with the reigning cardinal's permission.

I reported to Exxon by telephone and heard no more. Years later I learned that one of the board members who had worried about blasphemy had sat through an advance screening and remarked that *Mass* impressed him as not only reverent but also deeply felt.

We had barely launched the theater series on the air when Tryg, who was not a great theater buff, asked what I thought about adding music to Exxon's television commitment. I am sure he knew that I would be all for it. The hard question was what and where to find it. "If you undertake music," I said, "it should be the best." Tryg's next question: "Like what?"

Several years earlier, in the course of a European trip for *The Times*, I had seen in Munich portions of a film of Bach's B minor *Mass*. Musically it was impressive. What made it especially exciting was the way in which the visual element added to the impact of Bach's masterpiece. The performance had been filmed in a modest baroque church in a small Bavarian town. The camera, when it did not focus on the performers, lingered on the delightfully naive and devout frescoes and statuary that filled the church, providing a lovely visual complement to the tender and soaring music.

That film popped into my mind as Tryg put his question. "What would you think of the B minor *Mass?*" I asked, realizing that I was probably aiming too high. But Tryg's answer was "Why not?" With Tryg's hearty approval, I got in touch with Klaus Hallig, American representative of Unitel, the Munich company that had made the film, and he arranged for a screening.

A number of Exxon representatives and their guests attended the screening. Among them were musicians. Peter Mennin, president of the Juilliard School and a leading American composer, sat through the opening Kyrie, then rose to go to another appointment. "What's the problem?" "It's wonderful," he called out.

Tryg was delighted with what he saw, and so was Stamas. Other executives did not agree. When we returned to Exxon headquarters, one chap took me aside and berated me: "What does stuff like that have to do with company policies?" Nevertheless, Exxon bought the rights for a telecast, and Tryg wisely decided, with WNET and PBS agreement, that the broadcast should be on Good Friday night.

There was a problem to be solved. The film ran some minutes over two hours, and the broadcasters needed to round out the last half-hour to fill the two-and-a-half-hour slot allotted to the show. We checked with Unitel. Karl Richter, conductor of the Munich Bach Choir Orchestra, could speak English, and he would be willing to appear on film in introductory material. But who would provide the script?

I was dispatched to Munich. I borrowed a typewriter at the Unitel office and wrote five pages about Bach, his time and his music with major attention to the *Mass*. Richter, I had been told, was a fine organist and harpsichordist, and I provided for illustrations at the harpsichord.

Fritz Buttenstedt, production manager for Unitel, made a late-afternoon appointment with Richter at the Vierjahreszeiten Hotel, and we met Richter in the lounge. He was a lean, intense man, and his greeting was cool. I outlined my plan, to begin with him seated at the harpsichord. He would read the script as if he were extemporizing, pausing from time to time to illustrate at the harpsichord.

Richter nodded intensely as I spoke. When I handed him the script, his discomfort seemed to increase. Suddenly he paused, glared at Buttenstedt and flung the script to the floor. As a professional writer, I had some experience of rejection but had never encountered anything so violent and final. I looked at Buttenstedt, but he was busy talking to Richter in German. As he picked up the sheets of the offending script, Fritz sought to calm our conductor. When Richter smiled rather stiffly, Fritz proposed that Richter take the script to his room and study it overnight. Richter refused. Nevertheless, Fritz told him we would meet the next morning at ten at the studio. As we left the hotel, I asked Fritz what was the use of being at the studio if Richter was not there. "Don't worry," said Fritz. "He'll be there."

Richter was there, but not at ten. He arrived at noon. While we waited, Fritz had an assistant write out the text on a series of blackboards. When he finally appeared, Richter was just as up-tight as he had been the previous evening. Asked to seat himself at the harpsichord, he did so reluctantly. The director went through some preliminaries as if he took it for granted that Richter would at least read the script, whatever he chose to do about harpsichord illustration. At last everything was go, and the director pointed at Richter. At that signal Richter attacked the harpsichord, and the studio reverberated with Bach.

Had those glorious affirming phrases effected the magic change? I shall never know; I never had an explanation from Richter or anyone at Unitel. Suddenly he was a thorough professional, reading the script as if it were his and illustrating eloquently. When we were finished, Richter told me how much he had enjoyed meeting me, asked whether I had an extra copy of the script for him and inscribed my copy with a lavish compliment.

The broadcast on Good Friday night was a distinct success. Bach's masterpiece had great appeal to two constituencies—the religious and the musical. Tryg had also proposed that in a break between sections of the *Mass*, there should be an announcement requesting people who wanted more musical programs of similar quality to write. The response was extraordinary.

Tryg, with Stamas's support, read it as a mandate. Some days later he and I were on our way to Munich, where we spent a week screening films of musical programs. We selected a large number as candidates for a possible expansion of Exxon's television commitment and arranged to have them sent to New York. A screening room was engaged for a full day, and excerpts from these programs were shown as Exxon executives, their guests and representatives of WNET came and went.

The following day Tryg presided over a large meeting, seeking reactions to the screening and, if possible, a consensus. A few comments were enthusiastic, many were cautious and several were hostile. One of the films was of a luminous performance of Verdi's *Requiem* with Herbert von Karajan conducting the orchestra and chorus of La Scala in Milan, with a quartet of glamorous soloists—Leontyne Price at the height of her powers, Luciano Pavarotti in his refulgent prime, Fiorenza Cossotto, a richly voiced contralto, and Nikolai Ghiaurov, a distinguished basso cantante. One executive voted against this film on the ground that the women in the chorus were unattractive and were dressed too plainly. Evidently he had not realized that they were in black because this was a requiem; nor had it occurred to him that faces like these adorned some of the great Italian paintings of the Renaissance. Another man dismissed the Verdi *Requiem* as boring. Poor chap!

Though Exxon decided to add five musical programs to its next television season, the Verdi *Requiem* was set aside. I thought it was the wrong decision, but I was comforted by an agreement that we would include the Mozart *Requiem* instead. To present a work of such quality on television seemed to me a delightful swap. But I brooded about the loss of the Verdi masterpiece.

Several years later the Berlin Philharmonic, led by Karajan, visited New York, and the Verdi *Requiem* was on one of its programs. I happened to be in a box at Carnegie Hall with Stamas, and when the stirring performance was over, he turned to me and said, "Why can't we have a piece like that on 'Great Performances'?" He had not attended the 1974 meeting and had not realized that members of his staff had found fault with the work. Turned down for the 1974–75 season, it became one of the outstanding broadcasts of 1977–78.

With the addition of music to our mix, we initiated a second season, another step toward achieving the breadth and diversity that became the hallmark of "Great Performances." By the third season, that of 1975–76, the mix was complete. "Dance in America" and "Live from Lincoln Center" became components of the series. It is my strong conviction that at its best, "Great Performances" provided the nation with an astonishingly consistent and noteworthy representation of the richness and diversity of the performing arts.

By 1975–76 "Great Performances" became the official umbrella title for the series, and it now ran fifty-two weeks a year in a stable time slot in prime time. The theater component continued to rely on drama in America, but an indication that change was on the way was the introduction of a mini-series made in Britain. The six-part "Jennie: Lady Randolph Churchill," starring Lee Remick and Ronald Pickup as the Churchills who were Winston's parents, turned out to be a delightful winner. I suspect that Mobil, funder of "Masterpiece Theater," felt that this series belonged in its domain. I know there was some behind-the-scenes hassling involving executives of Exxon and Mobil before the issue was decided in favor of "Great Performances."

Jac never let up in his determination to offer theater by and with Americans, and I salute him for it. But compelling drama is where you find it. In the very opening season, there was a play by an Englishman, one D. H. Lawrence. *The Widowing of Mrs. Holroyd* was acceptable because it was done by an American company, the excellent Long Wharf Theater of New Haven led by the gifted Arvin Brown. With effective performances by Joyce Ebert, Geraldine Fitzgerald and Frank Converse, this production was a reminder that Lawrence's theater work was not as negligible as the pundits had told us.

It would be impossible to list the achievements of "Great Performances" without running on for pages. I do not even touch on the "Shakespeare Plays," that ambitious cycle of the entire Shakespeare canon, which was co-sponsored by Exxon, Metropolitan Life and Morgan Guaranty Bank and which ran for seven years, often in the "Great Performances" time slot. I had my favorites among the single plays.

Elie Wiesel's *Zalmen or The Madness of God*, from the Arena Stage in Washington, for its moral passion and the power of Joseph Wiseman's performance as a rabbi of a congregation in Moscow seeking to cleave to his truth in the face of Communist threats.

Tennessee Williams' *Eccentricities of a Nightingale*, an affecting early version of *Summer and Smoke*, produced in collaboration with San Diego's Old Globe Theater, with sensitive performances by Blythe Danner and Frank Langella.

Arthur Hopcraft's adaptation of Rudyard Kipling's pathetic autobiographical story, *Baa Baa Black Sheep*, of his childhood separation from his parents in India, produced by Granada in England.

Julian Mitchell's *Abide with Me*, a tender and amusing tale of the relations between a domineering ninety-year-old, played splendidly by eighty-nine-year-old Cathleen Nesbitt, and a young, humble live-in servant, produced by the BBC.

On Giant's Shoulders, a wrenching and exalting drama about a young man deformed as a result of his mother taking the drug Thalidomide during pregnancy, with the young man, Terry Wiles, playing himself courageously, and with Judi Dench as his foster mother. When I began to screen this BBC production, I thought I would be put off by the appearance of Terry, a stunted young man without arms and with flippers for feet. After a moment's squeamishness, I found myself drawn to his cheerful determination to make a life for himself. I could understand the refusal of some station managers to show the piece in its regular time slot during one of the recurrent pledge weeks. Their fear was that their audience would be repelled, tune out and fail to make the hoped-for contributions. But the stations that adhered to the schedule reported that pledges ran higher after this broadcast than at any other times during the week.

The adaptation by Philip Reisman, Jr., of *Life on the Mississippi*, the first of a group of Mark Twain dramas that producer William Perry's drive and enthusiasm transmitted to television with a fond grasp of the author's America.

Paul Scott's *Staying On*, a warmhearted Granada production of a story about a couple of leftovers of the British raj after India won independence, with delightful performances by Celia Johnson and Trevor Howard.

A Circle in the Square production of Shaw's *Heartbreak House* with Rex Harrison, Rosemary Harris and Amy Irving leading a cast that played with Shavian flair.

A Long Wharf Theater production of Athol Fugard's *Master Harold—and the Boys*, in which Zakes Mokai, John Kani and Matthew Broderick memorably conveyed the painful strains between whites and blacks in South Africa.

Judy Allen's *December Flower*, a touching story about caring, with delicious performances by Mona Washbourne and Jean Simmons, in a Granada production.

Scene from a 1959 production of Shaw's *Heartbreak House*, with (from left) Pamela Brown, Diane Cilento and Maurice Evans.

David Storey's *Early Days*, in which Ralph Richardson in his last role, as an old man full of guilt and regrets, was both mischievous and heartbreaking. A BBC production.

Wilde's *The Importance of Being Earnest*, in a BBC production with a lively cast headed by Wendy Hiller as the indestructible Lady Bracknell.

A Christopher Neame dramatization of Graham Greene's *Monsignor Quixote*, in a Thames production, with Alec Guinness and Leo McKern irresistible as a modern Quixote and his Sancho Panza.

I have said that Exxon never attempted to censor, but that is not to deny the uneasiness caused by certain words and images that might appear on the home screen. Wendy Wasserstein's *Uncommon Women and Others* was a source of perturbation. We had seen the Phoenix Theater production, and we agreed—Jac and the people at Exxon—that the dialogue among the women recalling their days as college friends at Mount Holyoke needed toning down. Miss Wasserstein did her own editing, and when I read her new version, I offered several suggestions. One line about which I had doubts was "Have you ever tasted your menstrual fluid?" Jac promised to do something about the troublesome line. Somehow it remained in the script and was spoken on TV. Exxon received indignant letters and sought to appease the protestors. I wonder whether the caller who was assured—I do not know by whom—that the play would not be repeated before 6 P.M. was placated. Say for the production that it brought together an uncommonly good cast that included Meryl Streep, Swoosie Kurtz and Jill Eikenberry before they went on to greater prominence.

I do not blame Exxon's executives for being sensitive to complaints from viewers. So many are ready to take umbrage at the slightest innuendo, let alone any vivid expression or image that is interpreted as an obscenity. In *Staying On* there is a moment when Trevor Howard shouts "Balls!" at Celia Johnson. In *December Flower* Mona Washbourne, sitting on a commode, expostulates with satisfaction, "I'm shitting a brick!" In *Monsignor Quixote* Guinness as a naive priest is led into a brothel, where he toys with a condom and blows it up into a balloon. Should something be done about these sources of possible embarrassment? Exxon did not intervene, and the sky did not fall down.

There was more concern about a scene in the BBC production of Edna O'Brien's *Mrs. Reinhardt*, about a woman who is escaping temporarily from problems in her marriage and who catches the eye of a young man on the make. Helen Mirren as Mrs. Reinhardt is in her hotel quarters taking a shower when the young man, played by Brad Davis, enters through an open window. One can see legs and a bare back through the glass window of the shower stall, and then one watches as the young man forces his way into the stall and begins to discard clothing. Mrs. Reinhardt is seen lifting a leg suggestively. Could this bit of business stand? We all agreed that a tiny cut was in order.

The biggest flap occurred ironically as a result of a scene in the ninth episode of "Brideshead Revisited." This eleven-part mini-series was acclaimed rightfully as one of the finest achievements of television, but in some of Exxon's highest echelons, it was virtually unmentionable. The reason? The sequences in the ninth episode when Jeremy Irons as Charles and Diana Quick as Julia are making very active love. Vivid bedroom scenes of this sort are almost *de rigueur* in the movies nowadays, and they have also become a commonplace on British television. But to many American viewers they remain offensive, and the "Brideshead" scene provoked a lot of letters of protest to Exxon, including torn credit cards.

The flap could have been avoided. It was my habit to screen all tapes when available well in advance of airtime. The tape of the ninth episode reached me only a few days before it was to be broadcast, and I alerted several Exxon executives late one evening that the bedroom scene might cause trouble. They screened the episode the next morning, and to their credit they decided they had no right to interfere with the product of artists they respected. Poor judgment perhaps in the eyes of their superiors concerned with corporate public relations, but an honorable posture, since artistic responsibility belonged to Granada, producer of the mini-series, and WNET.

There was another ironic twist in the presentation of "Brideshead Revisited." It was a WNET decision to invite William F. Buckley, Jr., to be the host of the mini-series, and to some of us at Exxon he seemed an unfortunate choice. Since Evelyn Waugh's novel and the mini-series drawn from it deal in part with a Roman Catholic family, the use of a prominent American Catholic seemed logical. But Buckley was a leading voice of right-wing conservatism, and though he did not inject his political views into his introductions, his presence at the top of each episode was bound to displease people who disliked what he stood for.

In the perspective of time, "Brideshead Revisited" looms ever larger as one of television's greatest triumphs. It began at Granada as an idea for a five-part series. John Irwin and I were in London on one of our scouting trips and were lunching at Granada. We had had pleasant relations with this company. Thanks to the enthusiasm of Robert Kotlowitz, WNET's vice-president for programming, Granada had undertaken a four-part series based on Dickens' *Hard Times*, his spare, unrelenting novel of the plight of the workers in Lancashire's cotton mills, and had turned it into unforgettable television. We were asked what we thought of the Waugh novel as a subject. We confessed we did not remember it but promised to read it in the next few days. When we did, we phoned to say we liked the proposal, and when we returned to New York, we informed Kotlowitz and Venza, and they proceeded to sign up.

The making of "Brideshead Revisited" was a saga in itself. Derek Granger, the producer for Granada who had nurtured the project for a long time, ran into a multitude of problems, the most difficult of which were job actions by unions that delayed production for months. The first director, Michael Lindsay-Hogg, who had other contracts to fulfill, had to leave the series after presiding over the shooting of less than half. Granger took a big risk in assigning Charles Sturridge, a young director with relatively little experience, to finish the job. John Mortimer's brilliant adaptation grew from a five-part to an eleven-part series. Granada poured increasingly large sums of money into the project. Its casting in major roles—Irons, Anthony Andrews, Claire Bloom, John Gielgud, Laurence Olivier—and in minor ones was impeccable.

I remember sitting with Andrews at a dinner that Exxon gave a few days before the opening broadcast and observing that Granada had shown laudable percipience in choosing him for the role of the charming, feckless Sebastian. I had seen the early tapes and knew his performance could be a big winner. But on what basis had Granada guessed? Andrews laughed. "You will not believe it," he said, "but for a time it was touch-and-go whether I would be Charles and Jeremy would be Sebastian."

The costs of making "Brideshead Revisited" mounted as problems increased and the series expanded. While conceding that a contract was a contract, the owners of Granada pleaded with Exxon and WNET to make extra payments. In the end, though the payment was raised substantially, Exxon and WNET got one of the great bargains of television history, and it wasn't until almost ten years after the completion of the much acclaimed series that Granada could say it had finally paid off its costs.

"Masterpiece Theater" depended almost entirely on mini-series made in Britain, and it was no secret that Mobil was unhappy it had let "Brideshead

Revisited" get away. The truth is that it never was in the running for it any more than "Great Performances" had a chance at some of the "Masterpiece Theater" successes. But there was continuing competition, with representatives of both programs making frequent scouting trips to London.

The series I most regret losing to Mobil and "Masterpiece Theater" was "The Jewel in the Crown," a rendition of Paul Scott's *Raj Quartet* that borrowed the title of the first volume in the set and was another brilliant achievement by Granada. Granada had already made a version of Scott's *Staying On*, a sequel to *The Raj Quartet*, and "Great Performances" had presented it on American television. At a London meeting Sir Denis Forman, managing director of Granada Television, spoke of annoying difficulties his people had run into while filming in India and wondered whether they should go ahead with *The Raj Quartet*. Had I read it? I had. Should they do it? Judging by the quality of Granada's "Staying On," I said it might be a good bet. Later he took me aside and asked the question directly: would Exxon underwrite it? I said I did not know, but I urged, "Do it anyhow." "The Jewel in the Crown" was the sparkling result.

Jeremy Irons and Stefane Audran in "Brideshead Revisited," 1982.

"Great Performances" lost three other series I did not regret. My friend Mark Shivas, a gifted producer who had made such fine single plays as *Abide with Me, On Giant's Shoulders* and a wry, amusing treatment of Tom Stoppard's *Professional Foul,* undertook an ambitious and promising mini-series based on the Borgias. The BBC was the producing company, and after conversations with its production executives, we thought we had the inside track. But Mobil moved fast and committed to the series, which it never broadcast. Was it too scabrous for American tastes?

Another BBC project for which WNET—and therefore Exxon—bid vigorously was a mini-series based on F. Scott Fitzgerald's *Tender Is the Night.* I recall sitting in a BBC office while Venza negotiated. With a pained expression, he raised the price he was prepared to pay, but the BBC negotiators insisted they could not say yes or no until they had a call from Los Angeles. It seemed that Showtime was on the verge of offering more money. Showtime did outbid "Great Performances" with an offer of additional hundreds of thousands of dollars with which American stars could be engaged. In my opinion the televised "Tender Is the Night" might have been a lot better with fine actors than with some of the stars engaged with the extra money.

A third project we lost was "The Fortunes of War." Frank Hooke, an executive at Esso Australia, an Exxon subsidiary, had been urging us to think about a mini-series based on six Olivia Manning novels that made up *The Balkan Trilogy* and *The Levant Trilogy.* We and WNET read them and agreed with Frank. In time the BBC committed to the project and assigned Alan Plater to do the scripts and James Cellan Jones, whose work as director of "Jennie: Lady Randolph Churchill" we admired, to direct. David Loxton, in charge of drama at WNET, and I had problems with the scripts, as had David Elstein and Eric Abraham of Richard Price Television, a partner in the enterprise. We met at an intense meeting with Plater, Jones and BBC people in London, and it was my unhappy duty to say I could not recommend that Exxon proceed with the deal until there were thorough script revisions. Jones argued, "Not even if I give you assurances that it will come out all right?"

"Great Performances" and WNET, which had put up some front money, withdrew. Mobil took over. When the series was completed and began airing in Britain, Jones sent me a packet of British reviews, all complimentary, with a note saying, "Eat your heart out." I took pains to look at every episode on "Masterpiece Theater." My heart was hardly touched.

We managed to find some first-rate mini-series in different veins. The BBC's "Tinker, Tailor, Soldier, Spy," based on John le Carré's novel, was a thriller of exceptional subtlety, with Alec Guinness, master of understatement, leading an accomplished cast. From Thames Television we acquired the three-part comedy "The Norman Conquests," by Alan Ayckbourn, with its genial inanities and its disarming philandering in the bosom of the family, with Tom Conti as a sly, lovable Norman the philanderer and Penelope Keith, one of Britain's fine comediennes, as a haughty yet willing victim. Insisting on a change of pace, Venza offered the BBC's latest version of Bram Stoker's perennial *Count Dracula*, a production as unsubtle as "Tinker, Tailor" was subtle.

Eager to prove that we in the United States could turn out a mini-series of merit, Venza undertook to transform Eugene O'Neill's monumental play *Mourning Becomes Electra* into a five-parter. I confess I had my doubts. Some years earlier station WGBH in Boston, another PBS producing center and the entry station for "Masterpiece Theater," had approached Exxon with a proposal to develop a mini-series based on Hawthorne's *The Scarlet Letter*. I thought the idea had possibilities and recommended financial support. The scripts were faithful, and the sets constructed near Newport, Rhode Island, had the flavor of early New England. But alas, the cast did not measure up to the demands of the Hawthorne story, and the direction lacked the concentrated tension that this forbidding tale must have.

Venza was more successful with O'Neill. He had good leads in Joan Hackett, Roberta Maxwell and Bruce Davison, an able director in Nick Havinga, a solid adaptation of O'Neill's text by Kenneth Cavander and an effective setting in a fine, pillared mansion he located in upstate New York. If I felt any dissatisfaction with the ambitious undertaking, it was with O'Neill himself, who sometimes tended to be too wordy for his own good.

As the hunt and the competition for the knockout mini-series intensified, it occurred to me that we were neglecting producers on the Continent. In Paris Kotlowitz and I screened some scenes from a work in progress, a five-part series devoted to the life of Molière. Here was the dusty, sprawling, brawling Paris of the playwright's time, recreated with amazing fidelity to the period. Here was the court of Louis XIV with its powdered wigs, its flowing skirts and daring décolletage and its mannered formalities. Here was Lully seeking to please, and Molière intent on speaking in his own voice even as he also sought to retain His Majesty's favor. Kotlowitz and I kept in touch with this project through its brilliant conceiver and director, Ariane Mnouchkine, and her proud father, Alexandre Mnouchkine, a successful producer of feature films. When we saw the finished series, we knew we wanted it on "Great Performances."

But how to present it? After all, it was shot in French. The consensus was to try dubbing into English. We were well aware that some critics and many viewers look askance at dubbing; they are properly troubled when the lips of the actor on screen and the voice off screen are not synchronized, and a serious loss of credibility results. But what about subtitles? They are effective on foreign films in movie houses. The trouble with the home screen is that it is small, and subtitles are often difficult to read.

We opted for dubbing. I have to admit that it was far from perfect. I am sorry that "Molière" did not have the success it deserved. We had no better luck with a dubbed version of a six-part series based on Stendhal's *The Charterhouse of Parma*, with an international cast headed by Marthe Keller. The dubbing, however, was not the only shortcoming; the production tended to be perfunctory. We had guessed wrong.

We were eminently right, however, in electing to present "Buddenbrooks" and "The Life of Verdi" in dubbed versions. There was a lot of resistance at PBS and WNET to acquiring these series. So what if the original *Buddenbrooks* was the work of one of Germany's great writers? And what if the series achieved a remarkable grasp of the rise and decline of a notable family, emblematic in a way of the nation itself? The German production was excellent, and in John Gielgud it had a fine, illuminating host. Even the dubbing was superior. But nearly everyone was dubious about the prospects of "Buddenbrooks" in America, and it was decided to air its nine episodes in late spring and early summer. The doubters were confounded. The reviews were laudatory, and the ratings were as high as those for the most successful mini-series on PBS.

Dubbing did not hurt the popularity of "The Life of Verdi." I should add that the success of this six-part series was particularly pleasing to me. From the outset I was fascinated by its possibilities, and there were times when I seemed to be virtually alone in believing in it.

My interest began when the late Dario Soria mentioned casually that RAI, Italy's government-controlled radio and television complex, was thinking about doing Verdi's life. He introduced me to Renato Pachetti, the head of RAI's American offices, who arranged to have a set of scripts in an English translation sent to me. Whoever had written them knew what he was about. Here was the truth of Verdi's humble beginnings, his rejection by the Milan Conservatory, the tragic, early death of his wife and two children, his faltering start as a composer, his successes and disappointments, his unsought role as a symbol of his country's passion for unity and independence, his union with soprano Giuseppina Strepponi, his mistress and then his wife, and, of course, his music.

I have always cherished Verdi the man for his uncompromising integrity. From Gatti-Casazza and Arturo Toscanini, who had known him personally, I had heard admiring stories. I fear that as a young music critic I tended to patronize his music, but as I grew older I learned to appreciate its simplicity and directness and the way in which it spoke unfailingly to the heart.

Promising as were the scripts, would they be realized? Thanks to Renato Castellani, the promise was richly fulfilled. It was months before I learned that he had written them himself. As director he spared neither effort nor RAI's money to get every detail right. I made a trip to Cremona to watch some of the filming. At great expense Cremona's opera house had been altered temporarily to look like Milan's La Scala in Verdi's time. On another trip to Italy I watched some scenes being shot in the studio in Rome. My Exxon colleagues and I encountered Ronald Pickup, the English actor, who in beard and makeup seemed to be a ringer for Verdi as he sat on a bench and sipped a cup of tea. He

Ronald Pickup in "The Life of Verdi" in the 1980s.

wanted to know if we had seen any of the finished footage. We nodded. He continued casually, "What's it like?" Didn't he know? His answer, "Not really."

Negotiations with RAI were begun and broke down. Meanwhile CBS undertook its ambitious cable commitment devoted in part to programming like that on "Great Performances," and it bought the rights to "Verdi." After large losses, CBS abruptly terminated its cable undertaking, and once again "Verdi" was available to us. A deal was struck, not without grave misgivings at WNET and Exxon. One of my colleagues made no secret of his distaste for the project and of his warning that it would be a disaster. A few days before the broadcast of the first episode, Stamas stopped me in a corridor to say that he was worried about "Verdi." I tried to reassure him; I said I could not, of course, guarantee its success but was confident that a lot of people would like it.

The late Peter Weinberg, who was Venza's associate in charge of music programs, and I had decided that the series started too slowly. In my viewing of many prospects made abroad I had concluded that too many mini-series began at a crawl. In a none-too-jocular formulation, I had once proposed the rule of thumb, *Throw out the first episode.* What we did with the Verdi series was to telescope the first two one-and-a-half-hour episodes into a single two-hour one. Weinberg and his staff accomplished the task seamlessly, and our first episode ended not only with a stirring example of Verdi's early music but also with his first meeting with Strepponi.

"The Life of Verdi" was a huge, unexpected triumph. Pickup as Verdi and Carla Fracci, the lovely ballerina turned actress, as Strepponi seemed to be the characters restored to life. The look of Verdi's world was accurate and colorful. And there was the music! And the performers of the music! Castellani contrived to use the recorded voices of some of the finest singers of our time: to name only a few, Callas, Di Stefano, Christoff, Pagliughi, Corelli, Tebaldi, Taddei, Lauri-Volpi, Tagliavini, Bergonzi. And as an additional asset, there was Burt Lancaster, the attractive host. It was Weinberg's happy inspiration that Lancaster, known to be an opera buff and an admirer of Verdi's music, would add to the appeal of the series, and I have no doubt that he did.

I wish we could have done as well with Richard Wagner. Under the direction of Tony Palmer, an ingenious and ambitious film and television man, a consortium was formed in Britain to finance a grandiose mini-series on the life of Wagner. Based on an early script by Charles Wood, which I had read when other interests were promoting the project, I thought the proposal had possibilities. What Wood had written was truthful. Nor did Palmer fail to film the truth. He did not minimize Wagner's gigantic egotism, nor did he ignore his abuse of love and trust or his vicious anti-Semitism.

But in going for a spectacular blockbuster, Palmer achieved a grandiosity that undermined his series. He cast a worn-out Richard Burton as Wagner, which was a sad blunder. As the young Wagner, Burton was hopelessly unconvincing; he did better as the aging Wagner. Bear in mind that the first three episodes of the nine-part series dealt with the young Wagner. Rarely has any mini-series assembled such a cast of glittering names, among them Vanessa Redgrave, Laurence Olivier, Ralph Richardson, John Gielgud, Marthe Keller, Gemma Craven. The soundtrack, all Wagner, was conducted by Georg Solti.

Venza and Loxton thought the series could be saved by drastic surgery. Loxton and his staff trimmed the original nine hours to four, eliminating many embarrassing scenes. But apart from the music, "Wagner" worked only sporadically.

Georg Solti conducting in the late 1970s.

"Great Performances" did infinitely better by Wagner when it presented the entire *Ring of the Nibelung* as the epic masterpiece was produced at Bayreuth. To acquire the rights was an act of courage by Exxon. I know perfectly well that not everyone there applauded the decision. I remember a discussion with Stamas and associates when, after confirming the decision to go ahead, he closed the meeting with the comment, "If we don't do it, who will?"

It was a decision not taken lightly. When Unitel contemplated the possibility of such a television venture, it asked Exxon and WNET whether "Great Performances" would be interested. There had been so many conflicting reports and so much controversy about Bayreuth's latest interpretation of this massive tetralogy that a television version seemed an immense risk. Patrice Chéreau, the young French director and designer who was Wolfgang Wagner's bold choice for a radical restaging, was assailed for treating *The Ring* as if it had Marxist implications, the way George Bernard Shaw had interpreted it in his book *The Perfect Wagnerite*. Pierre Boulez, the conductor, noted for composing and performing difficult new music, was faulted for his supposedly analytical, intellectual approach to Wagner.

At Exxon's request I attended the cycle in Bayreuth. I had seen a lot of Wagner and *The Ring* at the Metropolitan Opera in the glorious days of Flagstad, Melchior, Schorr, Bohnen, Branzell and colleagues, and I had been in Bayreuth for earlier, traditional cycles. I was not enchanted with some of Chéreau's ideas. Wotan in a tailcoat was offputting. Some of the sets—for example, the suggestion of an urban slum in the last scene of *Götterdämmerung*—seemed odd. But I was tremendously impressed by what Chéreau had achieved in the relationships of the characters. The scenes between Wotan and Brünnhilde, his loved and loving daughter, had a warmth and tenderness I had never seen before. There were countless subtle, human touches. The gods, their charges and their victims were not merely distant myths; in their passions and motives they were like us. As for Boulez's conducting, it too had a different dimension: thanks to its clarity and balance, it had an eloquence of its own.

Kotlowitz's support was invaluable in getting agreement to broadcast *The Ring*, but not even he could persuade the PBS authorities in Washington to schedule the cycle properly. It was my hope that "Great Performances" would follow the BBC scheme of presentation on ten successive Sunday evenings, beginning with the intermissionless *Das Rheingold* and following with one act each from *Die Walküre*, *Siegfried* and *Götterdämmerung*. The cumulative effect was tremendous. A commercial channel launched a highly touted mini-series opposite the BBC and lost that competition by a wide rating margin. I believe that *The Ring*, if scheduled with a concern for continuity, would have done a lot better in the United States than it did.

The PBS people in Washington, however, no doubt abetted by station managers in some parts of the country, were fearful. They began with the one-hour introductory program especially prepared to provide a background for *The Ring* and Bayreuth, and followed it the next week with *Rheingold*. Then a month or more elapsed until we got the next music-drama, another month or so before *Siegfried* and another long interregnum until the last music-drama. Those responsible for this irresponsible scheduling were severely criticized in the press and in letters from outraged viewers. WNET sought to make amends by offering each of the music-dramas complete in the course of a week.

Opera had become an event on the "Great Performances" schedule with a *Pagliacci* in the second season, and it remained a strong element in every season thereafter. When "Live from Lincoln Center" was added to the mix, there were annual broadcasts from the New York City Opera. Exxon would have been delighted to include "Live from the Met," but Texaco, which had been sponsoring radio broadcasts from the Met for decades, chose to expand into television and eventually became a co-sponsor of "Great Performances."

The scope and quality of opera on "Great Performances" remain a source of pride to me, as they should be to PBS and Exxon. When and where could audiences of millions in the United States have access to the three extant works of the first great composer of opera, Monteverdi? In 1981–82 "Great Performances" offered *Orpheus*, *The Coronation of Poppea* and *The Return of Ulysses* in a single season, a feat that no American opera house could boast of. In performances directed by Jean-Pierre Ponnelle and conducted by Nikolaus Harnoncourt, they spoke to us across the centuries with timeless humanity.

Ponnelle was an important contributor to "Great Performances." His staging of opera for television as well as his direction in opera houses in Europe and the United States was frequently—I might say, consistently—attacked by the music critics. And Ponnelle, who died too soon at the age of fifty-six in 1988, may have delighted in outraging them. His use of the camera to make dramatic points was often startlingly untraditional. I admired the freshness of his approach even if I had reservations about some of his ideas.

His *Butterfly* was a case in point. When I first screened it at Unitel headquarters in Munich, I was enchanted with all but one sequence. The opening with its dreamlike mistiness, in which we meet Pinkerton floating through a scene that might have been an old Japanese painting brought to life, was a magical evocation of place and time. The notion of using slow motion for the end of the second act when Butterfly, Suzuki and Trouble strew blossoms for the possible return of Pinkerton was brilliant, enhancing the impact of the music. With Mirella Freni, Placido Domingo, Christa Ludwig and Robert Kerns in the cast and Herbert von Karajan conducting, the performance musically was one of the finest I had ever heard. Yet I could not recommend its acquisition.

Ponnelle's treatment of the duet at the end of the first act troubled me: it was totally out of keeping with the tender rapture of the music. Ponnelle had Pinkerton tearing off Cio-Cio-San's clothes and all but raping her. Perhaps he had a point about Pinkerton's basic purpose. But the crudity of the action belied the gentle ardor of the music. Unitel accepted my criticism and, at considerable cost, reshot the scene. The "Great Performances" broadcast won praise everywhere and an impressively large audience in every section of the country.

Ponnelle's other contributions to "Great Performances" encompassed three operas by Mozart—*The Marriage of Figaro, The Magic Flute* and *La Clemenza di Tito* (a *Don Giovanni* from the Salzburg Festival—not directed by Ponnelle—

Jean-Pierre Ponnelle, 1984.

with the American Samuel Ramey in the title role was on a similarly high level); two by Rossini— *The Barber of Seville* and *La Cenerentola;* and Verdi's *Rigoletto,* in my view Ponnelle's finest opera film. Ponnelle also gave us "A Celebration of Seville," in which he and Domingo brought off a visual and musical tour de force, with Domingo singing and playing both Figaro and Almaviva.

The mention of *La Clemenza di Tito* leads me to reflect on the patronizing attitude of some music critics toward television. Long regarded as hack work ground out by a harried composer in the last troubled year of Mozart's life, this opera was revived by Ponnelle and his conductor, James Levine, with an appreciation of its musical riches even though they were imprisoned in the formalities of opera seria. When it was presented on "Great Performances," it was an achievement of importance. Some time later the Ponnelle-Levine production entered the Metropolitan Opera, and some critics wrote as if it were a total novelty to an American audience. Had they not noticed that television with its audience of millions had been there ahead of the Met?

The range of opera on "Great Performances" was proudly wide. In addition to those already mentioned, we presented Beethoven—*Fidelio;* Richard Strauss—a stunning *Rosenkavalier,* a powerful *Salome* with Teresa Stratas as an alluring Salome and *Elektra;* Johann Strauss—an echt Viennese *Fledermaus;*

Placido Domingo in a musical tour of Seville, 1983.

Wagner—*Tannhäuser* and *The Flying Dutchman;* Verdi—*Macbeth, Otello* and *Falstaff;* Puccini—*Tosca* and *La Rondine; Cav* and *Pag* in Zeffirelli productions; Saint-Saëns—*Samson and Delilah;* Bizet—*Carmen;* Gounod—*Faust;* Tchaikovsky—*Pique Dame;* Humperdinck—*Hansel and Gretel.* Nor did we neglect more recent works: Janáček—*Cunning Little Vixen;* Weill—*Street Scene* and *Down in the Valley;* Britten—*The Turn of the Screw;* Moore—*The Ballad of Baby Doe;* Menotti—*The Consul, The Saint of Bleeker Street* and *Goya;* Barber— *Vanessa;* Carlisle Floyd—*Willie Stark;* John Adams—*Nixon in China.*

J. Kenneth Kansas, an Exxon colleague, and I flew to Houston for the premiere of *Willie Stark.* The question arose, should the opera be taped for "Great Performances"? A decision was delayed to find funds for a TV version. Harold Prince, the director, thought the generally negative views in the press were the cause of our hesitation and uncertainty. An old friend, he took the liberty of sending me a sharp note insinuating that we were chickening out because of those reviews. In an equally curt reply I assured him that we had not traveled to Houston to see the opera only to wait for the reviews before deciding whether to recommend inclusion in "Great Performances." When we did include it, I did not get an apology from Hal.

Eager to keep its definition of a great performance wide and open, "Great Performances" was delighted to embrace R. G. Blechman's brilliantly imaginative animation of Stravinsky's *A Soldier's Tale.*

Opera was, of course, only part of the commitment of "Great Performances" to music. In addition to the wealth of resources contributed by "Live from Lincoln Center," programs were made and bought in Europe as well as in the United States. Our conductors included Leonard Bernstein, Herbert von Karajan, Georg Solti, Eugene Ormandy, Bernard Haitink, André Previn, Zubin Mehta, Lorin Maazel, Mstislav Rostropovich, Claudio Abbado, Aaron Copland and Gidon Kremer. Among our soloists were Artur Rubinstein, Maurizio Pollini, Rostropovich, Rudolf Serkin, Claudio Arrau, Itzhak Perlman, Isaac Stern, Emil Gilels, Vladimir Ashkenazy, Pinchas Zukerman, James Galway, Benny Goodman and André Watts.

"Great Performances" offered generous samplings of the classics—Handel, Haydn, Mozart, Beethoven, Brahms, Schubert, Schumann, Mendelssohn, Strauss, Chopin, Tchaikovsky, Rachmaninoff, Mussorgsky, Stravinsky and so on and on. Particularly ambitious was a cycle of Mahler conducted by Bernstein, who had probed deeply into this composer's psyche as well as his creative workshop. Major works of Bach were on the agenda; after the initial gingerly entrance into music with the B minor *Mass*, there were the *St. John Passion* and the *St. Matthew Passion*, the *Christmas Oratorio* and the Brandenburg Concertos. Copland conducted a program of his own music with the Los Angeles Philharmonic, and Maazel paid tribute to a distinguished immigrant turned citizen, Ernest Bloch, in a program with the Cleveland Orchestra that included the rarely heard *America*, a large-voiced salute by the composer to his adopted country, broadcast, naturally, in 1976 during the bicentennial year of the nation's independence.

It took a while, but eventually "Great Performances" found occasion to include chamber music—not a great deal, to my regret, but enough to give a large audience in prime time an opportunity to savor its delights. The Chamber Music Society of Lincoln Center provided the personalities and the programs for most of these concerts via "Live from Lincoln Center."

"Live from Lincoln Center" became the vehicle for other notable developments. The most striking was the transformation of Luciano Pavarotti into a national attraction on the order of a rock, film or athletic superstar. It began with a late afternoon solo recital at the Metropolitan Opera House. Using his large white handkerchief as an indispensable prop, the tenor revealed a thoroughly engaging personality as he sang a collection of arias that have become his standards over the years. The reaction from America was that Pavarotti, a genial fat man with a rich, lyrical tenor, had won big. "Live from Lincoln Center" and "Great Performances" certainly treated him like a winner. They brought him back in a succession of joint appearances with Joan Sutherland and Marilyn Horne, and with a group of talented singers whom he was displaying and with whom he managed further personal display. Where could he go after that? Obviously to Madison Square Garden at $150,000 a concert and to a starring role in an unfortunately poor film. At this date, 1994, he is still singing at the Metropolitan Opera and making frequent television appearances.

Beverly Sills did not require television to become a nationally known and respected personality. She had been an accomplished prima donna long before she became a TV host. She sang leading roles in New York City Opera productions in the "Live from Lincoln Center" series, and when she retired from singing to take over the management of the company, she was always there on camera, smiling broadly, to talk about the opera and to share her pleasure in the lively company. In January, 1994, she took over the reins of Lincoln Center.

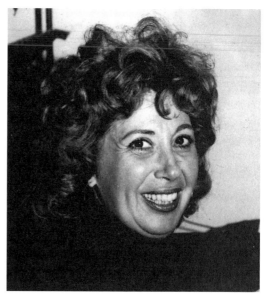

Beverly Sills, 1975. Photograph by Don Hogan Charles.

Itzhak Perlman turned a mishap into widespread affection for his presence of mind and his geniality. He was playing first violin in a Tchaikovsky sextet when a string broke, and he seized his neighbor's fiddle and seemed ready to carry on while that musician hurried off to replace the string on Perlman's violin. Evidently it took him a while to find a new string, and the music stopped. Instead of sitting on the stage of Alice Tully Hall in an uncomfortable silence, Perlman, in a confidential tone, began ad-libbing as if he were chatting with friends in a private home. By the time his violin with a new string was returned to him and the music resumed, everyone in the audience was in a wonderfully receptive mood. And Perlman was on his way to becoming a national celebrity not simply as a musician but as a genial TV host in, among other appearances, broadcast concerts from the White House.

By the time Artur Rubinstein appeared on "Great Performances," he was well into his eighties. His prowess at the piano remained extraordinary, and it was a privilege for the TV series to share it with a large national audience. By great good luck, we also had an opportunity to provide that public with an intimate view of the man—wise and witty and heartwarmingly mellow. I speak of the program "Artur Rubinstein at Ninety." Unitel had filmed the pianist in his late eighties in Grieg and Saint-Saëns concertos with the London Symphony under Previn, and his performances were as authoritative and committed as they would have been in his prime. They were, in fact, his last performances, for he was going blind. It occurred to us that we could use them as the basis of a tribute on his ninetieth birthday. Robert MacNeil, a knowledgeable and sensitive interviewer, was sent to Paris in the autumn of 1976, and his conversation with Rubinstein occupied almost a half-hour of an hour-and-a-half broadcast.

Rubinstein talked about music, about his early years and difficulties, about the qualities that make an artist, about himself as a Jew in a Europe that only too recently had experienced the Holocaust and about his belief, despite endless horrors and cruelties, in mankind. He was still capable of a ringing affirmation: "I learned to love life simply because I became aware of the fantastic interest in the beauty of life under all circumstances."

Though absorbed in his dialogue with MacNeil, he could be aware of lesser matters. Ken Kansas and I had come to Paris from Munich and were late in getting to Rubinstein's Avenue Foch home. When we were ushered in by his wife, we tiptoed to be sure we did not interrupt his conversation with MacNeil. I had spoken softly to Mrs. Rubinstein, but his hearing was as acute as ever. He stood up and said, "That's Howard's voice," and embraced me. We were old friends, but I had not seen or spoken to him in years.

A few days before the program was to be aired in January, 1977, Rubinstein came to lunch at Exxon. Without recourse to a diary, I remember the day because it tells so much about this nonagenarian. It was January 20. Still firm in stride but walking cautiously because of his failing sight, Rubinstein greeted his hosts, Stamas and his associates, and before he could be offered an aperitif asked whether there was a TV set at hand. What would he want with a TV set at lunchtime? "Simple," he said. "I'd like to hear Jimmy Carter's inaugural speech."

"Great Performances" devoted a program to Vladimir Horowitz in his home, "Last of the Romantics," and another to Toscanini that included homemade movies as well as moments from the maestro's NBC telecasts. Zubin Mehta as the principal conductor of the New York Philharmonic was on camera frequently not only as a performer but as a lively host.

Leonard Bernstein, with his aptitude for talking about music, was an illuminating guide to and interpreter of such composers as Mahler and Brahms. On one delightful occasion, he did not speak at all but served as pianist for a program of Brahms sung beautifully by Christa Ludwig, and it was she who discussed Brahms, *Lieder* singing and her career.

Bernstein, in a program that was pure serendipity, showed us a way to do musical comedy. Venza and Exxon were eager to encompass some of the matchless examples of American achievement in lyrical theater, but the costs were beyond the budget of "Great Performances." Even the commercial networks did not venture into this enormously expensive region. From Britain "Great Performances" did acquire an attractive production of an American musical, *She Loves Me*, by Sheldon Harnick, Jerry Bock and Joe Masteroff, but when we sought the rights for *Porgy and Bess* and *Show Boat*, we ran into difficulties. We did get a production based on a revival of Loesser's *Most Happy Fella*, and one of *Sweeney Todd*.

Bernstein had an idea. Eager to do a fresh audio recording of music from his own *West Side Story*, he assembled an outstanding operatic cast headed by Kiri Te Kanawa, José Carreras and Tatiana Troyanos and elected to be his own conductor. Why not, he proposed, move TV cameras into the recording studio and tape the proceedings? Klaus Hallig, aware that American musical theater had a

Leonard Bernstein (at center) during a recording of *West Side Story* with Kiri Te Kanawa (left), Tatiana Troyanos and José Carreras, 1984. Photograph by Sara Krulwich.

large public abroad, agreed to Unitel's underwriting of the production costs. But would it work? Would it be suitable for "Great Performances"?

Was it suitable! It was a smash hit. The cameras recorded amusing and revealing details: the conductor's impatience with the sound crew, his patient request that Carreras try again with an interpretation that wasn't right, Carreras's unmistakable irritation, the informality of the performers' costumes and of the entire scene. Seldom had a score first performed in a Broadway theater been played and sung by such an outstanding ensemble of singers and instrumentalists, with the composer himself to make sure the interpretation did not take on airs.

Encouraged by this success, Venza set out to do something comparable with Stephen Sondheim's sophisticated, sparkling score for *Follies*. He persuaded the New York Philharmonic to join forces in a concert version, presented in part almost informally like a run-through, on the stage of Avery Fisher Hall, and then like a party shared by a full house. Among the performers were Carol Burnett, Elaine Stritch and Alexis Smith. This was not *Follies* as it had held the stage in the course of its too brief Broadway run. Nor was it *Follies* as produced in London, where the obsession with overwhelming, active machinery evidenced in hits like *Cats, Les Misérables* and *Phantom of the Opera* infected so many productions. What had been so impressive in the brittle, sardonic and literate musical in Harold Prince's Broadway production and so disaffecting in the vulgar London version was a tremendous challenge to television, which brought it off successfully.

"Great Performances" did not manage to get Kern or Porter or Rodgers or Youmans or Burton Lane, but it did have generous portions of Gershwin in a pair of programs conducted and narrated by Michael Tilson Thomas, including excerpts from *Of Thee I Sing* and *Let 'Em Eat Cake*. We had an ASCAP show, a specially made tribute to Ellington, another to Harlem's Cotton Club, and a program devoted to Miles Davis. I was especially fond of a revue titled "Taking My Turn," in which an octet of oldtimers sang and talked engagingly about their desire and capacity to carry on.

Of contributions to the performing arts, none has been more creative or significant than what "Great Performances" has done for dance in all its manifestations. No area was neglected. There was ballet, modern dance, tap dance and hoofing, gymnastics and discussions of all the forms and techniques. "Dance in America" through "Great Performances" played a vital role in developing a large new audience for the dance. For this achievement, Venza and his associates at various times—Rhoda Grauer, Merrill Brockway, the late Emile Ardolino and Judy Kinberg—deserve the nation's gratitude.

Not everyone in the dance world rejoiced at the prospect of dance on TV. The obvious objections: dance was movement in space and could not be encompassed on the home screen. How could cameras and directors be quick enough to capture the leaps, pirouettes, writhings, of a brilliant performer or group of performers without blurring the images? How many cameras would be needed, and where would they have to be placed to communicate the breadth and continuity of a design in movement?

These are legitimate and difficult questions. It took time and repeated discussion and analysis to persuade George Balanchine to accept television for his company, the New York City Ballet, and for his dances after an initial unsatisfactory experience with television in Europe in the early 1970s. It took a lot more time to convince Jerome Robbins, and he has agreed to only a few televised productions thus far.

My chief regret is that the outstanding dance companies of the world—such as the Bolshoi, the Kirov, the Danish and others—were not represented. "Dance in America" was launched at the instigation of the National Endowment of the Arts, with Exxon agreeing to contribute to the funding and to integrate these programs into "Great Performances." The Endowment stipulated that "Dance in America" must be limited to American dance; otherwise federal funding would not be available.

"Great Performances" did present two programs by Britain's Royal Ballet, thanks to Venza's negotiating skills. We also had "Boxes," in which the Sydney Dance Company from Australia offered a "rock dance spectacle." This was one time when I would have preferred less successful negotiating skills.

Don't think that everyone in the government system for support of the arts went along cheerfully with the commitment to "Dance in America." When the Corporation for Public Broadcasting was requested to make a grant to this "Great Performances" component, a member of its staff shook his head, partly in jest, as he examined a WNET submission and said, "So much money for tights?"

In Balanchine, "Dance in America" had the best in the world. The New York City Ballet, which he and Lincoln Kirstein created, was as good as any company anywhere, and it was right to accord this troupe and its reigning choreographer pride of place. No other company appeared so often, not even the American Ballet Theater when its leadership was taken over by Mikhail Baryshnikov, after that superb dancer appeared as a guest of the New York City Ballet under Balanchine's direction. No choreographer was represented as comprehensively as Mr. B., though Robbins and Peter Martins have had their dances presented in the TV series.

Mr. B. began his official collaboration with "Dance in America" by insisting on reconceiving his works for TV. The result was a series of programs that provide a modest summation of his career. He had also hoped to create works especially for television, and finally "Great Performances" accorded him the opportunity. The result was the magical "Spellbound Child," Balanchine's version of Ravel's and Colette's charming little opera, *L'Enfant et les Sortilèges*.

Several of us from Exxon—Eliot R. Cattarulla, then Stamas's deputy and later his successor as vice-president for public affairs, Lauren Katzowitz and I—flew down to Nashville to watch the grand old man of dance fashioning this new work. The stage was that of the Grand Ole Opry, which was spacious and well enough equipped to accommodate so large an enterprise. The musical portion had been pre-recorded, and Mr. B. was pushing hard in the face of time limits to refine the dance sequences. There in the midst of a throng of young dancers was the choreographer, demonstrating steps and movements of the arms and attitudes of the body, as if he were to be on camera himself. Working

George Balanchine (left) during rehearsal, 1972. Photograph by Jack Manning.

with calm concentration, he moved his dancers individually and in groups, often taking them by the arms and placing them in positions and attitudes that conformed to images in his mind.

Kermit Love, who contributed so much to the Muppets and to "Sesame Street," was Balanchine's choice as designer, and his costumes, masks and collapsing and expanding furniture added their measure of innocent wonder. What emerged was not just a ballet, not just an opera, but a unique theater work that evoked comparisons in my mind with the world of Lewis Carroll.

We learned in Nashville that Mr. B., having relished his experience with "The Spellbound Child," was ready to attempt other works combining music, dance, drama and illusive settings in fresh directions, but it never happened again. The cost of "The Spellbound Child" was about $850,000. The budget of "Dance in America" could not provide such funding. But it did guarantee that every dance company of consequence in this country had a chance—and sometimes more than one—to show its wares to the nation on television.

My involvement with "Dance in America" was limited. Venza and his associates, Kotlowitz and Cattarulla, had so much more experience with and special fondness for and sensitivity to the dance, that my advice was rarely sought or needed. At Exxon, however, there was a question about the program for the first season. The Joffrey Ballet, the Pennsylvania Ballet, a company led by Twyla Tharp and Martha Graham's Dance Company were the scheduled events. One day a worried Stamas asked me whether the opening dance season should include the Graham company. He had never seen it himself but had been warned that this was unappealing, even ugly dancing. I shook my head. Whatever it was, it was none of these things. "In fact," I said, "we cannot *not* have Martha Graham. She is one of our greatest creative figures." The morning after the Graham company's initial appearance on "Great Performances," Stamas sought me out to say how much he had been impressed and moved by the Graham company and how pleased he was that this great lady was in the series.

The scope of dance on "Great Performances" was a faithful reflection of dance in America. Among the companies represented were those of the Dance Theater of Harlem, Merce Cunningham, Paul Taylor, Pilobolus, the San Francisco Ballet, Alvin Ailey, Eliot Feld, Katherine Dunham, Trisha Brown, Laura Dean and Mark Morris. A special program brought Nureyev with the Joffrey Ballet recalling Nijinsky and his dances. Another special program was devoted to the career and work of Agnes DeMille.

Artwork from a booklet celebrating the tenth anniversary of "Great Performances" in 1982. Copyright © 1982 by Educational Broadcasting Corporation. Reprinted by permission of WNET, Channel 13, New York.

Twice during my years as an Exxon advisor, I traveled around the country being interviewed by the press and on television. The first trip took place before "Theater in America" made its TV debut, the second when "Great Performances" with all its components had become a reality.

During the latter circuit I was interviewed by David Richards, a writer for the late *Washington Times-Herald.* It was a lively question-and-answer session, principally on the role of the arts in television, past, present and future, and the editors saw fit to publish the report on the front page. It was a time when oil spills were in the news; there had been several serious ones, notably the massive disaster that fouled parts of the French coast. My interviewer asked me what I thought of oil spills, and I replied that I was not a spokesman for Exxon, only a consultant dealing with television and the arts.

"Come, now," the interviewer said, "you must have an opinion about oil spills."

"Of course I do," I said. "They are dreadful, deplorable."

When I returned to New York, a Stamas subordinate demanded to know who had authorized me to talk about oil spills. I explained that the reporter had persisted in his questioning, and I would have seemed an idiot if I had insisted I had no opinion on such an issue. "Anyhow," I added, "you know and I know that oil spills are awful, and from now on I shall be strictly an advisor, not a traveling salesman for Exxon and its role in 'Great Performances.'"

Nevertheless, I was and remain inordinately proud of Exxon's role in "Great Performances" and of whatever I contributed to that accomplishment. I cannot understand how a great corporation, which had taken so much pride in its contributions to education and the arts and which had gained so much good will throughout the nation as a result of its participation in "Great Performances," could pull out. Obviously it could not have been to effect a big saving. At its peak the Exxon contribution to "Great Performances" could not have cost as much as $10 million a year, and this for a corporation that was netting more than $4 billion a year.

Such decisions leave one wondering. As for oil spills . . .

20

A Great Artist! A Great Lady!

MARIAN ANDERSON, the celebrated contralto, died at the age of ninety-six in Portland, Oregon, on April 8, 1993. In the following weeks obituaries were published and broadcast around the world. Thoughts of Marian crowded my mind.

In early 1955 Sol Hurok, the most daring, venturesome musical impresario of our time, called and urged me to help Marian Anderson with her autobiography. Hurok had brought her back from Europe twenty years earlier and had reintroduced to her own country a singer of such stirring vocal amplitude and such personal dignity that she had become a dominant figure on the American musical scene. When the Daughters of the American Revolution barred her from appearing in their Constitution Hall in Washington in 1939 and she sang instead for more than fifty thousand from the Lincoln Memorial on Easter Sunday, she became something more than a fine, admired singer. In her career and person, whether she liked it or not, she became a powerful precursor of the civil rights movement that grew to maturity in the 1960s.

When Hurok broached his suggestion, I declined. I had done a bit of ghosting years earlier. In the thirties I had worked with Giulio Gatti-Casazza on his memoirs. In the forties I had helped Frances Perkins with her book, *The Roosevelt I Knew.* Though I had high regard for Marian as an artist and a friend, I was too busy with my own work. Hurok persisted: "At least have lunch with her."

"All right, but where?" He understood what I meant.

Marian Anderson singing at the Lincoln Memorial, 1939.

"At the St. Regis," he said. "I'll see to it that there will be no problem."

It is almost impossible to realize four decades later that black men and women, even distinguished ones, were not welcome in elegant hotels in 1955. But Hurok had attended to the matter. Marian and I met in the lobby and were escorted to a table in the St. Regis dining room. We were served as pleasantly as everyone else, but I could not fail to notice that we were constantly being stared at, perhaps because Marian was a celebrity, perhaps because a black here was a rarity indeed.

In her modest, diffident way Marian said that she was being urged to tell her story in a book, that she was uncertain whether she wanted to, that she did not know whether she could write and that in any event she did not have time to find out. Would I help? I replied that I, too, was hard-pressed for time and did not see how I could manage it. "Surely," I said, "someone else can be found."

She shook her head. She knew me, I had written many pieces about her; we had met from time to time and had gotten along well.

"But I really can't," I said.

She had told Hurok that she had no taste for starting so difficult and delicate a task with someone she did not know well; now she would tell him to forget about it.

I felt guilty. Like Hurok, I had been advising her that she ought to do it. From her vaunted position as the best-known and most highly regarded black singer, she could at long last tell it as it had been—what it was like to make a career in the face of all the handicaps and hardships that a black skin was heir to in the United States, including Jim Crow audiences, colored restrooms, no admittance to hotels and restaurants on the road. I began to waver in my resolve not to ghostwrite again. Was it her aim to be candid, sparing no one from the truth? She nodded emphatically. Well, I would give it further thought and let her know. We agreed that if I could work with her, we would do so in the summer during our vacations.

The details of our agreement were fashioned in a conference at the home of Rex Stout, who happened to live in Danbury, Connecticut, in a hilltop house not far from mine. George Bye, my literary agent, drove up to represent me, and Rex, who as long-time chief of the Authors' Guild knew more about book contracts than many publishers, spoke for Marian. I should add that in all the years since that meeting, not a word about that contract ever passed between Marian and me, not that the mention of money could have affected our friendship.

In July Marian and I began our sessions in a studio that stood some distance from the house and barns of her Danbury farm. We set up a tape recorder, and she undertook to answer my questions. I found that I was dealing with the personality familiar to the public. She hardly ever spoke of herself as "I," resorting instead to the impersonal "one" or to "we"—not the royal "we," but another retreat to impersonality. But what gave me pause was that she was telling me things I had read or written myself. There were no revelations.

I was distressed. On the third day of useless talk, I stopped the tape recorder and said that what she had confided thus far to the tape recorder and me could easily be found in a press kit or in the files of *The New York Times*. She seemed stunned. "If you really want your book to be a contribution of consequence," I said, "you will have to tell a lot more, if not all." She indicated that she would reflect on my remarks and give me an answer in the morning.

When we reconvened, it was clear that she had decided not to hold back. In the days that followed she tried hard to be forthright and frank. There were moments of backsliding. As she began to dredge up a painful memory, her hand almost automatically reached for the stop button on the tape recorder. I did not protest, but let her stop the tape recorder. Then, when I got home, I made full notes of incidents she could not bear to have recorded, like the time in Philadelphia when as a girl in her teens she sought entrance to a music school and was turned back by a receptionist who informed her that they didn't take Negroes. I incorporated these episodes into her story.

After about a month of conversations, I had the tapes transcribed and, using what spare hours I could find away from my job, completed the manuscript. I submitted it to Marian. She phoned me after she read it. She was clearly unhappy. Much too sensitive about my feelings, she talked around the subject, until I finally suggested that she did not like what she had read. No, it wasn't that, but yes, it was a bit different from what she had expected. However, I was not to be upset; she would check with friends. Some days later I had a call from Rex Stout, an ebullient man who rarely minced words. He had just read the manuscript and had given Marian holy hell. "A damn fine job," he roared, "and it sounds just like her."

Satisfied at last, she asked Nora and me to a July Fourth party, where we met

Anderson with her husband, Orpheus Fisher, greeting Rex Stout in 1963.

a stimulating group of her black friends. We, in turn, invited her and her husband, Orpheus Fisher, to dine with us. They came and were correct and distant. Our two young boys joined us at the table, and she, charmed by the boys, relaxed and began to tell stories and laugh heartily.

A condensed version of the manuscript appeared in the *Woman's Home Companion,* and when the book was issued by Viking in 1956, it bore a brief acknowledgment (as had *The Roosevelt I Knew*) of my "editorial and critical assistance." I did not wish any further credit. I had done my best to reflect Marian's phrasing, attitudes, judgments and personality.

I am happy to report that the book, *My Lord, What a Morning,* rolled on like the river Jordan in one of the spirituals she sang so movingly. After the civil rights upheavals of the 1960s, other black Americans wrote about their lives with more anger and more brutal bluntness. More power to them! But that was not Marian's way.

Still, in what she could bring herself to reveal, she made a breakthrough, even as her career was a model for other black men and women. Perhaps her book had the same somber impact as a remark made by Roland Hayes, the black tenor, who preceded Marian in forging an international career. He once prefaced a spiritual he was about to sing by recalling that his mother used to say that when she got to heaven, all she would want to do was sit down. As the audience laughed, he held up a hand and said, "Not funny."

Stout, a man of impeccable candor, once told me he had spoken bluntly to Marian about her career. "You are lazy," he said. "You don't practice enough." He was right. At the end her voice had not worn well, nor had her interpretive powers deepened.

But in the glory years of her career, she was a marvel. Her voice when I first heard it in that memorable concert at Town Hall in 1935 was unforgettable in its richness throughout its range. My enthusiastic review of the debut concert appeared in *The New York Times* of December 31, 1935. As the politicians like to say, I stand by it.

> Let it be said at the outset: Marian Anderson has returned to her native land one of the great singers of our time. The Negro contralto who has been abroad for four years established herself in her concert at the Town Hall last night as the possessor of an excelling voice and art. Her singing enchanted an audience that included singers. There was no doubt of it, she was mistress of all she surveyed.

The simple facts are better than superlatives, for superlatives are easily abused. Fact one, then, should be the sheer magnificence of the voice itself considered as a musical instrument. It is a contralto of stunning range and volume, managed with suppleness and grace. It is a voice that lends itself to the entire emotional gamut, responsive to delicate nuance and able to swell out with opulence and sonority.

Fact two should be Miss Anderson's musicianship. In a program that encompassed a full group by Handel, another by Schubert, a Verdi aria, a Finnish section and a concluding group of Negro spirituals, she revealed a penetrating command of style. She understood not only the difference in approach between the songs of Handel and Schubert and Sibelius, but the divergences of intent in music by the same composer. Each song was treated as an artistic unit, set forth with care, study and intelligence.

But without deep feeling these other assets would not achieve the grandeur of interpretation that was Miss Anderson's last night, and that should be item three. For Miss Anderson has the transcending quality of all authentic art—a genuine emotional identification with the core of music. Schubert's "Der Tod und das Maedchen" and "Allmacht" were ennobling in their grandeur. And how many singers have communicated the transfiguring rapture of John Payne's "Crucifixion" as Miss Anderson did last night? It was music-making that probed too deep for words.

To all these things must be added the native good taste of the artist and the simplicity of her personality. Here was a woman of poise and sensibility. The fact that one foot, injured in an accident on board ship in the voyage home, was encased in a cast was never permitted to intrude on the listener's consciousness. She sang with a consciousness of her ability and with a relish of her task that were positively infectious.

It was possible for those of pedantic minds to find minor matters to quibble over, such as the occasional edge in top tones or imperfections of enunciation in foreign languages. They need not be labored here. In the presence of such art, pedantry might well be spared.

Limitations of space forbid a detailed discussion of each song on Miss Anderson's program, where columns could be devoted to it with profit. A hint of felicities of phrase and style culled without sequence must be added, however: the sweep of Handel's "Ah spietato," the delicacy of Schubert's "Liebesbotschaft," the purity of the contralto's amazing low tones in "Tod und das Maedchen," the coloratura work in Sibelius's "Die Libelle" that remained always in the frame of the song, the laughing quality and exquisite tone coloring in the little Finnish folk song that was an encore after the Suomi group.

Miss Anderson will undoubtedly give many more concerts this season, and there will be opportunity for extended comment on her resources. The reticent accompaniments of Kosti Vehanen must not be overlooked.

In the last four years, Europe has acclaimed this tall, handsome girl. It is time for her own country to honor her; for she bears gifts that are not to be feared. Born of poor parents in Philadelphia, Miss Anderson has made something of her natural endowment. If Joe Louis deserves to be an American hero for bowling over a lot of pushovers, then Marian Anderson has the right to at least a comparable standing. Handel, Schubert and Sibelius are not pushovers.

Marian Anderson was a proud woman, well aware of how much her career spoke for the need for equal rights for black performers. Yet she did not like to be regarded as a civil rights symbol. In the 1980s, when the project of a Marian Anderson Award was proposed to her by June K. Goodman, who did so much to bring it to reality, June asked me to help persuade Marian to agree to the idea. I went to visit her and told her it would be good for the fight for equal rights for black artists. She scowled as I spoke. Clearly the idea did not please her. However, many years earlier, she had readily and happily agreed to make a long-delayed debut at the Metropolitan Opera (as Ulrica in *Un Ballo in maschera* on January 7, 1955), knowing it would be an exemplary occasion of national consequence. In the end she agreed to the award project too, though it was an uncharacteristically public statement about her beliefs and convictions.

The Marian Anderson Award Fund continues to grow. Based at the Charles Ives Center for the Arts at Western Connecticut State University in Danbury, Connecticut, and supported by contributions, large and small, it had raised over $400,000 by early 1994. Continuing Marian's efforts to bring new talent into the community of music, it gives an award of $25,000 to greatly promising American singers chosen by a distinguished jury of vocal experts, to allow them to continue their studies and development. Recent recipients have been Denyce Graves and Nancy Maultsby, mezzo-sopranos, Sylvia McNair, soprano, and Philip Zawisza, baritone.

Anderson making her debut at the Met as the fortune-teller Ulrica in *Un Ballo in maschera*, 1955. Photograph by Sam Falk.

As a pertinent postscript, I include some comments I wrote for the first program launching the Marian Anderson Award Series on August 12, 1989:

> I was not there on April 9 fifty years ago when Marian Anderson, on a clear, cool day, stood in front of the statue of Abraham Lincoln that dominates his memorial in Washington, and sang to an audience of thousands. Nor was I there fourteen years later when Marian Anderson sang to a capacity audience in that very Constitution Hall where, in 1939, her performance had been denied by the Daughters of the American Revolution because her skin was black.
>
> But I was there in December, 1935, when Marian Anderson sang at Town Hall in New York. Some years earlier she had won a modest prize, had appeared in a concert at Lewisohn Stadium where the New York Philharmonic played outdoor concerts in the summer, had made little progress in the United States and had left for Europe where she had steadily built a career. Despite glowing reports of her achievements abroad, there seemed to be no eagerness on the part of American concert managers to re-introduce her to her native land. Was it because they

believed that there was not much of a market for a young black singer? Impresario
Sol Hurok, a maverick and risk taker, took the trouble to hear her abroad, signed
her and brought her back.

I was at Town Hall because Olin Downes, senior music critic of *The New York
Times*, had chosen to attend a performance at the Metropolitan Opera. He made
the wrong choice, and he directed readers of his review to take note of the report
on the Anderson concert. And that report was, though I dislike the clichés used to
describe reviews, an out-and-out rave. It was so excitedly laudatory that I took a lot
of good-natured ribbing from colleagues—so young and so susceptible?

Let me try to recapture the impact and emotion of the occasion. On the sea
trip back from Europe, Marian had tripped, fallen and sustained a leg fracture.
Would she appear at Town Hall? Nothing would stop her. She would not be able
to make entrances and exits. No matter. The curtain, almost never used for concerts, was closed when the audience gathered. When it was drawn, there stood this
impressive figure in the bend of the piano, and there she remained throughout the
performance.

And what a performance! I have not bothered to check out my review. I don't
need to. The quality of the voice—dark, velvety, powerful, gentle, enormous in
range—lingers in my inner ear. I remember the reverence that filled her singing of
Schubert's "Ave Maria," the intense drama in Schubert's "Der Tod und das Maedchen," the passion and sorrow that informed the spiritual "The Crucifixion."

Though this concert was not an American debut for Marian Anderson, it had
the effect of one of those once-in-a-lifetime instant successes. And so it remained
in a long, brilliant career through which she became a hope and a symbol for other
aspiring minority artists. When the Metropolitan Opera at long last in 1955 broke
its unacknowledged prohibition against black singers, it was Marian Anderson
who was invited to sing. She sang with the authority that marked a career of shining integrity. A great artist! A great lady!

Having talked of the beginnings, I must add a few words about the end, the
June 7, 1993, memorial service for Marian Anderson at Carnegie Hall. The stage
was adorned by two magnificent vases of flowers sent by Van Cliburn and four
beautiful photographs of Marian provided by her nephew, the conductor James
DePreist. We were a host of friends and admirers gathered to say farewell. We
listened to well-considered words by Isaac Stern and by DePreist and to some
of her recordings. The emotions engendered by the Town Hall concert came

flooding back as I heard her singing Schubert's "Ave Maria" and "The Crucifixion," with its concluding "Were you there when they crucified the Lord, and he never said a mumbling word," and she repeated the last sentence, lingering on "not a word, not a word," in her lowest crepuscular tones. I thought once again hers was the true, grieving voice of a race.

21

Support of the Arts

I AM A STRONG believer in government support of the arts and take pride in the fact that through my news and critical articles in *The Times*, I contributed to a public discussion of the subject. During the Kennedy Administration there was an important beginning when the young President named August Heckscher to be his arts advisor. Jacqueline Kennedy provided significant momentum to the idea that the government and the White House should show off the nation's creative people. Lady Bird Johnson took up the baton with energy and enthusiasm. It was LBJ who proposed and won creation of the two Endowments for the Arts and Humanities. He got appropriations of $5 million for each through Congress and appointed Roger L. Stevens the first chairman of the Arts Endowment.

Roger was a dynamic and resourceful executive. Under his leadership a lot of good was accomplished through his wise allocation of the $5 million. Naturally there was heated opposition in Congress to this program, as reflected later on by self-anointed authorities on the arts like Senator Jesse Helms. During the Nixon Administration the appropriations for the Endowments soared into the range of $500 million a year. The people who deserve a great deal of credit for this accomplishment were Leonard Garment, a former Nixon law partner and later a member of the White House staff, and Nancy Hanks, who at Garment's recommendation was Nixon's appointee as chair of the Arts Endowment. A charming lady from Fort Worth, Texas, she became a persuasive spokesperson for the arts with often recalcitrant members of Congress.

President Kennedy hosting a White House concert in 1961. Alexander Schneider, with violin, and Pablo Casals, with cello, are at left.

Gordon MacRae and Carol Lawrence, left of Lady Bird and President Johnson, sang at a White House dinner in 1968.

We should not forget the role of the Rockefeller family in providing leadership for a new national acceptance of the importance of the arts in American life. John D. Rockefeller III was the dynamo who helped create the Lincoln Center for the Performing Arts. His brother Governor Nelson Rockefeller of New York was a forceful contributor to the new idea that government—federal, state, city and county—had an obligation to support the arts and to encourage their dissemination. Their brother David was influential in creating the Business Committee of the Arts among chief executives of our largest corporations.

Occupants of the White House learned long ago that creative people of all sorts would be attractive additions to the guest list on state occasions. Concerts from the White House were developed by the Kennedys and continued by the Carters, the Reagans and the Bushes. I believe and trust that the Clintons will carry on. The establishment of the National Medal of Arts for a lifetime of achievement was a good step toward raising the consciousness of Americans to an appreciation of careers like those of Leonard Bernstein, Aaron Copland, Martha Graham, Agnes DeMille, Marian Anderson, Helen Hayes, Isaac Stern, Rudolf Serkin, Mary Martin, Leontyne Price, Eubie Blake and George Balanchine.

Governor Nelson Rockefeller in 1971.
Photograph by William E. Sauro.

David Rockefeller, chairman of the Chase Manhattan Bank, in 1972. Photograph by William E. Sauro.

Louise Nevelson with Ronald and Nancy Reagan after receiving the National Medal of Arts in 1985. Photograph by Paul Hosefros.

I have a personal roll of honor of many who worked hard in developing American appreciation of the arts and their practitioners. At its head are Leonard Garment, Nancy Hanks, Jacqueline Kennedy and Lady Bird Johnson. Not to be forgotten are Lincoln Kirstein, who almost single-handed, with his patronage of George Balanchine, created and financed an American school of the ballet; Leonard Bernstein, who with the New York Philharmonic proved to young people and their elders that music could be fun, exciting and inspiring; and Eric F. Goldman, a Princeton professor, who served as an intellectual advisor to LBJ. Goldman proposed a kind of White House festival of the arts which lasted a number of days and included performances by leading actors, musicians and dancers. It got some unwelcome notoriety during the Johnson years when the poet Robert Lowell wrote an open letter declining his White House invitation because of his opposition to the war in Vietnam. (As a guest and *Times* representative I checked around and found that many of us shared Lowell's position on the U.S. role in Indo-China.)

If it were in my power to award a prize for gallantry in support of the theater, I would award it to Lucille Lortel for her highly expensive effort to keep Lee Blessing's fine play *A Walk in the Woods* running. When this work, underappreciated by the New York press, was on the verge of closing, she personally undertook to keep it going at great cost. She also produced it in London with Alec Guinness in the cast, to greater approval than it had enjoyed in New York. Lucille has had a long history of devotion to the theater. The productions she has backed, like Marc Blitzstein's English version of the Brecht-Weill *Three Penny Opera*, are an eloquent endorsement of her good taste. I salute her judgment and courage.

A Walk in the Woods was not only entertaining but also prescient. Not long after its appearance, Ronald Reagan, who had called the Soviet Union "the evil empire," and Mikhail Gorbachev walked together in Red Square.

I must not neglect to express my admiration for the Ford and Rockefeller Foundations for the ingenious programs they instituted to stimulate creative activity in the arts. W. MacNeil Lowry of the Ford Foundation was particularly resourceful in this area. He and his staff found ways to encourage artists and artistic institutions to function in improved ways. One of their best programs sought to help artistic institutions deal with their budgetary problems. This

Lucille Lortel, 1985. Photograph by Marc Raboy.

program was guided by Marcia Thompson, who succeeded in turning it into a permanent organization. My former *New York Times* colleague Howard Klein served as an arts program officer at the Rockefeller Foundation, which established a commissioning and recording program for the works of American composers in conjunction with the Louisville Symphony Orchestra, helped enormously by Charles Farnsley, the energetic and delightful mayor of Louisville.

Lowry once convened a conference of men and women deeply involved in the arts and artistic institutions in an effort to get fresh ideas for Ford Foundation programs. I recall that Archibald MacLeish, poet and playwright, turned to me and asked, "What can we do to improve criticism?"

My answer: "You must educate publishers and chief editors about the importance of the arts so that they will look seriously for people who can bring knowledge and sympathy to the task."

I must not forget that many large corporations have established foundations that make grants to the arts and artistic institutions. I have watched how conscientiously the Exxon and *New York Times* foundations study and carry out their responsibilities in these areas.

While praising these foundations, I should emphasize that they have become possible thanks to the leniency of the tax laws. In other words, you and I as ordinary taxpayers must take up the burden of providing the necessary funds in our tax payments, since wealthy families and corporations are able to evade their proper taxes by setting up foundations!

I should like to see the great, vastly richer foundations follow the lead of the Aaron Diamond Foundation in its policy to continue making grants until its core funds are spent, instead of investing capital in the hope of gaining substantial profits. Thus unexpected large sums will be freed for gifts to art institutions.

A Family Album

With my wife Nora and Bill in 1945.

Bill with his baby brother Phil in 1948.

With Phil, Nora and Bill at Bayreuth in 1958.

In Brussels in 1958 with Nora, who died in 1985 after a long illness.

Phil (at left) and Bill at our Danbury, Connecticut, home in 1960.

With Philip's family—Gregory and Philip at left, Michael and Felicity at right, June 1994.

With Bill's family—Alex and Phoebe at left, Bill and Jane at right, June 1994.

With Lori, my second wife, in 1994.

A photograph taken by Lori as this book went to press.

Index

Illustrations are indicated in **bold** type.

342   *Index*